A BELIEVER with AUTHORITY

The Life and Message of John A. MacMillan

Paul L. King

✛ CHRISTIAN PUBLICATIONS, INC.
CAMP HILL, PENNSYLVANIA

CHRISTIAN PUBLICATIONS, INC.
3825 Hartzdale Drive, Camp Hill, PA 17011
www.cpi-horizon.com
www.christianpublications.com

Faithful, biblical publishing since 1883

A Believer with Authority
ISBN: 0-87509-917-3
LOC Control Number: 01-130454
© 2001 by Paul L. King
All rights reserved
Printed in the United States of America

01 02 03 04 05   5 4 3 2 1

*To my wife Kathy
and to my children
Sarah and Christopher*

Contents

Foreword

The authority of the believer is a doctrine that is closely allied to the quintessentially Protestant doctrine of the priesthood of all believers. The authority of the believer focuses on the individual and his/her position in the heavenlies with Jesus Christ. Indeed, the doctrine of the authority of the believer celebrates the fact that along with the Ephesian believers, we are seated with Jesus Christ in the heavenlies, with Christ at the right hand of the Father (Ephesians 2:6).

We know as well from Scripture that God gives some believers a ministry of a particular doctrine (1 Corinthians 14:26). John A. MacMillan was such a man.

He was a husband, a father, a minister, a missionary, a businessman and a writer. But more than all of that, MacMillan was a man with a doctrine. That doctrine clearly was the authority of the believer. When he read Isaiah's comment "concerning the work of my hands, command ye me" (Isaiah 45:11), he not only understood but dared to believe. He was not brushed aside by doubtful interpretations. Instead, he seized what has been called the "throttle of omnipotence" and discovered the powerful workings of God that are unleashed by spiritual authority.

Paul L. King, whose doctoral work explored the immense body of MacMillan's writings, has provided in this book a biography which introduces us to the man and his message—*and* to the glorious doctrine of the authority of the believer. I heartily commend this writing as one of the most significant in our day. It is eminently worth reading.

—K. Neill Foster, PhD

Acknowledgments

There are numerous people who have contributed in many ways to enable my dissertation and this book to be accomplished. More than anyone else, my wife Kathy and my children Sarah and Christopher have helped me with this project, assisting with research during working vacations. My daughter's expertise in statistics was valuable in statistical authorship analysis in the dissertation. My wife has been my best critic in submitting the chapters. My student assistants Caroline Frame and April Williams also provided valuable insights and aid.

Dr. Loren Calkins, former District Superintendent of the Southwestern District of The Christian and Missionary Alliance, encouraged me to stir up my gift for writing and to submit some of the work I had done to Christian Publications, which resulted in a published article, coauthoring for the book *Binding and Loosing* and the book contract for this project. Dr. Charles Farah, retired professor and son of a Christian and Missionary Alliance pastor, also encouraged me to write for publication and to pursue my doctorate, as well as providing mentoring and challenging me spiritually and intellectually.

Special thanks go to Dr. K. Neill Foster, who praised my work and gave me helpful criticism in producing both the dissertation and the book.

Many people helped with the research: Dr. John Sawin, C&MA historian, who led me to numerous sources of information; Dr. Joseph Wenninger, Archivist at the C&MA headquarters in Colorado Springs; Dr. Lindsay Reynolds, Canadian C&MA Historian; Sandy Ayer, Director of Library Services at Canadian Bible

College/Canadian Theological Seminary; Mike Guy, Librarian and Archivist at the OMF headquarters in Denver, Colorado; David Pratley, Clerk of Session, St. John's Presbyterian Church, Toronto, Ontario; Linda Poston, Director of Library Services, Nyack College; Marion Howe, staff member, Nyack College; Barb Taylor, Archival Assistant, Victoria College, University of Toronto; Steve Adams, Editor of *Alliance Life*; Rev. Robert Niklaus, C&MA Historian and Director of Communications.

Jane MacMillan, John MacMillan's daughter-in-law, provided me with a treasure of information and resources—especially John's journal from 1923-1928 in China and the Philippines and Buchanan's family notes and many memories. Also Alan MacMillan John's grandson, shared his recollections.

Thanks to everyone else who contributed information through correspondence and conversations which have been cited in this book: Anita Bailey, Keith Bailey, Thomas Bailey, Richard Barker, Rexford Boda, T. Robert Brewer, Otto Bublat, John Ellenberger, Rev. and Mrs. Howard Emary, Regina Jagst Fischer, Neil Fye, Richard Gifford, F. Paul Henry, Richard Herritt, Marian Howe, Ross Ingraham, Maurice Irvin, Don Kenyon, L.L. King, Betty Knopp, Rev. and Mrs. George Lang, Jerry McGarvey, Gerald McGraw, Ed Murphy, John Nevius, Bob Niklaus, Lindsay Reynolds, Lloyd Robertson, Albert Runge, John Sawin, Jay Smith, John Stizaker, Paul Valentine, Cliff Westergren, James Zeigler.

Introduction

When I speak in churches on the authority of the believer, one of the first things I do is ask the congregation, "How many of you have heard of John MacMillan?" Invariably, only a few hands are raised. This is true even in churches of The Christian and Missionary Alliance (C&MA), in which MacMillan played a significant leadership role.

The original source of teaching on this vital doctrine comes from John A. MacMillan and his classic holiness roots in the Higher Life and Keswick movements.

This book is adapted from my doctoral dissertation, which was a case study of the life, ministry and impact of MacMillan—missionary, writer, editor and professor. In 1923 this forty-nine-year-old Presbyterian layman and his wife became missionaries to China and the Philippines with the C&MA. Nine years later, after many dramatic experiences with spiritual warfare, he wrote a series of articles in *The Alliance Weekly*, the periodical of the C&MA, entitled "The Authority of the Believer." Eventually they were published in booklet form, distributed widely and also republished in other periodicals. MacMillan had a remarkable and extensive ministry in spiritual warfare, spanning more than thirty years.

Today the concept of the authority of the believer is taught widely, yet seldom do its proponents give credit to or faithfully follow the principles taught and practiced by MacMillan. Who would be better to study and emulate than one of the prime trailblazers who taught and lived the principles?

Some background regarding The Christian and Missionary Alliance is helpful in order to understand the context of

John MacMillan's ministry and teachings. Founded by A.B. Simpson in 1887 as an interdenominational organization emphasizing missions, holiness and healing, the Alliance does not identify itself with the charismatic/Pentecostal camp.

The position of Simpson and the C&MA is that although God is still bestowing all the gifts of the Spirit today and the baptism or filling of the Spirit is subsequent to conversion, the gift of tongues is not the evidence of the baptism with the Spirit.

Since gifts are sovereignly bestowed by God "as the Spirit wills," it is not God's plan that all speak in tongues. Gifts may be desired, but should not be sought after. In addition, though some teachings and practices of Simpson and the Alliance appear to be similar to those of the modern faith movement, the C&MA disavows any identification with modern faith teachers because they deviate from earlier classic holiness faith teaching.[1]

This project is forged out of my personal involvement in the exercise of the authority of the believer and ministry of deliverance through nearly thirty years of pastoral and educational ministry. In 1998 I coauthored a book with Dr. K. Neill Foster on one particular aspect of spiritual warfare and the believer's authority.[2] Since John MacMillan's teachings and experiences are discussed in that volume, this book is a natural follow-up.

The church needs sound theology and practical application of the authority of the believer, spiritual warfare and spiritual discernment to hurting Christians. MacMillan's life and ministry is a model of the balanced exercise of the believer's authority.

By exploring the life and ministry of John MacMillan, we can discover how he practiced the authority of the believer in his own life. We can examine his model for conducting the ministry of deliverance and exercising spiritual discernment. Other significant insights into Christian living can also be observed from his life and gleaned from his writings.[3]

Marion Howe, a long-time faculty member of Nyack College, a student of John MacMillan and a colleague of his son Buchanan, wrote, "If the Alliance had saints, he surely would be one of them."[4] Retired Nyack College professor Donald Kenyon writes that MacMillan "represents a generation of Alliance 'history' long forgotten by many and totally unknown by others. . . . MacMillan is one of the true links with Alliance beginnings."[5]

It is important that John A. MacMillan receive proper recognition for his seminal thinking and writing on the authority of the believer. This biographical study deserves attention because of its value to Christian leadership in the church. Some of the insights to be gained from MacMillan include:

1. An appropriate theology of demonic influence and attack.
2. Practical ways to deal with demonic forces.
3. Appropriate situations for exercising a believer's authority in daily living.
4. The extent to which the authority of the believer can be exercised.
5. Guidelines for appropriate guidance.
6. Principles and procedures for discerning whether a manifestation is of God, Satan or the flesh.

This book presents a biography of John MacMillan. Those who desire more detail on MacMillan's life, ministry and teachings can consult my dissertation.[6]

Hebrews 13:7 advises, "Remember your leaders, who spoke the word of God to you. Consider the outcome of their way of life and imitate their faith" (NIV). It is the intent of this book to (1) remember this Christian leader, (2) consider the impact of his life and ministry, and (3) encourage imitation of his faith as a model in exercising the authority of the believer.

ONE

Formative Years

W
HO WAS THIS MAN, John MacMillan? And what made him the man of God and spiritual warrior he became? Although information about his life as a child and young adult in Canada is sparse, we can nevertheless discover from his family heritage insights into his spiritual formation.

John Alexander MacDonald MacMillan was born in Tillsonburg, Ontario, Canada, on October 27, 1873, the youngest of eight living children of Buchanan MacMillan and Betsy McNee.[1] John descended from a strong Scottish Covenanter heritage. The MacMillan clan is believed to have descended from Methlan, son of a thirteenth-century Buchanan chief.[2]

John's grandfather, Allan MacMillan, born in 1791, was a Gaelic-speaking Highlander who, soon after the Napoleanic Wars, emigrated from Scotland to Canada. He and his wife Mary settled in Eastern Ontario and raised a large family. Their second son was Buchanan, John's father, born in 1819, the year of Queen Victoria's birth. He became a boyhood friend of John Sandfield MacDonald, who later rose to to prominence as the first premier of Ontario. Buchanan grew up in a Gaelic-speaking home, but apparently did not pass the language on to his children, except for a few words and phrases. In his youth, Buchanan aspired to become a doctor, but as he was never able to fulfill that dream, he became instead a skilled carpenter and cabinetmaker.

John MacMillan described his father as "a stern, but kindly Presbyterian." For many years John's father opposed having a piano in the house, but eventually relented "on the condition that it should not be played on Sunday." John's son Buchanan recalled, "My father cherished a deep respect and affection for his father, whom he resembled—except for the beard!"

We know little about John's upbringing. He apparently enjoyed his childhood, but the declining health of his parents required that he assume, at a young age, a major portion of the family responsibilities. John had to drop out of school at the age of sixteen due to financial difficulties and go to work at Jarvis Street Collegiate Institute, a high school located in downtown Toronto. Years later he reflected back on those days:

> Childhood is our time of illusion. We live in the land of vision, and of dreams, and of pictures. Many of us look back with pleasure to those early days. We have come with regret out of the land of the make-believe into the world of the matter-of-fact. There is much in its stern realities that is painful. To be grown up is not all that we anticipated it would be.[3]

However, John was not bitter about his past, but according to his daughter-in-law Jane he was proud of his Scottish heritage and loved to tell Scottish stories and jokes. His writings often make reference to such stories,

as well as to great Scottish preachers. His father probably read to him *The Scottish Chiefs*, the fascinating story
of the early history of Scotland, just as John read to his
son. In one of his editorials years later, John alluded to
those childhood stories with poetic flair as he explained
the etymology of the word *slogan*:

> The word comes from the Gaelic *sluagh-gairm*, which
> means literally "army shout." When the writer's
> Highland ancestors came face to face with their foes
> on the field of battle, their only knowledge of tactics
> was to draw the claymore, fling away the scabbard,
> and rush to the attack, with the fierce clan slogan
> rending the air.[4]

It may well be that John's warrior ancestry was di-
vinely engineered in the providence of God as preparation for spiritual warfare. In a sense, it was "in his genes."

John was also fond of making reference to *Pilgrim's
Progress* in his writings, so it is likely that he listened
again and again to the classic allegory at his father's
knee. It may have thus been at a young age, while reading of Christian's struggle with Apollyon, that John became aware of the reality of spiritual warfare.

In John's teenage years, the MacMillan family attended the Presbyterian Church and lived across the
street from Knox College. Pioneer Presbyterian missionary Jonathan Goforth graduated from Knox College
about that same time, and although they certainly met
later, it is unknown if the teenage John MacMillan became acquainted with him then. John later reported of
hearing Goforth speak about the revival in Korea and
wrote a lengthy obituary of Goforth in 1936.[5]

Buchanan MacMillan died in 1895 at the age of seventy-
six, leaving John, at the tender age of twenty-two, as the man

of the house. His mother died about 1900, reducing the household to John and his spinster sisters.

Even though he could not study formally, John developed a relationship with the principal of Jarvis Collegiate, who, according to his son Buchanan, was revered in the annals of Toronto education. Through the encouragement of this leader, he was able to complete a "certificate of education," probably similar to today's G.E.D. program. Like A.W. Tozer, his successor as an editor of *The Alliance Weekly*, MacMillan never formally completed high school or attended college. But, again like Tozer, he was self-taught and well-read, with a depth and breadth of knowledge.

MacMillan expanded on his limited education and sharpened his critical thinking skills by attending debates and lectures at local theological schools, such as Knox and Wycliffe Colleges.[6] He became proficient in Hebrew, sitting in lectures by renowned Princeton Old Testament and Semitic languages scholar Robert Dick Wilson, probably when he was a visiting professor in one of the colleges in Toronto.[7] Since MacMillan conversed frequently with rabbis and others in the Jewish community, he may also have learned Hebrew from them. He also became knowledgeable in Greek, perhaps studying on his own, taking classes through Knox or Wycliffe College, or through his friend and pastor Rev. John Neil. His writings show a remarkable aptitude for both languages.

At some point, John became a "printer's devil" for Ryerson Press. Another of his early jobs was working for a mail publishing establishment. He usually worked from 7 a.m. to 6 p.m. six days a week. During times of heavy demand on the firm, he would read proofs for railway timetables for thirty-six hours without sleep. In his free time, long before the concept of independent correspondence studies, he engaged in self-instruction, voraciously reading a wide variety of literature, ranging from the classics to theological studies to Greek and Hebrew studies.

Through these experiences, he learned the printing trade and went into a business partnership about 1902 with John Arbuthnot, Jr. and three other men. Arbuthnot's father was a printer and an elder at Westminster Presbyterian Church along with MacMillan.[8] When the elder Arbuthnot died in 1902, his son evidently inherited the business and invited MacMillan into the partnership. Initially, they called their new venture "Arbuthnot and MacMillan," but later shortened it to "Armac Press." Eventually, MacMillan bought out Arbuthnot's interest, continuing as president of the thriving business.

Armac Press blossomed into a growing venture and by 1914 listed thirty-four different types of printing services on its letterhead. It also became the printer of *China's Millions*, a monthly magazine of the China Inland Mission. Through his contacts in Christian publishing, MacMillan became acquainted with William Henderson and Dr. R.V. Bingham, the early editors of the periodical *The Evangelical Christian*, which was birthed in 1887 under the name of *Faithful Witness*.[9] Dr. Bingham had been a Salvation Army captain in his youth, became involved with the C&MA in Canada for a time, then founded the Sudan Interior Mission. He became editor of *The Evangelical Christian* in 1904, a periodical esteemed highly by MacMillan for many years.[10]

John MacMillan maintained an active schedule, shouldering the varying responsibilities of a businessman, a lay minister in his church and community, and the breadwinner for his family. Though his burden often became heavy, he discovered that "the real secret of enjoyment at such times is the ability to leave behind all those responsibilities which have pressed, and sometimes worried, during the days of business or home cares."[11] He learned this secret from an elder businessman:

> We were acquainted with one old Swiss watchmaker, the head of a firm of some size, who, in the times of business difficulties, which were very real and pressing, used to say that, when he left his factory, he took nothing of the day's work to his home—it was locked in his office. This he was enabled to do by a firm determination in his earlier days, which had grown into a habit as life advanced. But this means he was enabled to face the serious problems of the morrow with a rested mind and body.[12]

Ultimately, though, MacMillan believed that trust in God was the key to balancing his responsibilities and maintaining health and prosperity. He remarked years later that "The Christian who has learned to cast his burden upon the Lord has a better prescription for rest."[13] John MacMillan's spiritual development is key to understanding his assurance and authority as a believer. To that we turn in the next chapter.

TWO

Spiritual Development
and Ministry

ALTHOUGH DETAILS OF HIS early years are sketchy, it is apparent that John MacMillan's godly home and church life nurtured and molded him spiritually from young childhood. It is also evident that he received Christ as Savior early in his life. He later wrote articles emphasizing the importance of early conversion, obviously alluding to his own experience.[1] Certain phrases in his writings, such as "Growing up in an atmosphere of heavenly affection, the acceptance of the Saviour is natural at an early age,"[2] are decidedly autobiographical.

John's spiritual precociousness was evident in his teen years. Confirmed as a member of West Presbyterian Church in 1887, he became actively involved in church activities.[3] He held official positions in the church as a teenager, including serving as a steward. In an article many years later John recorded a lasting memory of his early church experience:

> The pastor requested at one time that, instead of in-
> stantly moving [at the end of the service], each mem-
> ber sit down and reverently ask that the power of the
> Holy Spirit might follow with blessing the Word spo-
> ken, and then that all might quietly leave the audito-
> rium. The result was excellent, and also lasting.[4]

An atmosphere of worship sensitive to the moving of
the Holy Spirit was impressed upon his heart and would
continue to impact him throughout his life.

The MacMillan family was evangelistic in their faith.
They deeply desired for others to come to a saving knowledge of their Lord. For a time, John's cousin, George
MacMillan, lived with them.[5] As a result of their influence, he joined West Presbyterian Church by profession
of faith. Neighbors down the street from them also became members, apparently due to the MacMillans' faithful witness.[6]

When they moved to another part of Toronto, the
MacMillan family became active in Westminster Presbyterian Church, where John's mother Betsy became involved in the Women's Missionary Society in 1896.[7] His
mother's interest in missions was no doubt foundational
to the development of John's missionary heart.

John's son Buchanan reports that his grandfather
"liked his 'toddy,' and the glass decanter for his whiskey
was an heirloom in my aunt's home. However, in later
years he gave it up." His father's decision had a strong influence on John; once, asked to join a friend in a saloon
for a glass of beer, MacMillan said that he did not feel
the least bit of temptation and turned down the invita-
tion. He had made a commitment to be a non-drinker.[8]
Speaking out against the use of alcohol and tobacco was
a frequently repeated theme in his later writings.

By the age of twenty-four, John had become an elder at Westminster and was very active in church work. His early passion for ministry and missions was evident in his personal work with Chinese immigrants, his financial support for Chinese missions, his promotion of missions work and his recruitment of workers. It appears that only the need to support his aging mother and his sisters prevented him from going to the mission field himself. In 1900 John took on additional responsibilities, including the position of secretary for an interdenominational committee for the Belmont Mission and the superintendency of the Davenport Road Mission School.[9]

The book *In His Steps* could have had a major impact on John's life, since his elder board voted to make it recommended reading for everyone.[11] The main character in the classic book was involved in the publishing business, similar to John, and it would appear that he ran his business with the principles and ethics advocated in the book.

A significant event is noted in the June 24, 1904 session meeting at Westminster Presbyterian: it was recommended that two Chinese immigrants, Chu Zuong and Chin Bow, be baptized.[11]

John became a close friend and colaborer with Dr. John Neil, pastor of Westminster. An eloquent expository preacher, Dr. Neil was highly respected among the clergy of Toronto and eventually became moderator of the Ontario Presbytery.[12] Dr. Neil had such high regard for John that in 1908 he and the Westminster board of elders appointed him to be the representative elder to the presbytery.[13] By his mid-thirties MacMillan had become known and respected as a prominent Toronto civil and religious lay leader.

In 1912 the board asked Dr. Neil and John MacMillan to attend a "picture show" to determine if it was "detrimental to church work or work among the Chinese."[14] The result of that investigation was not recorded, but in editorials years later, MacMillan had little positive to say about movies or the theater.[15] In 1946 he declared, seemingly prophetically, "The movie should be reformed, or it should go. It is based wholly on financial profit, and has little consideration of the social or spiritual welfare of its patrons, young and old."[16] He was insightful in his understanding of its potential negative impact, though today his views might not be widely respected.

Toronto was a meeting place of great evangelical leaders, especially of the Higher Life and Keswick holiness movements—the groups in Reformed circles that corresponded to the Wesleyan holiness movement. Toronto also became a leading city in the emerging fundamentalist movement, with well-known leaders like Alliance-affiliated P.W. Philpott and T.T. Shields, pastor of Jarvis Street Baptist Church.[17] This fundamentalist influence on MacMillan is seen later in his frequent writings against modernism—what we today call liberalism. And yet, though he identified himself as a fundamentalist, he was also sometimes critical of the movement.[18]

One precursor to the fundamentalist movement was the nearby annual Niagara Conference on prophecy (1883 to 1897), a Keswick-like nonsectarian event led chiefly by Presbyterians such as A.T. Pierson. These conferences and the teaching of fellow-Canadian A.B. Simpson influenced several Presbyterian leaders in Canada to abandon the typical Presbyterian postmillennial viewpoint of the Second Coming in favor of premillennialism.[19] They also no doubt played a part in MacMillan's adoption of premillennialism, and it is possible that he may have attended some of these meetings.

As a young man, John MacMillan would have had the opportunity to drink deeply of the preaching and teaching ministry of well-known holiness leaders of his day. South African Dutch Reformed holiness leader Andrew Murray and Presbyterian Keswick leader A.T. Pierson preached together at a convention in Toronto in 1895.[20] Since MacMillan was actively involved with Presbyterian churches advocating higher-life teaching, it is possible that he attended their meetings.

MacMillan later recommended Murray's writings along with A.B. Simpson's as "among the best."[21] He also published articles by Murray on healing.[22] In particular, he refers to Murray's teaching on humility, which was published from a series of messages Murray preached in the same year he spoke in Toronto.[23] As a young man he could have had access to Murray's book *Holy in Christ*, which was published by the Willard Tract Depot in Toronto in 1888, a location MacMillan visited upon occasion.[24] Of A.T. Pierson he asserted from personal experience of hearing him speak on some occasion, testifying that he was an "outstanding teacher of the past generation" and "a great expositor."[25]

MacMillan also could have had contact with popular Methodist holiness leader George B. Watson, who later affiliated with the C&MA, when he spoke in Toronto in June 1896.[26] He had significant impact on MacMillan's life, for John later expanded upon Watson's idea of "throne power" and other holiness themes taught by Watson.[27]

One of the strongest spiritual influences on MacMillan's life was Jessie Penn-Lewis, a leader in the British Keswick movement and subsequently the overcomer movement. During her speaking tour of North America, she and her husband visited Toronto for a few days in August 1900, staying at the China Inland Mission home. Since the home was located just blocks from the

MacMillan residence, and John worked closely and cooperatively with the China Inland Mission in Chinese missions, it is possible that he first became acquainted with
Penn-Lewis and her ministry then.[28]

Penn-Lewis presented a teaching on "The Warfare with
Satan" at the China Inland Mission Convention in London in 1897, in which she heralded the concept of the believer's position in Christ according to Ephesians
1:20-22.[29] That same year A.B. Simpson also wrote about
the believer's position in Christ from the same text.[30]
MacMillan's classic book *The Authority of the Believer* is an
expanded exposition of this Scripture,[31] so either at this
time, or later, through the influence of Penn-Lewis and
Simpson, John MacMillan began to develop a strong consciousness of the believer's authority.

Sometime during his years in Canada, John MacMillan
attended a meeting in which Keswick speaker G.H.C.
Macgregor shared an experience of a personal revelation
from the Lord "which brought him to his feet as one
dead."[32] Although we do not know exactly what this revelation entailed, MacMillan recounts that he was awed by
the testimony. As a result, he gained an appreciation for
the genuineness of subjective supernatural experience in
the believer's life, though he also recognized the need for
objective balance as well. Keswick and higher-life meetings
could be both quietly reflective and also at times enthusi-
astic and emotional. So it was with John MacMillan.
While he ordinarily displayed a quiet, reverent demeanor,
he was also known on occasion to break out with a shout
of "Amen!" or "Hallelujah!"

MacMillan's Contact with the C&MA

We do not know when MacMillan first became familiar
with the ministry of A.B. Simpson and The Christian and

Missionary Alliance (C&MA), but with Simpson's Toronto Presbyterian connections it is quite possible that it occurred early in MacMillan's life. About 1889 the C&MA began to be organized as an interdenominational parachurch ministry in Toronto, emphasizing missions and the higher-life message of the fourfold gospel—Jesus Christ as Savior, Sanctifier, Healer and Coming King.[33] Simpson, a native Canadian, came to Toronto to preach twice a year for nearly twenty-five years, often preaching in Presbyterian churches,[34] so there could have been many opportunities for MacMillan to hear him speak. John recounted with fond memory some of what he periodically called the "thrilling" experiences of Alliance meetings in which A.B. Simpson was present:

> Those who have felt the "holy hush" and the consciousness of the divine presence in meetings where Dr. Simpson, and others of like spirit, were speaking, recall them as blessed memories. In a most real way, "Heaven came down our souls to greet," sinners were saved, saints were sanctified, and there was abounding joy. In a striking manner men felt that the "Dayspring from on high" had visited them. We praise God for the memory of such experiences.[35]

When MacMillan experienced the sanctifying baptism of the Spirit is not known, but he wrote much about the importance of this blessing from God. Buchanan mentioned that while his father attended Westminster Presbyterian Church, he had a "deep spiritual experience" which led to his overwhelming interest in missions. While a young businessman, he attended a missionary convention about the turn of the century, which MacMillan testifies changed his life.[36] This may have been the Dominion Convention, sponsored by the C&MA, which was hosted by Zion Congregational Church from 1902-1909, just blocks from the MacMillan home.[37] Simpson's Fourfold Gospel was presented at these conventions and could well have been the occasion of his baptism with the Spirit, often called in holiness circles the "crisis of sanctification."

Regardless of when it occurred, he considered the experience so vital that he later quoted R.A. Torrey, saying, "Now if those men [the apostles], with such exceptional training, were not allowed to enter upon their work until they had received the baptism with the Holy Spirit, should we dare to undertake that service until we have been so baptized?"[38]

Because the C&MA practices believer's baptism by immersion, we know that at some point in his Christian life he was immersed, but we do not know when. However, eventually he became convinced, as did fellow Presbyterian A.B. Simpson, that:

> The great weight of testimony holds that immersion is the original form. The disappearance of the candidate under the water and his re-emergence are regarded as symbolizing death and resurrection. . . . That view naturally invalidates the baptism of infants, who can have no share by the exercise of faith in the ceremony.[39]

Though MacMillan did not join an Alliance-affiliated church during these years, his missionary and deeper-life fervor would have put him in the same circle of association as several Alliance luminaries who frequently spoke in Toronto. Carrie Judd Montgomery, for instance, spoke at the Toronto C&MA convention at Parkdale Tabernacle in July 1910.[40] Her influence on MacMillan is evidenced by that fact that years later, as associate editor of *The Alliance Weekly*, he published articles by Montgomery, including one on his favorite subjects—spiritual warfare and discernment—in an article entitled "Witch-craft and Kindred Spirits."[41]

Sometime during this period MacMillan developed a friendship with pioneer Alliance missionary Robert Jaffray. Though Jaffray was born the same year as MacMillan and attended the same public schools in Toronto, it is unknown whether they ever met during childhood.[42] However, in 1903, a member of the Jaffray family joined Westminster Presbyterian, where MacMillan served as an elder, so the Jaffrays and the MacMillans were acquainted by then.[43]

MacMillan also became acquainted with A.W. Roffe, a district superintendent of the Alliance work in Canada (1919-1925), possibly after Roffe moved into the newly completed Missionary Rest Home, just west of Toronto, in February 1914.[44] He soon established a warm and enduring friendship with him, referring to him years later as "my kinsman."[45] This close relationship with Roffe may have been one reason MacMillan joined the C&MA mission in China. The two men continued to correspond while MacMillan was in China, and later served together on the C&MA Board of Managers.

Ministry as a Layman

In a missionary convention just after the turn of the century, perhaps even the same one as mentioned above, the treasurer of the missionary society in his annual report contrasted the total expense with the number of converts baptized on the mission fields, and estimated the cost of saving an unbeliever. MacMillan reminisced about himself and this experience, as he typically did in the third person:

> The idea fired the imagination of a young business man in attendance. Debarred himself from going to

the field, he determined to invest all that he could spare in the most priceless of all commodities—human souls. For a number of years he carefully kept a record of the probable number of those to whom his gifts had brought the saving message of life eternal. Later, the door to missionary service unexpectedly opened, and he gladly left his business and friends, and went forth to China. There he was blessed with a fruitful ministry, and was used to establish and extend the work. Afterwards, however, he acknowledged that the number visibly brought to the Lord by his personal efforts had not equalled those whom he had reckoned as saved through his offerings on the basis above mentioned.[46]

What an affirmation of the value of giving to missions!

Buchanan writes that his father planned to become a missionary to India but did not because of family responsibilities—in particular, his unmarried sisters. MacMillan believed that caring for one's family is a scriptural responsibility that supersedes a call to ministry. Years later he wrote:

How definitely the Lord urges the care of parents upon their children. It is a spiritual charge that cannot be laid aside. Yet not a few in our day say, "my responsibility to those who brought me forth is Corban; I have been called to the ministry of the Gospel, or to the mission field. This calling of God comes first." Brother, you have heard wrongly. Until parents and those who have a rightful claim of dependence upon you are provided for, you are chargeable before the Judgment Seat of Christ with their care. If He really has given you a commission abroad, He will make provision for them, and thus relieve you. But until then, wait; do not run ahead of His working.[47]

MacMillan put into practice what he preached and God honored his patience and faithfulness years later. Since he could not go himself, he served on the home board of Gwalior Indian Mission for several years, and was active in ministry to the Chinese in Toronto. R.P. McKay, head of the Canadian Presbyterian Board of Missions, at one point asked MacMillan to go to central China to become business manager for the Presbyterian Chinese mission in Szechwan, but he had to decline once again due to his responsibilities. By 1904 (age thirty-one) he had become the general secretary of the Chinese Mission Work in Toronto. This was a position he would hold until 1922 when he prepared to sail for China with the C&MA.

MacMillan was very concerned and outspoken about the need for supporting missions. In the church where he was a member he reported on missions giving:

> A goodly sum had been contributed, but the average per member had not been high. In placing the figures before the congregation, it was pointed out that seven-tenths of the membership had not contributed at all. Thus the proportions of these had been met by the three-tenths who had recognized their obligations.[48]

Even though he was unable at that time to serve on the mission field overseas, he possessed a heart for missions, and continued to give generously, to encourage others to give and to promote evangelistic and Bible study ministry among the Chinese.

The Chinese work that John directed continued to bear fruit. In 1910 MacMillan reported that seventeen classes were meeting and that seven men had been baptized during the year. By 1920 the work had grown to twenty-six schools with eighteen baptisms that year.[49]

John's diligent and capable leadership was demonstrated in the great expansion of the ministry.

While working among the Chinese, MacMillan was concerned about the creeping disease of the social gospel, which watered down the message of salvation. Once he was approached by a YMCA leader about working together in educating the Chinese. MacMillan told the official, "We are seeking to evangelize these Chinese—your object is to Canadianize them." The official responded, "There is no difference." MacMillan commented on this later, "In the same way, the average social worker seems unable to discern the gap between educating a moral pervert, and bringing to him the saving gospel of Jesus."[50]

As a layman, MacMillan openly shared the gospel with businessmen in Canada. He gave a Jewish business leader a booklet entitled "The Day of Atonement—and No Atonement" and asked him, "How is it that you Jews have for nineteen hundred years observed the Day of Atonement without any sacrifice?"

"I have sacrificed," he retorted. "From before sunrise till after sunset, I touch neither food nor drink."

MacMillan responded, "Granting that to be a sacrifice for you, or at least an act of self-denial, it does not meet the demand of the Law." The man acknowledged this, and he listened thoughtfully as MacMillan read to him Isaiah 53 of the sacrifice made by the Messiah to provide for redemption.[51]

On another occasion he visited the store of a Jewish businessman and gave him a copy of a Christian paper. The businessman accepted it, asking, "You Christians believe that Jesus is coming back again, do you not?" When MacMillan replied, "Yes," the man responded eagerly, "Tell me about it." For more than two hours MacMillan shared with him from the Old Testament Scriptures of the prophets regarding the coming of Jesus as the Messiah.[52]

MacMillan especially enjoyed making evangelistic contacts with Jewish people. He learned Hebrew and studied rabbinic literature to open doors for witness. A Jewish mission was located in Toronto, so it is possible that he assisted with their work as well.[53] On one occasion, after MacMillan had spoken in Toronto at a "Home for Aged Women" on Isaiah 53, he engaged in a conversation with an eighty-four-year-old blind woman, the daughter of a London rabbi. She remarked sincerely and earnestly, "Oh! I wish I could believe as you do!"

MacMillan asked, "What is your difficulty?"

She replied, "Our rabbis tell us, sir, that the Servant spoken of in this chapter is not a person at all, but our nation, Israel."

He answered, "It is true that in some places Israel is spoken of as Jehovah's servant. But the nation is never called by God, 'my righteous servant,' as here (Isaiah 53:11). Israel never deserved that title, but rather that of 'stiff-necked and rebellious.' Only of the coming one was the title 'righteous' true." He observed that she was "hungry for peace" and "acknowledged the truth of the remarks and seemed deeply interested, but she was hindered by her friends from hearing more of the Word."[54]

Even though he was a layman, John MacMillan nonetheless participated in city union ministerial meetings. One such meeting discussed physical healing, arguing the pros and cons. One denominational minister summed up the tenor of the discussion by stating, "We all need to have more faith in God." As a Presbyterian elder, MacMillan himself came to believe that elders of the church were to lay hands on the sick and anoint them with oil in faith, according to James 5:14-15,[55] likely influenced by the preaching of A.B. Simpson.

MacMillan was always alert to opportunities to share spiritual truth and relate it to everyday life. In discussing Deuteronomy 11:20, which speaks of writing the words of God on the doorposts of one's house, MacMillan gave a practical application of this verse from his ministry in Canada: "On one occasion, at a summer camp, a young French Catholic asked [me], with some wonderment, regarding Scripture texts which had been placed upon the wall. These formed a testimony to the truth, and an opening for conversation."[56]

He also related another insightful story about a young European student in a Canadian theological college who, when reading the King James Version of Romans 8:1, commented, "There is something wrong; that last clause should not be there."

The professor responded, "You are right; it is an insertion, and does not appear in the earlier manuscripts. But why have you asked the question?"

The student answered, "Because it is not in accord with the teaching of the apostle in the chapters which go before. Paul tells us earlier in this epistle that we are justified freely through God's grace, by the redemption which is in Christ Jesus. Our walk follows our being justified, but it has nothing to do with our justification."[57]

MacMillan's comments on this incident reflect his emphasis on spiritual understanding and discernment:

> His spiritual insight detected what most of us pass over without thought. Not many who peruse the Word are as quick to discern the inner meaning of what is written as was this young European, who was studying in a strange land and in a strange language. But his heart was open to the promptings of

the Spirit, and his mind had grasped the spiritual fulness of redemption in all its richness and completeness and power.[58]

Sometime during his ministry in Canada, though we do not know when, MacMillan first encountered demonic forces. He writes,

We recall a well-known Methodist minister in Toronto, who claimed that he could communicate with his deceased wife, who would come to him in his study, and with whom he would have at such times full freedom of communication. But the invariable end of such contact is the entangling of the seeker in the coils of demonism.[59]

He was also strongly influenced by the writings of British scholar George Pember on spiritualism and the occult. Pember's book, *Earth's Earliest Ages and Their Connection with Modern Spiritualism and Theosophy*, originally published in the late nineteenth century, was reprinted in Toronto about 1909, so it is possible that MacMillan was familiar with his work by then, if not earlier.[60]

It is apparent that John MacMillan comprehended the priesthood of the believer as a young adult. He understood that though a layman, he had a strong consciousness of his call to minister and he exercised that ministry widely and extensively. Lack of clergy ordination or opportunity for full-time ministry did not hold him back. Years later he would write: "The genuine anointing of the Holy Ghost bestows an authority for ministry that can be conferred by the hands of no bishop. . . . No human hands can authorize or commission to the work of the ministry, save where the Spirit of God has Himself endued with power and with suitable gifts."[61] Again he wrote of the importance of the call of God:

To every pastor and preacher who would speak with authority to men there must come a time in his ministry when the consciousness of his call from God is the most definite of all experiences, when he fully realizes that he belongs to Him by purchase and by personal surrender, when he acknowledges himself to be in truth "the bondslave of Jesus Christ," with no will or desire save to serve Him in obedience.

By such a messenger "the whole counsel of God" cannot but be spoken. It is part of his very being. The burden of it lies heavy on his heart: "Woe is me if I preach not the gospel." He feels an inescapable responsibility to God and to men. The souls of his fellows he realizes to be in his keeping. But, while it is a burden, it is also a delight, for he is a servant of Christ and rejoices in ministry for Him.[62]

As a result of his own experience and ministry, he did not denigrate the role of a lay person, but acknowledged that every believer is called of God to minister and has a valuable purpose in the plans of God:

Simon [Peter] had placed his all at the disposal of the Preacher. . . . This is what the Saviour is seeking from all His saved ones. The desk of the businessman, the bench of the worker, the kitchen of the housewife—all these, like the fishing boat of Simon, may become places from which Christ can address the lost. We know some of such people through whose offices and workshops and homes the Master speaks daily to all and sundry who draw near. Many of the hearers would receive the message in no other way if this opening were unavailable.[63]

Buchanan summed up the nature of his father's spiritual development and ministry with this tribute:

He was constantly active in the Lord's work in a variety of ways. He developed a virile, strong, disci-

plined, consistent Christian character that I have
never seen surpassed, and rarely equalled. . . . His
discipline was tempered with a rare degree of Christ-
like gentleness and sympathetic insight that won
him an ever-widening circle of friends, and of those
who harbored a deep sense of admiration and gratitude for his understanding and spiritual counsel.

THREE

Isabel Robson—
A Divine Match

THOUGH JOHN MACMILLAN ENJOYED a vibrant ministry as a single layman, the Lord had more in store for him. Part of God's sovereign plan included a helpmate for John, one that shared his heart for reaching the Chinese.

Isabella Agnes Robson (also known as Belle or Isabel) was born August 14, 1872 (or 1873), in Ontario.[1] She was the third of five children of Thomas Robson and Katherine McRea. Like John MacMillan, she came from a noble Scottish heritage (or, as her son Buchanan put it, "sprang from sturdy Border stock") and was nurtured in a strong Christian home. Known affectionately as "Tibbie" to her father, she grew up in the Presbyterian church and committed her life to Jesus Christ in May 1885. Her love for children was demonstrated through a six-year ministry as a Sunday school teacher.

When she moved to Toronto, she became a member of Central Presbyterian Church, whose pastor, Dr. D. McTavish, was a friend of A.B. Simpson.[2] She assisted with the Chinese Christian work in Toronto as a young woman. She also received training as a nurse and served ten months in that capacity in Toronto before leaving for China as a missionary.

Isabel undoubtedly became acquainted with The Christian and Missionary Alliance when Simpson spoke at a missionary conference at Central Presbyterian in January 1895. This was the same year she left for China with the China Inland Mission (CIM), now known as OMF International. It is possible that in China Isabel became acquainted with missionaries such as Dr. R.H. Glover (who later became foreign secretary of the C&MA), Robert Jaffray and Jonathan Goforth, since they were Canadian Presbyterians from Toronto like herself, and the C&MA, CIM and Presbyterian missions in China all worked cooperatively.[3]

The December 1895 issue of *China's Millions* in Toronto featured a photo of Isabel and six other female missionaries who left for Shanghai in October.[4] She quickly fell in love with the Chinese people, especially the children. In May 1896 Isabel wrote from the island community of Ta-ku-t'ang (Chinese for "the big maiden mountain"),[5] in Kiang-Si province, where she was teaching school children and women's classes and dispensing medical care:

> Each Sunday afternoon I take the little ones and endeavour to teach them something. It is the first step, and I long to be able to do more. Nearly every day since coming here I have had one or two patients, and sometimes more, with sore eyes, abscesses, etc. Mr. Yao, the evangelist, or Mrs. Cameron, talk to the patients about Jesus, either whilst I dress their sores or afterwards. Many of these people come from villages round about.

She also expressed a burden for lost souls and a yearning for a deeper Christian life:

> The most zealous of these idol-worshipers must
> feel an empty, aching void in their hearts. Oh! That
> they knew in truth that none but Christ can satisfy.
> He has taught me a little of the "depths of the
> riches," that I had but tasted in the homeland. Mrs.
> Cameron and I have been feeling lately that the "be-
> ginning of days" has come for Ta-ku-t'ang, and our
> hearts are full of praise.[6]

By the summer of 1897 this young woman had proven
herself not only faithful, but capable of leadership. She
was put in charge of the mission station at Ta-ku-t'ang
with a native evangelist working under her guidance
among the raftsmen and boatmen.[7]

Isabel's ministry in China undoubtedly included repeated contact with the deeply respected founder of CIM,
J. Hudson Taylor. Though he was aging, he actively continued to oversee the ministry. In January 1899, however,
Taylor developed influenza which progressed into bron-
chitis in February. He made some recovery, but was still so
ill with incapacitating headaches and dysentery that he
and his wife Jennie left for CIM's coastal health station at
Chefoo on May 24 to spend the summer recuperating.

Isabel and two other woman missionaries accompanied
the Taylors to Chefoo. Since Isabel was trained in medicine, she may have served as the elderly missionary's personal nurse during his convalescence. In spite of his poor
health, Taylor spent long hours in prayer during that summer,[8] giving Isabel the opportunity to observe firsthand
the deep devotional life of this great man of God. The experience undoubtedly influenced her own devotional life,
which, in God's providence, contributed to the ministry of
her future husband and his emphasis on prayer.

Isabel experienced periods of danger during her ministry
in China. During the Boxer Rebellion of 1900 she was sta-

tioned in Ts'ing Kiang-Pu, a military center. The city of
Kao-Yiu broke out in rioting on June 25; other cities soon
followed. Isabel and the other missionaries were quickly
evacuated and sent to Shanghai, where they remained for
a few months until the danger had subsided.[9]

Isabel's China ministry was interrupted in 1905 by a
dangerous bout with typhoid, and she withdrew to the
sanatorium at Chefoo for convalescence. When even the
refreshing climate of Chefoo was not a sufficient tonic, she
departed for North America in the fall of 1906.[10] As a result of her illness she lost much of her beautiful hair, but
after her recovery, Buchanan was told, she "retained her
extraordinarily young appearance, for in her early forties
she looked nearly thirty, without a line in her face."

It is disappointing to be forced to abandon a ministry
due to failing health, and Isabel may have wondered why
the Lord did not choose to heal her while she was in
China. But God, who causes all things to work together
for good, had other plans in mind. The divine chess Master, who knows the plays of life from beginning to end,
was maneuvering circumstances *in* her life to fulfill His
greater purposes *for* her life.

After her recovery Isabel was appointed "missionary on
the home staff," and became the Canadian editor of
China's Millions magazine in Toronto.[11] In this role, she
was in charge of the editorial work, along with preparing
the magazine and its mailings. Her service of more than a
decade on the field and her day-to-day contact with Hudson Taylor and others in CIM made her well suited to the
job. Under her editorship, *China's Millions* featured missionary reports, testimonies, articles about holiness and
Christian living and stories about evangelism, revival,
healings and spiritual warfare, on the mission field and on
the home front.

Whether John MacMillan and Isabel Robson became acquainted before she went to China is unknown, but it is certain that they knew each other soon after her return, since their paths crossed so often. John's company, Armac Press, served as the printer for *China's Millions*. The headquarters of CIM was just half a block from the MacMillan home. Isabel worked with Chinese women in Toronto and John also labored among the Chinese through evangelism, Bible classes, counseling and meeting physical needs. Their common passion for Chinese ministry, combined with frequent contact as neighbors and business colleagues, fostered a romance which blossomed over several years.

Isabel may have even played a role in stirring John's interest in spiritual warfare and deliverance. An editorial written in *China's Millions* in June 1907, probably by Isabel, refers to the need to "try the spirits whether they are of God" (1 John 4:1), advocating the use of this passage of Scripture to test the spirits.[12] John would later make that scriptural test a cornerstone of his ministry of discernment in spiritual warfare. In addition, Isabel included two deliverance articles in the September 1908 issue of *China's Millions*, including one by three Alliance missionaries entitled "Demon Possession," describing their ministry of discerning and casting out evil spirits.[13] These articles could have been read by MacMillan and piqued his interest.

It is possible that Isabel herself may have observed or participated in sessions of deliverance. She was certainly acquainted with the story of Pastor Hsi's ministry of exorcism, written by Hudson Taylor's daughter-in-law.[14] In addition, she could have been familiar with the ministry and writing of Presbyterian missionary John Nevius regarding demon possession. Interestingly, MacMillan makes reference to both Nevius and Pastor Hsi in his writings.[15]

On March 2, 1914, Isabel spoke to the Young Women's Mission Band of Westminster Presbyterian Church, John MacMillan's home church, on the work among the Chinese women in Canada. With a compassionate spirit, she related that

> . . . their lives are so isolated that they feel very, very lonely in their strange surroundings. The last few months it has been easier to get access to the homes. Previously the husbands were very suspicious and would not admit the workers. The visits made come under three classes, visits for instruction, friendly visits, and sick visits. Our prayers were asked for the many boys who are here some without their mothers and for the mothers who feel so lonely here, particularly when there is sickness or death in the family.[16]

Her love for the Chinese had not abated, but had grown with added concern for the plight of the women.

During this time John and Isabel's hearts had knit into one, for just a few days after this address, John wrote a letter to Isabel's father, informing him of their intention to marry. We may smile at the formality of MacMillan's letter, but it was typical of his personality and writing:

> When one receives, from a total stranger, a letter couched in a familiar tone, he naturally wonders whether to be trustful, or to suspect that he is the object of a confidence game. . . . The only fact upon which I can fully rely as constituting a claim to your favour, is that your daughter (she said that you would recognize her best by the name of "Tibbie") has, after due consideration, decided that the writer is a fit and proper person to be entrusted with the care of her future happiness. This will, doubtless, be a surprise to you—it was to me. But that the statement is correct

will be verified by herself, although she asked that I
should be the first to apprize you of it.[17]

John described his admiration of Isabel to her father in
these words: "Her many excellent qualities—of which
you are fully aware—her devotion, her mentality, her
amiability, combine to form a character of which the
writer is quite unworthy, though she has been generous
enough to think otherwise." Her warm, godly personality was recognized by all, and especially by John.

CIM leaders described her as exhibiting a "gentle,
self-denying, gracious character."[18] After her death, an *Alliance Weekly* article characterized her as manifesting a
"singularly beautiful life. She possessed in a rare degree
the art of making friends, but there was no motive save
that they might know the Lord better. She dwelt deep in
the secret place of God, and walked humbly before
Him."[19] John MacMillan maintained later, "if I ever displeased her, she never let me know." Buchanan recalled
that "she was extraordinarily cheerful and exceedingly gracious and free from malice of any kind. She had the widest
intellect and sympathy, and a deep, natural and unaf-
fected spiritual life. A relative once remarked that she was
the most nearly perfect woman he had ever known."

On August 26, 1914, John MacMillan and Isabella
Robson were married at the CIM headquarters in Toronto, half a block from the MacMillan home. *China's Millions* reported that it was one of the few wedding
ceremonies that had ever occurred at a CIM home in
North America.[20] The joining together of John and Isabel
in marriage aptly fulfilled the words of Ecclesiastes 4:9:
"Two are better than one, because they have a good return
for their work" (NIV). Buchanan remarked of his parents
decades later in retrospect, "Theirs was an extraordinarily
close and rich union, entered into by unusually mature

parties—mature both in years and character. Both lived very close to Christ. I fear that only in later years, after my mother had been taken from us, did I fully realize the spiritual climate into which I had been born."

At this time Isabel left her position as editor of *China's Millions*. The magazine remarked at her parting,

> She has labored with great interest and zeal in its production, and, as its readers know, with marked success. It may be said that it is a difficult matter for many reasons to edit a missionary magazine. But Miss Robson has prayed and worked her way through all difficulties, to the blessing of many readers.[21]

Isabel's change in marital status did not discontinue her ministry to Chinese women, however; in fact, she appears to have expanded her concern to include immigrants from other countries as well. In February 1915 the new Mrs. MacMillan addressed Westminster's Young Women's Missionary Band once again, this time speaking on "The Importance of the Child." She shared from her heart about needy children in North America and other countries, and also described the ministry to Jewish children at the Christian synagogue in Toronto. Isabel rounded out her talk by referring to the writing of Amy Carmichael, entitled *Lotus Buds*, describing ministry with the children of India.[22] (Carmichael had contact with CIM prior to launching her own ministry in India.)

Within a few months after their marriage, Mr. and Mrs. MacMillan relocated to the east side of the Don Valley of Toronto, to a house with a beautiful southwestward view of the valley and the city. Their only child, John Buchanan (known as J. Buchanan or J.B.), was born in that house on December 4, 1915, and said of those early years, "My earliest recollections are, for the most part, of happy events. . . . I still recall the delight of watching a family of robins from the building of a nest to the flight of the young in a crotch of the tree outside our second-story bedroom window." Just a few houses away ran a streetcar, which Buchanan loved to watch go by.

In March of 1916 the MacMillans transferred their membership to St. John's Presbyterian Church, just a few blocks south.[23] Buchanan's earliest remembrances of church were at St. John's. Founded by Pastor McPherson Scott, St. John's was noted for its strong missions emphasis. The church had been involved with A.B. Simpson and the C&MA as early as 1895 when Simpson spoke at Central Presbyterian Church,[24] so it was natural for the MacMillans to be drawn to this active congregation.

Long-time member Lloyd Robertson recalls from his boyhood seeing the entire church packed with hundreds of people and the balcony filled. While he did not know the MacMillans personally, he does remember seeing their picture on a wall with photos of other missionaries from St. John's.[25] In light of the MacMillans' call to Asia with the Alliance, it is significant that today St. John's Presbyterian Church borders on an Asian section of Toronto. It is also both fitting and providential that St. John's Church today is the meeting place of the Vietnamese Alliance Church. It would please the MacMillans to see that their home church was host to the Far Eastern peoples they loved so much and the organization under which they served so diligently.

John was inducted as an elder at St. John's and continued to serve through 1922. He had accepted the eldership with the understanding that he would not be able to "take charge of an elder's district" due to his busy involvement with the Chinese ministry in the city.[27] The

demands of his work with immigrants also led to his frequent abscences at session meetings.

Isabel continued in visitation and counseling ministry
to the Chinese women, and also taught a Chinese
women's Sunday school class at Knox Presbyterian
Church as of 1921. Robert Jaffray's wife, with whom
Isabel was acquainted, also spoke at Knox in 1921 regarding the ministry of the C&MA among the Chinese.[27] Both
the C&MA and Knox Presbyterian were also involved in
Jewish missions in Toronto, another ministry interest of
John and Isabel.[28]

The earliest recorded instance of MacMillan's exercise
of his authority as a believer occurred some time during
this period when Buchanan was a young child. An urgent
message came to John at Armac Press that the house
next door to his was on fire. Calmly, "he committed the
crisis to God in prayer, claiming divine protection according to Psalm 91:10 that 'no destruction would befall
the house.' " He drove home to find that the fire had miraculously stopped at a wooden fence that separated the
two houses.[29] About two decades later, he wrote out of
his own proven experience about the authority of claiming divine protection from Psalm 91:

> True it is that the angel of the Lord encamps
> round about them that fear Him, with a view to
> their deliverance. But the child of God is personally
> responsible for the definite claiming of such protec-
> tion, and also for abiding within the circumscribed
> limits wherein it is effective.
>
> Faith is the channel along which the grace of God
> flows, consequently, there is the necessity for main-
> taining a constantly victorious spirit over all the
> wiles and the attacks of the enemy. . . . More and
> more, therefore, it is vital that every true servant of
> God learn the secret of dwelling "in the secret place

of the Most High," thereby in all the going out and coming of life, experiencing the security of those who "abide under the shadow of Shaddai."[30]

Another development in MacMillan's understanding of the authority of the believer emerged in 1921. Jessie Penn-Lewis published a booklet entitled *Prayer and Evangelism*, in which she explained how to exercise the authority of binding and loosing.[31] MacMillan, who was fond of her writings, could have read her booklet at this time, for he was certainly practicing the principles set forth in it by the time he ministered in China. He became so impressed with this particular booklet that twice as associate editor of *The Alliance Weekly* (1937 and 1941) he reproduced a portion of this booklet as articles entitled "How to Pray for Missionaries."[32]

MacMillan recalled hearing Paul Rader, pastor of Moody Memorial Church and successor to A.B. Simpson as President of the C&MA, speak on several occasions.[33] In 1918 he appealed for funds to reach 230 million unevangelized Chinese. The goal of $22,000 was more than doubled with a total of $47,176 raised (more than $500,000 by today's standards). This was the largest missionary offering to that point in Toronto's history.[34] John and Isabel must have been thrilled to see the response to evangelizing the people that they cared about so much.

In June 1919 Robert Jaffray and Paul Rader, newly installed as Vice President of the C&MA, spoke at the Toronto Mission Convention. *The Alliance Weekly* reported, "A committee of prominent business men, together with Revs. MacArthur and H. L. Stephens, were in charge of the arrangements."[35] Even though he was not officially a member of the C&MA at this point, MacMillan, with his keen interest in missions, could have been one of those businessmen.

MacMillan also became acquainted with the evangelistic and healing ministry of C&MA evangelists F.F. and
B.B. Bosworth. The Holy Spirit sparked revival through
their ministry in Toronto in 1921, and revitalized the
floundering C&MA work. C&MA historian Lindsay
Reynolds reports, "Everywhere people were talking about
the Bosworths, the Alliance and divine healing." One
newspaper reported,

> . . . hundreds sought healing from various ail-
> ments, and many remarkable cures, besides conver-
> sions, were witnessed. . . . In striking contrast with
> many evangelists who have visited Toronto, the
> preaching of evangelist Bosworth is characterized
> by an entire absence of sensationalism or any en-
> deavor to excite emotional outburst on the part of
> the hearers. He is a plain man and preaches the
> plain old-fashioned Gospel.[36]

In spring of 1922, Robert Jaffray was visiting Toronto
again. Paul Rader delivered the dedicatory sermon at the
newly organized Christie Street Alliance Tabernacle and
Jaffray "gave a stirring missionary address."[37] This time
Jaffray sat down for a heart-to-heart talk with John and
Isabel. He asked for the MacMillans to join the C&MA
work in South China, and urged John to take charge of the
publication work of the Alliance Press, which Jaffray himself had founded years earlier.[38] China was still in Isabel's
heart, and it must have been a great joy for her to be able
to return to her land of ministry when the opportunity
arose. For John it was a long-awaited fulfillment of his vision to serve on the mission field. This time nothing
blocked their way to China, and John's long-delayed
yearning to go to the Orient as a missionary was finally being fulfilled.

FOUR

Call to China

F OR THOSE WHO THINK midlife is too old to enter the ministry or go to the mission field, John MacMillan proved otherwise. Many who approach the age of fifty begin looking toward retirement. For MacMillan, however, that was the farthest thing from his mind. His greatest years of ministry were just beginning and would continue unabated for more than three decades.

MacMillan's work with the Chinese Bible Institute, combined with his printing and publishing experience, made his call to direct the publishing work of The Christian and Missionary Alliance in China an ideal and timely one. Isabel's ministry among the Chinese was also an integral part of that call. In God's plan and timing the two of them came together to fulfill God's will. What they were unable to accomplish individually, in God's purposes they achieved together.

Early Days in China

On January 11, 1923, under the joint auspices of the Women's Missionary Society and the Session of St. John's, a farewell reception was held for the MacMillans before they left for China.[1] Undoubtedly, it was a grand occasion with dozens of their friends and family saying their good-byes and sharing in the excitement of the adventure which lay ahead.

On January 16, John, Isabel and seven-year-old Buchanan left Toronto for China. Around this time John began keeping a personal journal, to which he periodically made entries until the day of his wife's death in 1928.[2] Graciously supplied by Jane MacMillan, it is a valuable resource for the history of the MacMillans' China (and their later Philippine) ministry. While much of the journal discusses routine activities of no great consequence or interest, it also provides many significant and meaningful glimpses into the life and ministry of the MacMillans during this time. Without it we would have only a limited picture of their missionary experience.

The family's first port of call was Japan, where they visited with missionaries and toured the country for a few days, stopping to see the famous Asakusa Shrine. John was dismayed to learn that Japanese Buddhists boasted of more than 100,000 temples, with 40,000 pilgrims a day worshiping at this shrine alone. His heart was burdened for the thousands of lost souls, yet he rejoiced in the opportunity to speak with a young Japanese believer who, when questioned about the resurrection, replied, "I know that the Lord rose again, because He has risen again in my heart."[3]

They arrived at Wuchow, South China, on March 1. John began ministry immediately, addressing the Bible school students two days later at the opening of their fall session. The next morning he preached at the Sunday worship service to a congregation of nearly 500. The following day he was asked to teach classes in the Bible school twice a week on Old Testament prophecy. Isabel soon became involved with teaching in the girls' school.

While Isabel was conversant in Chinese, John was not. He struggled with language study, becoming discouraged at first. Only a week later, however, he was more positive about his progress, so that by March 17, he wrote, "Have had more fellowship with the Lord, and victory the past few days, than since I left Toronto." Still, during most of his ministry in China, he used an interpreter.

MacMillan battled with physical illness and discouragement for some time after his arrival. Such difficulties could have kept him down, but he would not allow it, and sought to gain victory daily. Much of his discouragement resulted from his penchant for discipline and structure in his work and study habits. So highly did he value efficiency that he sometimes became frustrated, even depressed, if he did not have a productive day, as evidenced from entries in his diary:

> March 6, 1923—Have accomplished very little all day.

> March 22, 1923—Three weeks ago today we reached Wuchow—what is accomplished hardly is creditable for so much time.

While he was anxious to get on with the work, he demonstrated in these early days the balanced life he had learned, and made time for relaxation and enjoyment. He engaged in a hobby (photography), played tennis with Robert Jaffray and spent time reading *The Scottish Chiefs* to Buchanan. Still, it was probably hard for such a results-oriented man to relax when he was so disappointed with his level of accomplishment.

MacMillan soon began to see the spiritual battle behind his tendency toward discouragement, which showed that he was already quite aware of the authority of the believer in this early stage of his professional ministry. It is evident that by 1923 he had been immersed in teaching about the believer's redemption rights taught by A.B. Simpson and others in the C&MA and the Higher Life movement.

In the first month of his ministry in China he declared to himself on a day of discouragement, "Discouragement and depression are of the devil. Good cheer and victory are the right of those in Christ." A journal entry in May alludes to one of his favorite Scriptures, Psalm 91: "Unpleasant rumours afloat, but we are safe in God's secret place." In June he preached, obviously out of his own experience, on "boldness with God" in prayer. The concept that believers have covenant rights with God and walk in authority over the enemy had become deep seated in MacMillan's mind and heart. It inherently affected his everyday attitude and behavior.

MacMillan's chief responsibility was to oversee the work of the printery. He remarked regarding his work, "[I] am becoming more impressed with the splendid work being done through the literature being printed and disseminated to all parts of the world. May it increase tenfold by the blessing of God!" A year later Jaffray reported in his annual foreign report on the progress of MacMillan's publication work:

> The silent messengers that go forth from our presses to all parts of this great land of China, and to the Chinese scattered abroad, represent a ministry of far-reaching effect. The Gospel leaflets and the Gospel calendar have been circulated by tens of thousands. The tracts and books exhorting and encouraging the Chinese Christian as well as the larger

volumes, "Expositions of the Books of the Bible," and the regular issues of *The Bible Magazine* are all doing a quiet, secret work in the hearts of men. May the living seed fall into many hearts and bring forth fruit to His praise and glory.[4]

Within four months, he had proven himself in ministry and was ordained by the C&MA executive committee in China (a committee he later served on himself). A year after his ordination he and Isabel were honored as senior members of the missionary team, and he was asked to manage the Bible school as well as the publication work. Though pleased with the appointment, he was also concerned, in his typical selfless manner, that other veteran missionaries might be offended because he was a relative newcomer.

In August of their first year in China, John and Isabel faced the common but distressing experience of many missionary parents: sending their child to boarding school. They enrolled Buchanan in the CIM school in Chefoo, hundreds of miles away.

Their contact with the school allowed Isabel to renew acquaintances with her former CIM coworkers and helped to reassure the MacMillans that Buchanan would be well taken care of. Still, they agonized over the separation many times in the coming years. Due to distance and financial circumstances, it turned out that John was not able to see him for nearly a year. When they heard that Buchanan was sick with scarlet fever, or having trouble getting along with his classmates, or struggling with his studies, they yearned to be with him.

On one occasion, while at home during a break from classes, he begged them with tears not to send him back to school. It must have broken John's and Isabel's hearts to send him away. Deeply troubled, MacMillan sought the Lord in prayer about this. The peace of the Lord swept into his heart and gave him a sweet assurance that God would undertake for his young son. He remarked in his journal, "The Lord's assurance regarding keeping him is very real and gives one perfect peace. Though I would give much to see him also." Two months later he wrote, "News concerning Buchanan has not been cheering, but we are resting on the covenant." He had a strong sense that trusting God for his children was the right and privilege of the believer through the covenant. He had confidence in the covenant-keeping power of God. God indeed heard and answered John's prayers for his son and molded him into a fine man of God who became a distinguished professor of music at Nyack College.

Memorable Episodes

MacMillan's writings are peppered with the many notable experiences he had during his ministry in China, and he often used these stories to convey spiritual truth. Passing along the narrow mountain footpaths of South China in the darkness of night, under convoy of native soldiers, MacMillan observed that Chinese paper lanterns were held by the soldiers suspended from the end of a bamboo pole, close to the ground. This reminded him of Psalm 119:105: "Thy word is a lamp unto my feet, and a light unto my path." He commented,

> The illumination was not bright, but it was ample and steady. Inequalities (iniquities) in the way were revealed, and avoided; crossroads (transgressions) detected and passed by; and we arrived at our destination without missing the mark (sin). Had the light been wanting, we would have stumbled many times, and perhaps rolled to death down the steep hillside into the river.[5]

Making reference to Mary's anointing of the feet of Jesus, he remarked, "It is not an unusual custom in the East to have ointment put on the guests as they arrive. In China the writer has been handed a napkin soaked in perfume, wherewith to bathe his face and hands as he came to a native supper, the same being done to all the guests."[6] On another occasion, while visiting Columbo, Ceylon, MacMillan desired to enter a new Buddhist temple in order to view paintings depicting the life of Gautama Buddha. The officiating priest greeted him cordially, but insisted that he take off his shoes before entering. MacMillan noted that this was an ancient biblical injunction for entering holy ground (Exodus 3:5).[7]

In spite of its religious significance, he apparently did not consider it displeasing to God to acquiesce to this request. He may have considered it similar to Paul's attitude toward eating meat offered to idols. Through these and many other illustrations, in his messages and his writings MacMillan sought to bring the Scripture alive and relevant to modern-day life.

Although MacMillan was a seasoned and successful businessman, he had to learn how to do business the Far Eastern way:

> "Talking price" is the actual term used in China for the bargaining between people, and the results are at times amazing to the Westerner. On one occasion in South China, it was necessary to rent two native boats for a trip up a river to a city some 350 miles away. Two boat owners were brought by the mission's business agent to the Alliance Home in Wuchow. For some hours they discussed the problem of cost. One thousand native silver dollars was the amount asked, which was a bit excessive. After returning the next day, the owners accepted the sum

of ninety dollars in full satisfaction of the rent of
their boats and their own work on the trip.[8]

He also discovered that the Chinese people were quite
superstitious. He had arranged to take passage on a
riverboat at 8 a.m. on the date of the Chinese New Year.
With characteristic diligence, MacMillan arrived at 7 a.m.
to be sure he would not be late. The boat owners, however,
had consulted with fortune-tellers, who advised them that
the hour of 6 a.m. was luckier—so even though he arrived
an hour early, the boat had already gone![9]

Another example of such superstition was related by
MacMillan as follows:

> Once in China, when excessive rains were causing
> damage, we saw the idols brought out of their tem-
> ples and placed where they might view for them-
> selves the loss to their worshipers. But these were
> heathen people, who took the idea of a supreme be-
> ing seriously. They were untouched by the increas-
> ing latter-day philosophy which declares that "all
> things continue as they were from the beginning of
> the creation" (2 Peter 3:4).[10]

MacMillan explained the origin of such Chinese beliefs:

> The worship of evil spirits, called generally ani-
> mism, is frequently separated from visible and mate-
> rial representations of the objects of devotion.
> Demons may take as their abode huge old trees,
> rocks, caves, streams, etc., and cause the people to
> worship them there. What missionary has not come
> across altars reared at the foot of some ancient ban-
> yan tree, upon which sheaves of incense lifted smoky
> fingers in silent appeal to the dreaded spirits which
> inhabited it? Or, at the crossings of streams, inserted
> in the ground, will be found a few spears of incense,
> renewed as one traveller after another seeks to propi-

tiate the demon of the stream that he may be allowed
to cross unmolested. Great is the fear of these water
demons. We recall the case of an English sailor, who
fell into the West River at the City of Wuchow. No
foreigner was near, and as the unfortunate man swam
from sampan to sampan, trying to get help, he was
pushed back into the water by the superstitious na-
tives, until at last his strength was exhausted, and he
sank to his death in the swift current of the river.[11]

Conditions were often quite horrid in China, with grue-
some sights and frightening experiences. While walking to
the chapel one morning, John saw a dog digging up and
devouring the body of a child which had been buried in a
shallow grave. Another time, while on their way home
from window-shopping, the MacMillans noticed the body
of a man down in a valley partially eaten by dogs. Other
disconcerting events at the mission included a tiger loose
in the neighborhood, executions by the military and a
near-collision with another boat.

MacMillan also visited other C&MA mission stations
in China. While in North China, near Tibet, he developed
a life-long friendship with Robert Ekvall, missionary on
the Kansu-Tibetan border. Ekvall contributed several articles to *The Alliance Weekly* while MacMillan served as associate editor, including the poetic "Monologues from the
Chinese," which was later published in booklet form.[12]

Also while visiting northern China, he came in contact
with a missionary from another denomination whose faith
had been shaken by the overwhelming thought of millions
of Chinese going into eternity without Christ. The struggling missionary had given up his ministry and entered
into secular work, lamenting, "When I see the myriads of
souls about me, and realize that very few of these will ever
have opportunity of hearing the gospel, I cannot accept

the thought that they will suffer eternal loss. I do not know what to think or do. I have not the trust in God I had."

MacMillan, who had settled this same conflict in his own mind, advised him, "Brother, the problem of eternal punishment is something with which we have nothing to do. It belongs to the administration of an infinitely just God, who cannot do wrong, and whose love to the world has been fully vindicated. You and I have a commission to give the gospel to men, and have the enabling of the Holy Spirit to that end. It is ours to fulfil our ministry, and to leave the untouched millions to Him. All that concerns us is the question, 'Are we doing our utmost?' "[13]

Discouragement was often the lot of missionaries working in difficult circumstances with meager results for their efforts. While passing through Penang, MacMillan visited a missionary who told of the difficulty of evangelizing Muslims: "I have been in this district for upwards of forty years, and I know of only one convert from Mohammedanism in all that time. He was a boy in the household of a Presbyterian worker, and though baptized he had no testimony among his former co-religionists." MacMillan called the resurgence of Islam "a demoniacal rebirth," discerning that spiritual warfare was the key to breaking through such strongholds.[14]

On another occasion he counseled with another struggling missionary statesman who was facing opposition. He intimated to MacMillan, "Brother, I know how I could get rid of this constant trouble. If I would just surrender these plans, and cease going forward, Satan would leave me at peace." He recognized that those who press on to do the work of the Lord suffer the harassment of Satan. MacMillan knew well the same feelings and encouraged him to overcome by exercising his authority as a believer.[15]

MacMillan the Evangelist

MacMillan had a heart for souls and was the consummate evangelist, sharing his faith confidently and freely wherever he went. On his many trips up and down the rivers and coastal waters of China, he engaged in conversations with the ship's crew and passengers, steering the dialogue to spiritual issues. He had a way of diffusing an argument and transforming it into an opportunity for a positive witness.

One day, while traveling on a merchant ship, MacMillan struck up a conversation with the English captain, who remarked, "Padre, I think the Bible should be rewritten." Rather than argue, MacMillan countered with a question: "How would you go about to rewrite it, Captain?" The captain then disclaimed "any ability to undertake the task." As a result, MacMillan was able to turn the conversation around to give witness to the purpose and value of the Scriptures.[16] In another instance he silenced the arguments of an unbelieving captain by responding with Scripture—not in a preachy manner, but in an informal "chat."

MacMillan also practiced lifestyle evangelism, disarming opponents with his peaceable, congenial demeanor. One day, as he was passing through a city, a group of people called him "foreign devil," a common insult to Anglo-Saxons in China. He rejoined with a friendly wave of his hand. As a result, they smiled and waved back. In relating this incident, he commented, "Because the insult was overlooked, an understanding was arrived at. But so long as the representatives of each side have their hackles up, and are ready to snap back at the slightest fancied affront, there will be found plenty of causes of trouble."[17]

In another trip on one of the inland rivers of China, he struck up a conversation with the steamboat captain,

quoting the Scripture, "Except ye be converted, and become as little children, ye shall not enter into the kingdom
of heaven" (Matthew 18:3). A college professor was listening, and challenged MacMillan's interpretation of the
words. Not intimidated by the man's academic degrees,
MacMillan responded confidently and authoritatively,
"When a child is born into a home, he comes into a new
environment, and must learn all things from those about
him. In like manner, when a man is born into the kingdom
of heaven, he also enters a new environment, with which
he is wholly unfamiliar. He also must learn from the only
source of authentic information—in the Holy Scriptures."[18]

Captain Lossius of the *Chung On* was a leader among
the Christian Scientists. MacMillan boldly witnessed to
him, pointing out from the Scriptures "the absolute necessity of atonement by blood." His efforts at planting
seeds of the Word in the hearts of men bore immediate
and evident fruit on at least one occasion. In August
1924, while traveling from Wuchow to Shanghai on the
S.S. Wing-peng, MacMillan shared his faith with Captain
Malm, a Norwegian. As a result of his witness, the captain accepted Christ on the second night of the journey.
MacMillan kept up pastoral contact with Captain
Malm, dining with him and his wife and attending a
church service with them four months later.

In his ministry with the Chinese, his greatest soul-winning
endeavor came in April 1925, when he preached a series of
evangelistic meetings. On the first night twenty-four responded for salvation, the second night thirty-five, the third
night sixteen. Many days of intense and agonizing spiritual
warfare—more than three months—preceded this remarkable breakthrough. He was stirred in his heart by the response of Chinese hungry and thirsty for the truth of the

gospel: "We have seen the tears stealing down the face of a Chinese as he read the story of the Saviour on the cross, and heard him say, 'Every time I read this it makes me weep.' "[19] MacMillan's success in evangelism was birthed out of travailing and prevailing prayer—a life of spiritual warfare.

Spiritual Warfare in China

JOHN MACMILLAN WAS A man who continuously and earnestly sought more of God. He wrote in September 1923: "Soul longing for a deeper knowledge and experience of God." God rewarded his longing when a few days later, on October 5, a monthly day of prayer stirred hours of intercession. This was followed by a session of prayer beginning at 8 o'clock the next night, which lasted until 4:30 a.m. That marathon meeting turned into nightly intercession for more than six weeks. As a result, MacMillan recorded that "answers are coming fast," "the prayer spirit is widening" and revival was breaking out in the Bible schools.

He noticed that as he engaged in spiritual warfare he was personally experiencing oppression from Satan. At the same time revival broke out, a boy in the school manifested signs of demonization which defied deliverance for a time. Satan attacked on other fronts, as news arrived to John and Isabel that Buchanan, at the school in

Chefoo hundreds of miles away, had contracted scarlet fever. Three days later MacMillan received more hopeful news, and he cheerfully described the budding recovery in his characteristically poetic style, "Buchanan very bright; fever very slight."

By March of the following year, the revival had waned, and MacMillan was burdened about "the Satanic opposition now everywhere appearing in the Mission."

The Prayer Life of a Warrior

Spiritual warfare can only be conducted successfully when founded on close and frequent contact with the Commander-in-Chief. It was John MacMillan's habit to rise early in the morning, kneel in the presence of God, open his Bible and scan it prayerfully and thoughtfully. He often spent hours in prayer, sometimes arising at 5:30 a.m. One morning he rose before 7 a.m., but chided himself that it was too late. The next morning he awoke at 5:30 a.m. and spent an hour in prayer. John practiced fasting from time to time for protection, health and provision of financial needs. He was disinclined toward formality in prayer, regarding it as coldness of heart. Such prayer lacks intensity, he believed, and results in failure.[1]

At times he felt inadequate in his prayer life: "Am greatly impressed with need of prayerfulness, and one's own neglect. The Lord forgive and help to true faithfulness." At one point he confessed he was "exercised over coldness of heart for some time past." The next day he wrote, "The Lord pointed out this morning that I have been more exercised over my head than over my heart—a lesson which is very true."

After visiting a colony of lepers just after Christmas, he yearned for a greater exercise of faith: "Do we live full lives of faith? He said not that healing power should pass away, but rather that greater power should be manifest *because* He had ascended. We do not see it—but it is His Word."

In February 1924, he was challenged as he read the biography of Praying Hyde, the Presbyterian missionary to India who spent hours on his knees. A few months later, after being burdened in prayer about the spiritual state of the Mission, he acknowledged, "One's own need, however, is still greater. . . . One longs exceedingly to be so bare before God." After sensing a lack of power and intensity in his own life, he responded, "Prayer is the remedy—seven times more prayer, as Andrew Murray said."

There were even times he felt like a failure in prayer. In February 1925, he had interceded for his wife, and she was healed, but the illness was transferred to him. He wrote remorsefully, "I am slow to learn. . . . [I] have failed, but abide in Him." Following that, his journal reflects many more "days of conflict, physical and mental":

> March 8—More victory than for long time past, together with assurance that the path ahead is upward. This is testified in many ways. But there is also the knowledge that the onward path will be one of battle. In Christ triumph is absolute, but I must fight and fight hard through the Spirit of God.
>
> March 15—The past week continued to bring hard fighting—but the result is victory.
>
> March 21—One notices a record for some weeks past of defined warfare. It still continues. I am not discouraged, although the pressure has continued with greater persistence than at almost any previous time. But the victory is certain, and the enemy's rout assured.
>
> March 24—On Sunday morning was greatly relieved, but yesterday again the warfare was on. Today is somewhat easier, praise God. . . . Lord, teach

me, having overcome all, to remain a victor on the
field. One conquers and reconquers, but so often
fails to maintain the position won. "That ye may be
able to stand against all the wiles of the devil," is the
exhortation. To maintain the ground won is the secret of success in warfare! What good to win if the
ground is perpetually regained by the foe? "More
than conquerors" is the Scriptural method and measure of success.

March 29—A week of prayer and watchings, also
of advance, but much ground remains to be possessed!

April 5—Have made more decided advances since
last Sunday. In body am better, in mind clearer; I
cannot say that in spirit I am changed greatly, for in
spirit I have had constant victory through all the depression, physical and mental.

April 11—In body am feeling less oppression, and
am stronger in many ways.

It is obvious that he regarded prayer in trial as spiritual
warfare. These battles were the turning point for a mo-
mentous breakthrough spiritually. The very next day began the great evangelistic harvest mentioned above. The
enemy had an inkling of what was on the horizon and attempted to wear down and overpower the man of God,
quenching the Spirit and foiling God's plans for reaping
a harvest of souls. John MacMillan did not succumb to
the pain and depression, but persevered to the saving of
many souls.

He recognized that the greater and more earnest the
prayer life, the greater and more vehement the warfare:
"Prayer has been with increasing intensity, and knowledge, but the way is contested every step." He regarded
these battles as opportunity to become "open for larger
service." His words proved to be prophetic about him-

self. Little did he know what larger service lay ahead for his ministry.

In spite of all his trials, MacMillan was a man of praise. Though he suffered bouts of depression, he would not let himself remain in that state. As with other classic faith and holiness leaders of his time, he believed it was important to make a positive confession in faith:

> April 4, 1926—Am strongly calling upon God for deliverance from the physical weakness which is upon me. And He surely will.
>
> April 6, 1926—Will record to God's praise that the physical weakness is much bettered. I feel it to be a matter of the spiritual will laying hold of the Divine promises and of the fulness of the Lord Jesus.
>
> May 11, 1926—Find physical oppression again severe, but I have the victory, and am looking for its manifestation.

In a particularly trying time he wrote: "Truly the enemy is active. Not only am I penniless at home, but now almost $500 in debt. My body also is attacked. But God giveth the Victory!" He would record candidly his struggle and the attacks of Satan, but he would almost always follow with a praise to the Lord or a confession of God's victory, even when not evident.

The humility and sincerity of MacMillan's spiritual walk is capsulized in his personal thoughts: "After more than 36 years of Christian experience . . . I am yet but a little child." Yet again he intimated, "Tonight [I] realize a new knowledge of Him. I seem to be beginning to be a disciple." He who had counseled and mentored others, who demonstrated depth and fervency of prayer, who exercised with great power the authority of the believer, yet felt he was but a novice in the Christian life. He was always learning and growing, always seeking more of God.

Exercising the Believer's Authority in Spiritual Warfare

MacMillan and the other missionaries frequently encountered demonic forces. In his journal, for example, on November 17, 1923, he makes mention of a demonized boy in the Chinese Bible school. On February. 22, 1924, he speaks of the wife of a Mr. Luk as having been demonized, then dramatically healed. He explained the spiritual climate among the Chinese:

> In Taoism and Spiritism we see not so much the efforts of spirits to possess men, but the desire of men to be possessed by spirits, and the yielding of their bodies to them voluntarily as their instruments.
>
> A Medium is a person who thus submits his or her body for the entrance of the evil spirit. When possession takes place, various manifestations may occur. The speaking appears to come from another personality distinct from the individual whose lips are being used. When consciousness returns to the medium there may be entire ignorance of what has been said.
>
> What is known as *fung-shui* is met with in every part of China. It is closely connected with Taoism. The expression refers to the spirits of the air and the water, those who preside over those elements. Pagodas are built in elevated places for the control of these spirits. Lucky days, lucky spots for burial or for building, etc., are determined by the priests in accord with certain methods of testing the fung-shui of a district. Much of the local feeling manifested against innovations like the railroad, the telegraph, mining, etc., were due to the fear of these spirits.
>
> That form of Buddhism, in Tibet, known as Lamaism, is peculiarly demonistic. William Christie, missionary to Kansu Tibetan border, told me that he has been at festivals where numbers of men and women come under the power of the demons, and are

strangely affected. Some jump up and down, others
are shaken violently, some go into trances. He has
seen several strong priests holding down by main
force a man who was foaming. Some are simply hys-
terical and laugh and cry. Some speak messages,
which may be rational or simply a jargon of tongues.
A case in his knowledge was that of one woman, the
wife of a Christian, who refused to submit herself to
her father-in-law. He cursed her by the gods. Afterwards, she would be often seized and thrown down
violently while carrying water, or doing other work.
She died, and the man married another, who received
the same curse, with the same results, and also died.
Later, the Christian took a pagan wife, and forsook
Christianity, when the trouble at once ceased.

Both in Japan and China there are notions concerning the superhuman power of the fox and the
badger, which are supposed to possess people, so that
they are said to be "possessed by a fox."[2]

Authority over Dishonest Business Dealings

About a year after arriving in China, MacMillan received some unsettling news from his attorney. Apparently the company that had agreed to take over the
mortgage payments on Armac Press had reneged on the
deal, leaving MacMillan with a debt which today would
amount to thousands of dollars. Once a prosperous businessman, he was now, through no fault of his own, a pau-
per.

The news of the debt was especially troubling to the
MacMillans because they had sought to practice the principles of George Mueller according to Romans 13:8, "Owe
no man any thing." MacMillan commented in his journal,
"I am now in debt, contrary to the Word, but I herewith
set my hand to it that God is true, and that He will provide

abundantly in all these things." The MacMillans continued to pray and believe for a resolution to the injustice.

At the end of March 1926 he received word that,
through the buyout of his preferential stock, all outstanding debts had been paid in full, in answer to three
years of persistent prayer. A lawsuit against him was attempted later, but was blocked in 1929. Speaking with
authority, MacMillan prophesied, "Vengeance is mine,
saith the Lord." Eventually the business went bankrupt.
Through MacMillan's application of the believer's authority, he was vindicated and the dishonest contract-
breakers suffered the judgment of God.[3]

Authority Over Illness

While MacMillan was one of the pioneers of exercising
spiritual authority, he was by no means the first. The early
Christian and Missionary Alliance had a strong conception of authority in prayer from its founder, A.B. Simpson.
One of the missionaries described Simpson's exercise of
spiritual authority in prayer:

> Many years ago, an effective worker in South
> China was suddenly stricken with the most virulent
> form of smallpox. No hope was held out for his re-
> covery. But in the homeland, during the night, Dr.
> Simpson himself, quite unaware of the circum-
> stances, was awakened with a mighty urge to pray
> for his friend. Taking hold of God, he wrestled until
> relief was given to his own spirit. Out on the field, at
> that same time, the healing power of God came
> down upon the weakened body of the sufferer. His
> wife, traveling by native boat to the place, with the
> expectation that he was already with the Lord, was
> met at the landing by her husband, wholly recov-
> ered from the dread disease.[4]

Frequently MacMillan wrote in his journal of satanic opposition and viewed sickness and depression as satanic oppression requiring warfare. In September 1924 an Asiatic cholera epidemic threatened the mission. MacMillan claimed Psalm 91:3, "Surely he shall deliver thee from the snare of the fowler, and from the noisome pestilence." He prayed, "May we be enabled to keep the Home 'in the secret place of the Most High and under the shadow of the Almighty.' " During the next month they endured some oppression of body and depression of mind, but they emerged victorious and received divine protection from the plague. By November 6 he was able to say, "[I] find personally some of my former vigor of mind returning, for which I praise the Lord, and take fresh courage."

Brother Beatty, a fellow missionary, came to visit the MacMillans one night, sick in body and feeling discouraged. After words of encouragement, John and Isabel laid hands on him and commanded his release. Beatty slept peacefully through the night and felt much better the next day. The next night Beatty then laid hands on John and prayed for the healing of the cold which had clung to him for several days.

On yet another occasion, just after leaving a building after having anointed another missionary, MacMillan slipped on an incline by a spring and painfully twisted his ankle on a stone. Placing his hands on the injured spot, as was his custom in prayer, he prayed for healing. He records that he received an instant answer to prayer—no sprain or swelling, just a bruise, and he gave God the glory.

Authority Over Depression

MacMillan believed that depression was often an attack of Satan, and experienced many such attacks throughout his ministry in China. He always praised God continually

for the victory, even when it was not manifest. His counsel
to himself and others was that "a more positive attitude of
resistance would avail." He narrates the following anecdote which occurred during his ministry there:

> A young missionary lady in China, living with two
> companions in a river port, was suddenly seized with
> intense depression. So great was the effect upon her
> that the older missionary in charge sent word to the
> field chairman that she must be removed as she was
> causing harm at the station. Accordingly she was sent
> to the headquarters, where much prayer was offered
> for her without result, save that her depression
> seemed to increase. The case came under the observa-
> tion of the writer, who spoke strongly to her, saying,
> "Miss _____, you are doing wrong in keeping up this
> continued blueness of spirit; I want to tell you that all
> depression is of the devil." The words shocked her, as
> hitherto she had been petted and nursed with tender-
> ness by all in the headquarters. She showed her re-
> sentment, which was a most hopeful sign. He
> repeated his words; pointed out that the Lord com-
> mands all of His followers to rejoice in Him; some-
> thing she was disobeying. Then he indicated that her
> condition was due to her yielding to the lies of the en-
> emy, and that she must resist the devil. In a surpris-
> ingly short time she was back in her station, equipped
> this time to discern the attacks of the devil and to
> throw them off.[5]

Claiming Land for Jesus

C&MA minister-at-large Paul Valentine recalls hearing
MacMillan and Dr. Thomas Moseley, President of Nyack
College and a former missionary to Tibet, speak about supernatural experiences of spiritual warfare in China. One
such account they shared was that the C&MA missionaries would claim land from demonic control in Tibet and

bind the powers of darkness. On a certain occasion, the missionaries took possession of a piece of land and began moving logs. The evil spirits resisted the takeover by projecting a supernatural voice from a log. The voice in the log threatened, "Don't you dare move it!" The missionaries were not taken aback, but rebuked the voice. They then removed the log without any further incident and gained the victory over the dark powers.[6]

Binding and Loosing

Binding and loosing, taught and practiced by A.B. Simpson, Jessie Penn-Lewis, Carrie Judd Montgomery, and others, was practiced on the mission field as a part of the authority of the believer.[7] Dr. Jaffray related to MacMillan an incident in which he and some other missionaries encountered unusual antagonism. They had made particular plans during private prayer meetings which appeared to be revealed to the opponents in some mysterious, supernatural way. They discerned that dark powers were responsible, counterfeiting the revelatory gifts of the Spirit. So they took the precaution in subsequent meetings by binding the enemy and establishing a prayer covering over each project. As a result, they overcame the obstinate interference and succeeded in completing the proposals.[8]

It is apparent that binding and loosing was practiced regularly by Alliance missionaries in China at this time. MacMillan records in his journal that they were "binding here and loosing there, but the work to be done is stupendous. Yet it can be done. Satan can be routed out of the strongholds where he is so deeply entrenched. One fears at times, when seeing the power we are given over him. Yet, if we 'dwell in the secret place of the Most High . . .' " He leaves the sentence uncompleted, assuming the answer.

Again he writes in his diary with deep insight, "Men, as God's mouthpieces, vary in value; not according to their ability, but according to the measure of their entire surrender. There are times, even today, when, like Elijah, we may say: 'There shall not . . . according to my word'—when our hearts, in full comprehension of God, bind and loose in definite power."

The most dramatic illustration of exercising the authority of binding and loosing occurred in 1924 when several missionaries were kidnapped. The story, as recorded in the book *Binding and Loosing*, is recounted here:

> On May 22, 1924, four missionaries, including Dr. Robert A. Jaffray along with two others of The Christian and Missionary Alliance and Rev. Rex Ray of the Southern Baptists, left Wuchow, China by boat. Their purpose was to effect a rescue of other missionaries in the besieged city of Kweilin. Although the countryside was confused and disordered to a degree challenging belief, they headed north on the Kwei Kiang river. Along the way to Kweilin, their boat, the *Roanoke*, was taken captive by pirates. When the missionaries were asked for booty, Jaffray as usual took over. He demanded to talk to their chief.
>
> "We are missionaries," he told the chieftain, "You have no right to ask toll of us. We receive offerings to help us with our work. Come now, be reasonable. Give us an offering and let us go." The sheer brass of the man had its effect as he knew it would.
>
> Back in Wuchow, J.A. MacMillan and the other missionaries received word of the situation on May 26. On May 29, they received a wire to the effect that Jaffray and another missionary, Dr. Harry C. Mills, had been released in order to press, the robbers hoped, the ransom demands.

On June 1, Jaffray and Mills arrived back in Wuchow. MacMillan wrote that they had arrived "looking like a pair of bandits—dirty, unshaven, and with towel turbans. Both felt greatly the physical strain, and are wearied to the extreme limit."

Two missionaries were still being held captive, Rex Ray and Edgar Carne. Then on June 11, Ray escaped his captors.

That the missionary team had not been praying all along would not be true, but on June 20 MacMillan and the rest of the missionary team began concentrated prayer and intercession. That day, they received faith to declare Mr. Carne "loosed."

On June 22, a month after the ordeal had begun, two days after the particularly intense session of prayer, a telegram was received. Edgar Carne had been set free on the 20th—the very day of the loosing. MacMillan's cryptic comment called the release "a very gracious confirmation of our 'loosing' him on that day. Praise God."[9]

Authority over Demonic Derangement

MacMillan discerned that demonic activity sometimes masquerades as mental illness. He recounts this dramatic incident of taking authority over demonic spirits afflicting a mentally deranged man, causing him to attempt suicide:

> Coming down the West River, in the south of China, in 1926 there was a man on board being taken to Hong Kong for mental treatment. He was a foreigner and a member of the customs staff in Wuchow. Early in the morning, he leaped overboard, but was rescued and placed in a cabin on board. A little later he cut his throat from ear to ear. The boat dropped anchor, and native doctors came, sewed, and dressed his wounds. After they had left him, the

writer was asked to talk with him. He was lying on
the cabin bunk, with his hands secured by a rope. As
soon as the cabin was entered, and before any question was asked, he said: "They told me to do it."
"Who told you?" "The voices; they are talking to me
all the time. They told me to throw myself overboard;
and when I was taken from the water, they said there
was no hope for me, as I had tried to take my life, and
said I must cut my throat." Then, growing excited, he
cried, "They are talking to me now; they say I must
send you away. Go! Go!" He was quite beside himself. The answer was made: "These are demon voices
that speak with you. I am not afraid of them. I have
come in here to help you." After prayer, he quieted,
and no recurrence of the trouble occurred up to the
time he was taken from the boat to the hospital at
Hong Kong. He was not delivered, but the trouble
was under control while the worker was near. Here it
may be said that demons recognize at once anyone
who can exercise the authority of the Lord, and they
are afraid of him. But full deliverance in such a case as
this cannot take place without the consent of the one
attacked.[10]

Transition to Greater Service

In July 1925, due to political unrest, rioting, violence
and danger to foreigners, the missionaries were forced to
evacuate the headquarters in Wuchow, withdrawing to
the island compound near Hong Kong. They temporarily
turned the supervision of the work over to the Chinese
workers. When they returned three months later, they realized that the ministry of the C&MA missionaries in
China might soon come to an end. Jaffray and MacMillan
handed over the reins of leadership of the mission to the
native Chinese. It was a great step forward in the growth
of the Chinese church to supply its own indigenous leader-

ship.[11] Most of the missionaries were going back home or being redeployed. The MacMillans were uncertain of their future. But God had a plan He was preparing for them, just as He had been preparing them for His plan.

In 1925 Jaffray had gone on a reconnaissance mission to view the struggling C&MA operation in the Philippines. The C&MA had joined forces many years earlier with a Lutheran couple, Rev. and Mrs. David O. Lund, on the island of Mindanao. However, Mr. Lund had died, and Mrs. Lund proved to be an incapable and obstinate leader. Jaffray apparently was not well received by Mrs. Lund and some of the other missionary personnel. Then Rev. J.D. Williams had come to the country to provide interim leadership, but new, effective and permanent leadership was needed or the mission faced closure.[12]

Because of the leadership capabilities MacMillan had demonstrated in many kinds of difficult circumstances, Jaffray recommended MacMillan to take the helm of the Philippine mission as Field Director, and Williams extended a call to them in June 1926. Though John and Isabel had no other possibilities of ministry on the horizon, they did not rush to a decision. They prayed over a period of time and entertained counsel from others. By July 2 they determined that this was indeed God's will, and they accepted the call. MacMillan's words that great trials and warfare lead to larger service were about to be fulfilled.

CHAPTER

SIX

Ministry in the Philippines

URING THE MID-1920s, the C&MA mission in
the Philippines was teetering on the brink of
collapse. Dissension and strained relationships
poisoned the camp. The missionaries were demoralized
and talked of closing the mission. Many left the field in
1926, never to return. Several mission stations were left
without missionary personnel or qualified native workers.

In an attempt to salvage the floundering work, the
board of managers appointed John MacMillan field director for the Philippines. He was the right man for the job.
MacMillan had proven himself in China to be a capable
leader who understood the spiritual forces behind the
struggles.[1]

On Sunday, August 1, 1926, a special service of prayer
and testimony was held for the MacMillans in Wuchow.
Many members of the missionary team as well as the native Chinese expressed their deep appreciation for the
ministry of John and Isabel. Three days later, the C&MA
missionary team hosted a farewell reception for them on

the verandah of the missionary home. They had established special relationships during the past three-
and-a-half years, and they received a warm and gracious
send-off. John was presented with a set of *Meyer's Daily
Homilies*, and they received photos and financial gifts as
well. They sailed the next day, arriving in Manila August
13.

They arrived on August 22 at the city of Zamboanga
on Mindanao, the large southern island of the Philippine
island chain. He described the city as "a beautiful place,
set in groves of coco palms; every prospect pleases." He
was impressed with the colorful customs of the Moro
tribe: "A most picturesque procession—bright with col-
ors and costumes." After unpacking the next day, the following day he traveled to Mercedes to visit the boys'
school, addressing them in the morning chapel. That afternoon he met with all of the foreign missionary workers. Just as he had in China, he launched right into active
ministry immediately upon arrival at his new post.

Interestingly, after MacMillan had accepted the call
from Williams, foreign secretary A.C. Snead sent a cable
advising the MacMillans to remain in China. The cable
was delayed, however, and the message was not received
until after the MacMillans had arrived in the Philippines. John regarded the delay as providential. Later, a
cable arrived, granting them permission to stay in the
Philippines, but only temporarily.

MacMillan was unruffled by the uncertainty, remarking, "But God who sent, will be arbiter as to the length of
our stay." Whether Snead had second thoughts about
MacMillan's abilities, had another man for the job or
wanted to place the MacMillans in another assignment, is
unknown. Nonetheless, in January 1927, the board of

managers reaffirmed their decision to place John Mac-
Millan in charge permanently.[2]

Additional missionaries from the Chinese field were also
eventually redeployed to the Philippines to assist the
MacMillans in 1927: Rev. and Mrs. George D. Strohm in
April, and Rev. and Mrs. Desterhaft, Rev. and Mrs. A.M.
Loptson and Miss Bohleen in December.[3]

The Alliance work in the Philippines was comprised of ·
three divisions: Zamboanga Province (predominately Roman Catholic Filipinos), Cataboto Province (predominately pagan Subano tribe and some Catholics), and the
Sulu Archipelego (predominately Islamic Moro tribe).
The Zamboanga District had three chapels at the towns of
Tetuan, Zamboanga and Mercedes. The girls' school, the
mission home and headquarters was located at Tetuan
and the boys' school at Mercedes. Chapels were located at
Jolo and Siasi on two of the Sulu islands.[4]

The Ebenezer Girls' School was comprised mostly of
mestizas, children of American fathers and Filipina moth-
ers. The Mercedes Boys' School had more pure-blood Filipinos and some Moros as well. MacMillan taught Bible
classes twice a week at the boys' school, and preached in
the chapel at Tetuan on Sunday mornings and at
Zamboanga in the evening.[5] The presence of such a wide
variety of languages and tribes made the work so much
more challenging. MacMillan reported, "Perhaps in no
other section of the Alliance work is there such a diversity
of races and tongues and religions within so limited an
area."[6]

The awesomeness of the responsibility weighed
heavily on his shoulders in those early days: "The need
spiritually is great, and we feel the responsibility keenly.
Mistakes have been made in the past, and only God's
gracious leading can bring us to truly glorify His name

and extend His Kingdom here." It weighed upon him physically during his first week as well, as he confessed, "Am tried to the limit, and have no hope but in Divine aid, as work will be heavy henceforth." Two weeks later he wrote again,

> This morning . . . felt the Spirit's Presence and Power. Physically, am still very weary, and seem to have no reserve strength. But God "is able to make *all grace abound unto me*, that *I* having *all sufficiency* in *all things* may *abound* unto *every good work*." The responsibility of the evangelization of these fields is upon me peculiarly—therefore, I can look for grace.

Though the burden was great, he recognized that God is greater. His response to the need was, like Martin Luther, to spend even more time in prayer:

> This morning rose at 5 a.m. However, must rise at least an hour earlier to properly prepare for day. Much is to be done, and, only as the Holy Spirit directs, will it be accomplished to the glory of God. I want Him to be in the van[guard], leading and indicating; but we must follow closely that nothing of His will and words may be lost.

Interim field director J.D. Williams and his wife continued on for a few weeks to assist in the transition, leaving September 15 for Singapore. MacMillan praised them, saying, "They have done a good work, and are much beloved." They had spent about a year stabilizing the situation by providing needed leadership, reorganizing the mission, adding Bible subjects to the curriculum of the boys' and girls' schools and laying out plans for the opening of a Bible training school to equip native leaders for ministry.[7]

Isabel started teaching in the girls' school, began a Bible class for American women in the Philippines, visited homes, counseled together with her husband, and assisted in the services, sometimes preaching when John was ministering elsewhere.[8] They were able to make arrangements for schooling for Buchanan at the boys' school in the Philippines. He was the only North American boy in the school, but he adjusted better there than at Chefoo, and made several friends. John also bought him a monkey named Stella, and he was thrilled to have such an exotic pet. Buchanan described his years in the Philippines as the happiest of his childhood.[9]

John and Isabel became acquainted with noted linguist Frank Laubach, dining with him in Manila.[10] Laubach had been a veteran missionary to the Philippines and would later become famous for his writings on prayer as well as his work in literacy and evangelism. He became a lifelong friend of MacMillan and the Alliance Mission in the Philippines, visiting the Mission on other occasions.[11] They shared a common bond for a deep and rich prayer life, experiencing constant communion with God, as well as a burden for ministry in the Philippines. Laubach visited MacMillan decades later in the 1950s in his home at Nyack, New York.[12]

Ministry Problems and Opportunities

MacMillan tackled many problems early in his Philippine ministry, the first being morale. He immediately met with the workers to establish his leadership, build relationships, share his vision and encourage their faith. His winsome personality soon endeared the people to him. He personally devoted many hours to seeking the Lord in prayer regarding the needs of the field.

The owner of a neighboring property forced MacMillan into a dispute over property lines and ownership of several coconut trees. The man had secretly moved the landmark to include some of the trees, from which they had been taking fruit. MacMillan reported that he had the land surveyed, the boundary line adjusted and the landmark replaced, "much to the anger and chagrin of the transgressors."[13]

Presumably because of the Lutheran roots of the original leaders, the mission workers had not always shared Alliance doctrinal distinctives or carried out Alliance policies. MacMillan began teaching on such Alliance principles as the filling of the Spirit, sanctification, believer's baptism by immersion and divine healing—doctrines neglected in earlier years. In the strongly Roman Catholic province, many people came to MacMillan wanting to be baptized in order to be saved, or asking him to baptize their children. In most cases, he politely refused, but planted seeds by sharing the gospel of salvation by grace through faith, not by the work of baptism. While some turned away, others responded to the gospel message. He discovered that many people in the mission churches, though religious, had never been born again. In one meeting at the girls' school, three girls responded for salvation and eighteen desired to be filled with the Spirit.

Then there was the problem of Mrs. Lund. Rev. and Mrs. David O. Lund had founded the mission as independent Lutheran missionaries many years before. They eventually teamed up with the C&MA, carrying on the work mutually for many years. Rev. Lund died in 1925 and, by default, Mrs. Lund had taken charge, but she did not cooperate with the other missionaries. With the properties still in her and her husband's names, she wielded great policy-making power at the mission.

MacMillan met with her several times over two years to negotiate turning over the legal rights and property of the mission to the C&MA in exchange for a retirement allowance. She was very bitter about past matters, and MacMillan had to handle the issues sensitively.

Again and again they would come to a tentative agreement, then she would find fault and delay action or back out of the deal. Then they would have to go back to the table at square one with a proposal followed by a counterproposal. MacMillan acknowledged that in some ways she had been wronged and was willing to make some concessions. However, she could not be satisfied and wanted more.

At one point MacMillan asserted that if she did not make a reasonable agreement, the C&MA would withdraw the mission from the property and the province, leaving her with a property but no ministry or tenants. Rev. Snead came from New York to arbitrate on behalf of the board of managers. In spite of MacMillan's meek and gentle personality, she found fault with him and he was "personally . . . attacked with unusual savagery."

When a deal had finally been struck, Rev. J.D. Williams balked, believing it was too much of a compromise. In the end, she received a generous retirement allowance, agreed to leave the Philippines and turned the properties over to the C&MA. MacMillan said of the ordeal, "The whole matter shows demonic engineering for years." Through it all, he confessed, "[I] have the victory through 'the blood of the Lamb, and by the word of testimony.' Praise the Lord!"[14]

In the late 1920s the Philippine government began to impose stricter regulations on schools, making it more difficult and expensive to carry on the work. The C&MA concluded in 1928 that this was a sign from God to refocus the mission toward more evangelistic priorities and concentrate on solidly establishing the Bible school to train native workers for ministry. The mission eventually closed the girls' and boys' schools in March 1929.[15]

In the midst of these changes, MacMillan envisioned the potential of a great harvest, but the laborers were few. The work was made more difficult by the firmly ensconced religions of Islam, Roman Catholicism and paganism (mostly animism) and the many different tribal languages. In addition to dealing with Mrs. Lund, he battled the powers of darkness, established Bible studies and preaching points, and did much premarital and marriage counseling.

He regularly itinerated around to the various provinces, chapels and outstations, scoping out and pioneering new opportunities for ministry. Sometimes he walked more than ten miles in the hills to remote locations. Boat trips to islands in the Sulu Archipelago took days, often in stormy weather.

On his fifty-fourth birthday, when the Strohms held a reception in his honor, he reflected on his ministry: "May God help me. The years fly so fast, and one attains so little." In spite of all the problems, MacMillan maintained an optimistic attitude, making an appeal for workers in his 1926 annual report: "Opportunities are everywhere and calls to 'come over and help us' cannot be responded to."[16]

Training Workers

One of the most important ministries MacMillan had in the Philippines was that of inspiring others to enter the ministry. Armed with a vision to train national workers to minister and establish mission outposts, MacMillan challenged young men to take up the call. For one national believer, at least, the call was especially persuasive: "We knew a young farmer in the Philippines, whose call came to him imperatively as he walked behind his plow; he threw off the yoke from the carabao, left the plow in the furrow, and came to the missionary [MacMillan] who brought him to Bible school."[17] That man, Esteban Alfaro, became a mighty evangelist for the kingdom of God.

MacMillan seemed to take any occasion to issue a call for workers. While conducting the funeral of a Mr. Sebastian (whom MacMillan described as "a man of peculiar piety—a real light in a dark place"), he encouraged Sebastian's nephew Felix to train for the ministry. Felix seemed open to the possibility, but held back a little. A few days later the Spirit of the Lord moved upon his heart and he had a long discussion with Isabel about yielding himself to Christian work. This time he was eager to do so, but circumstances prevented him at that point.[18] About five months later, he willingly consented to preach at the first Spanish service in Tetuan. Another worker for the harvest was launched into ministry.

In another instance, a religious but non-Christian couple brought their young son to the chapel, asking MacMillan to dedicate him to the service of the Lord. John performed a service of dedication, praying for God's hand to be upon him to be used mightily of the Holy Spirit. Just as the elders had prayed for Timothy in the New Testament, so MacMillan laid his hands on the lad to impart a spiritual gifting for ministry. For a time, the boy chafed against the call, but eventually gave his heart to the Lord, and led his mother to true salvation. More than ten years later he became a powerful preacher in a pagan district of the Philippines with hundreds attending his meetings.[19]

The training these national workers received included opportunities for active ministry. Using students from the Bible school, MacMillan began a ministry at the San Ramon prison farm. Within a year and a half, they were

preaching to a large group of prisoners in three languages—Tagalog, Spanish and Ilongo—and the ministry
was bearing fruit.

MacMillan's business experience sometimes came in
handy when discipling his Bible school students. Once,
when he sent them out to distribute Bibles in the region,
they returned, complaining, "We can't sell these Bibles;
the people have no money." MacMillan responded,
"The reason you can't sell the Bibles is not because the
people have no money, but because you don't know how
to sell." He briefly trained them in basic sales tech-
niques, and from that day on they were successful. "In
fact," MacMillan recounted, "the sales were so good that
the American Bible Society in the Islands commended
the Alliance Mission for its splendid record of sales."[20]

On another occasion, "a Filipino convert asked
[MacMillan] for a sum of money that he might open a
stall in the general market, and thus support himself. It
seemed a laudable object; but, after prayer and thought-
ful consideration," MacMillan refused the request. "As a
result, the convert went northward for about thirty
miles, and secured a small piece of land on the outskirts
of a Moro village. Three months later he walked into the
presence of [MacMillan] who had declined to finance
him, with the report that through his witnessing the
chief and a number of the community had become interested in the gospel, and asked that a worker might ac-
company him back to bring to them fuller knowledge."[21]

Ministry to Catholics

As a result of his contact with the entrenched predomi-
nance of Roman Catholicism in the Zamboanga Province,
he had an unfavorable impression of the religion. He regarded the veneration of Mary as idolatry: "The whole sys-

tem of Mariolatry is man-made and demon-inspired."[22] He compared the variety of shrines honoring the Virgin Mary to the worship of Baal in various places in the Holy Land:

> In the different parts of the land, he was called by local names: Baal-zephon, Baal-peor, Baal-zebub, etc., and while each of their names was supposed to be the same Baal, people had rivalries as to the honor of the local god. In the Philippine Islands . . . the same was true of the Virgin Mary. Each district had its own virgin—the Virgin of Rosario, the Virgin of Antipolo, the Virgin of Pilar, etc., and the worshipers of these goddesses were at times most jealous of each of the other virgins.[23]

Oftentimes nominal Catholics came to him for baptism, marriage, burial or counseling, opening up opportunities to share the gospel. There were times when he felt that the mission was just barely making a dent in the hardness of the religion. But he also viewed their work as a ray of light in the darkness.

His ministry eventually began to produce enough significance to warrant opposition by the local padre. MacMillan and Esteban Alfaro had just returned from a conference in Cotobato, 250 miles away, when an earthquake struck the town of Mercedes. The local Catholic priest declared to his congregation that it was due to the arrival of the "Protestant pastor." With his typical dry wit, MacMillan reported, "He is evidently an expert seismologist, as he has propounded a theory as to the cause of the earthquake, which had quite escaped the scientists of the regular school."

MacMillan also reported that the priest had forbidden his members to have anything to do with the Alliance mission, commenting, "He is taking no chances of having the idols shaken from the altar and walls of his church."[24] He proclaimed that they were praying for a shaking of a different kind—a spiritual shaking.

MacMillan discovered that in the Philippine Islands "the Bible is practically a sealed book to the common people. We have been in many Catholic centres where the people have never seen a Bible, although they have heard of it, and were desirous of seeing a copy."[25]

In an editorial for *The Alliance Weekly*, MacMillan told the story of a converted Filipino in a government hospital reading a Spanish New Testament. He handed it to his neighbor in the next bed, who was examining it with deep interest when the padre from an adjoining barrio entered the ward.

"What are you reading?" he asked.

"La Santa Biblia" (the Holy Bible), was the reply.

"It is a bad book," said the priest. "Give it to me."

The reader, however, immediately handed it to the owner, who was able to answer the attack of the padre so effectively that he left the ward.[26]

The national Alliance workers also encountered aberrant beliefs from other missionary organizations. MacMillan related the story of a Seventh Day Adventist worker who visited a Filipino Alliance preacher in Zamboanga "to give him new light upon the truth." When asked the nature of the light which he brought, he replied, "There is no way of salvation except by keeping the commandments of God."

Immediately the preacher answered,

> That is strange. The thief of the cross broke the commandments of God, and had no further chance of obeying them; yet our Lord said to him, "Today shalt thou be with me in Paradise." Christ has redeemed us from the obligation of the Law, and we

> are now under Law to Himself. Our salvation de-
> pends not on what we do, but on what has been
> done for us. But, having been saved by the blood of
> the Lord, we now do for love's sake, and by the en-
> abling power of the Holy Ghost, the will of God as
> revealed in the Word for us.[27]

The wisdom of the preacher's answer demonstrates the strong training he had received from MacMillan and the other Alliance missionaries.

Ministry to Pagans

Half a century before missionary Don Richardson wrote about "redemptive analogies" in the stories and customs of primitive peoples,[28] MacMillan perceived similarities between pagan animistic religion and Old Testament worship:

> In the southern Philippine Islands, in some of the
> pagan tribes, there is found a 'spirit house.' It con-
> sists of one small house inside of a larger one. In the
> innermost the demon is supposed to dwell which is
> worshiped. We have wondered if this has some
> roundabout way descended from the tabernacle
> with its inner chamber for the Deity.[29]

This opened up an opportunity to establish common ground for sharing the gospel to these people.

MacMillan gave an example of one of the responses by the animistic peoples to the gospel:

> In the district of Margosatubig, in the south of the
> great island of Mindanao, an old Pagan came into a
> knowledge of the salvation of the Lord. He was
> weak in body and quite illiterate, but there seemed
> to be a strong opening up of his mind to divine
> truth. Some things that are often slowly learned
> seemed to come by intuition to him. Regarding it,

his son, a native worker, said: "I think God must
have taught him."[30]

Another pagan family who became Christians learned
to delight in prayer. "They prayed over everything they
did, including the planting of their coconuts and vegeta-
bles. Their heathen neighbors sneered at them for their
open testimony to the grace and love of God. But one
night the wild pigs made a raid from the nearby hills and
rooted up gardens and destroyed many young trees." Only
the Christian family's farm escaped the destruction. This
became a great witness to the neighbors of God's love and
protection.[31]

Ministry to Moslems

The Islamic Moro tribe posed a challenge to presentation of the gospel. MacMillan described them as "a virile,
hot-spirited race."[32] A door opened for MacMillan to witness to the Moros on their own island turf in April 1927.
The Strohms had just arrived from China, and they traveled to Lamitan on the island of Basilan to observe a Moro
wedding. There MacMillan met the Muslim headman,
who received him graciously. MacMillan found that if he
could build a relationship with the leaders of the vicinity,
they would become receptive to the sharing of the gospel
with the whole community. As a result of this contact, the
headman permitted him to preach twice to Moro audi-
ences, "the first opening of this kind."

On another occasion, two Muslims from the island of
Bilan-Bilan approached him one evening as he was sitting
on the porch of the the mission home. They had an earnest and stimulating discussion, and they "seemed
open-minded and eager to hear the Word of God." However, when MacMillan broached the subject of Jesus as the
Son of God, they "stumbled at that 'stumbling stone'—

the Deity of Jesus." They believed that Jesus was a Prophet, born of a virgin without a human father—but He could not be the Son of God. Even so, they asked that MacMillan and the Bible school students come to their island to to share this message to their people.[33]

MacMillan encountered many Sulu imams (Muslim prayer leaders or priests) and hadjis (people who had made a pilgrimage to Mecca) who admitted that they really had very little knowledge of the Koran. While he was standing on the deck of a boat crossing the Moro Gulf, he struck up a conversation with a Moro businessman. MacMillan asked him the nature of his business, and he replied that he was selling the Koran throughout the Sulu Archipelago. The man sold many books, but admitted that few people who bought it could read it because it was written in Arabic. The book was usually used as a fetish to bring good luck. MacMillan, who yearned to have the Bible in the languages of the people so that they could read and understand the word of truth, commented, "There is probably no better way of discrediting the Koran than by a fair comparision with the Bible."[34]

As time went on and MacMillan and the workers he trained made more contacts, openness to the gospel increased. On the island of Basilan one of the Bible school students was being transported in a little native "vinta" (outriggered boat) owned by a Yakan imam. The imam was familiar with Old Testament characters and stories, but had never heard the New Testament, and was fascinated. As the student shared the message of the life of Jesus and the cross, the imam began to cry out, "I have tears in my heart because of this story which you tell. I have never heard this before." The student worker gave him a copy of the Gospel of Luke in the Moro language. Sometime later he saw the man again, the imam confessed to him, "I believe this Jesus is the Son of God. I will tell about this to my people."[35] Through these trained workers two other Moro leaders came to believe in Jesus as the Son of God and shared their newfound faith with their people.

SEVEN

Spiritual Warfare
in the Philippines

FROM READING MACMILLAN'S JOURNAL, it is evident that by the time of his Philippine ministry he had grown even deeper in his walk with God. He began to rise even earlier to pray than he had in China and spent more time in prayer. Yet his responsibilities made it exceedingly difficult to maintain his prayer life with regularity.

Even two years after arriving in the Philippines, he complained of himself, "I am too spasmodic, for though I go forward, yet my prayer-drives have terminated too quickly. May God help us all to move forward to wide victory." On another occasion he wrote, "Personally have been much hindered in prayer, and the effect can be so quickly seen in conditions about. Friday, rose at 4:20 a.m. to try to have quiet. Yesterday, was lazy and did not rise till 5, which allows little time." He was not content with what we would consider an extraordinary life of prayer, yet he knew what he needed to maintain in order to accomplish the tasks before him.

Sometimes he felt well physically, but mentally inert:

> Am feeling somewhat more rested, but my mind is exceedingly dull. This must be battled against and overcome as a distinct ruse of the enemy. The body is not perfect, but the body is not wholly responsible. Every member may feel the renewing life of the Lord, and must do so, if the work of God is to prosper in my hand. To this I have been called, and this may be accomplished by His grace.

He was conscious of God's sovereign hand at work even in seemingly frustrating situations. On one occasion, he set out in a boat with other missionaries for one of the small island posts, but the boat's engine failed before they got far. Later a heavy rainstorm blew through. He viewed the stalling of the engine as God's way of protecting them from the storm. In his ministry, even when there seemed to be no results, he maintained a positive attitude, confessing, "I had claimed the promise of Christ definitely, and there will be fruit in due time."

In the summer of 1927, he experienced a dramatic breakthrough spiritually: "During the past ten days [I] have had definite consciousness in work of the Power of the Holy Spirit as never before. But it is but a foretaste of more to follow. And surely the need is tremendous." He had been earnestly seeking God for this fresh outpouring ever since he had come to the Philippines nearly a year earlier, and God rewarded his perseverance in prayer.

A brief note in his journal regarding his sister Lide's death provides us with another intimation into MacMillan's spiritual life. She died in September 1927, and he was greatly saddened by her slow and painful death. Significantly, at the same time he made note of her

death in his journal, he also mentioned the death of Jessie
Penn-Lewis in August 1927, which is a strong indication
of the extent of Penn-Lewis' influence on his life and ministry.

He experienced much less of the physical oppression
which had so frequently and severely plagued him in
China. In fact, before he left China he remarked, "Will
record to God's praise that the physical weakness is
much bettered. I feel it to be a matter of the spiritual will
laying hold of the Divine promises and of the fulness of
the Lord Jesus." He was learning to walk in divine healing more and more, which enabled him to broaden his
ministry as he took leadership in the Philippines.

He kept a heavy schedule, often working at a bustling
pace. He records in his journal after two months in the
Philippines: "Have been weary, but am learning the
power and purpose of our God the Life Giver." Again he
writes: "Felt greatly the need of spiritual reviving—more
prayer, more divine energy. Only constant receiving
from on High will avail to meet the demand here."

Nearly a year later he testified, "Am learning something of the grace which He gives physically in response
to our faith. Also somewhat more of the Spirit's power
and presence." A decade later, as a professor in the Missionary Training Institute at Nyack, New York, he
shared with his students one of the his secrets of receiving healing and maintaining health. He made it his practice daily to lay hands on various parts of his body,
praying for divine healing and health in each part.[1] In
this way he experienced the divine energizing he talked
so much about throughout his writings.

Exercise of Believer's Authority

MacMillan's exercise of the authority of the believer
and engagement with the powers of darkness increased

during his ministry in the Philippines. The opportunities for greater service also meant increased necessity of doing battle with the forces of evil. His ministry in the Philippines demonstrated in a greater manner the believer's authority over those forces.

On a Sunday morning about a month after the Mac-Millan's arrival in the Philippines, heavy rains caused flooding of the mission grounds. While returning to the grounds from a Sunday school class, John was musing over the service, remarking, "Great onslaught of old fleshly temptations. How clear that the flesh is not dead! But I am truly 'dead with Christ'—and I do 'reign with Him.' If the enemy suddenly assails the citadel, he cannot enter, so why should I fear his shouting outside?"

Suddenly, a large tree from the neighboring property fell in their direction. MacMillan described what happened next: "It was graciously guided of God, so that, although the space was comparatively narrow, it fell without damaging the chapel or house, apart from destroying the covering of the stairway to the upstairs door." MacMillan perceived in this startling occurrence of divine protection a spiritual message from the Lord: "The way out is blocked—is it not a gracious call to prayer, lest the great adversary block our efforts and shut us up in a small place? We have prayed for the binding of the strongman—we must watch and pray that the strong man does not bind us."

Authority over Addictions

Through MacMillan's ministry God displayed remarkable power in setting people free from addictive habits. In the Labangan district in the Southern Philippines, smoking was almost universal. Yet in that region, MacMillan enforced the church standard that no one who used tobacco could hold office. Instead of reacting negatively, one man spoke up. "If it is wrong for an officer to smoke, it is just as wrong for any Christian; I move that we give up growing tobacco in this district."[2]

On another occasion, a young man from the boys' school was caught chewing tobacco. His teacher sent him to MacMillan, who was the head of the school. The boy told him, "I cannot give it up, sir; I have tried again and again, and have failed." MacMillan responded, "Do you really desire to do so? The Lord Jesus is able to give you grace for victory." After talking with him further, they knelt to pray. MacMillan pled for him in prayer, and the boy "himself then took hold simply of the Lord."

Several weeks later when MacMillan was visiting the district where the young man had come from, he met him there and asked, "Are you having victory over the tobacco?" The young man responded, "I have not had a single taste for the tobacco since the day we prayed together in your office." MacMillan summarized this mighty work of God: "Thus God, in lands where the weed has been so widespread that practically everyone has used it, is Himself purifying and blessing the lives and bodies of His saved ones."[3] MacMillan later wrote strongly and repeatedly about the evils of tobacco and alcohol. After many encounters with such addictions, he discovered they often involved demonic oppression.[4]

Authority for Healing

MacMillan's ministry realized remarkable results as he prayed for healing in the Philippine Islands. A Subanan native came to MacMillan with his Bible open. He pointed to James 5:14 and asked, "Sir, what does this mean?" MacMillan explained, and the young man asked

MacMillan to anoint him with oil and pray for him. He described the boy' illness:

> The lad was suffering from a repulsive disease. The military doctor at Margosatubig had pronounced it a tropical disease unknown to himself, and the sufferer was brought to Zamboanga, where the two physicians verified the previous diagnosis. Their attempts to effect a cure were fruitless, and the young man was asked to remain in the hospital for observation. It was during his stay there that he had visited the chapel.
>
> Immediately after the anointing he left the hospital and returned to his home about one hundred miles away. In a few days his skin was clear, and it has since remained so. Other diseases, some pronounced malignant by the physicians, were healed in like manner.[5]

On another occasion a young man had a persistent cough and was thin and depressed. He went to the doctor and was diagnosed as being in the early stages of tuberculosis. He came to the mission asking for prayer. MacMillan and Strohm anointed him with oil, and he was immediately healed. Several months later he remained in perfect health and became a student in the Bible school.[6] MacMillan recounts another healing touch from God:

> A young Subano developed a swelling on his arm at the elbow. The arm was stiff and could not be straightened. . . . An x-ray examination was given at the Zamboanga General Hospital, where the doctor told him it was a malignant tumor, and advised amputation. Miss Holsted urged him to come for prayer, but though he is an earnest Christian, he was not ready for such a step. He had heard of a native herb-doctor, and going to his house, he stayed with him for a time. Nothing bettered, he appeared one

> night at the evening service of the chapel, asking for
> prayer. Later, in the presence of the students, he was
> anointed and prayer offered. A few days later . . .
> while down at the river, he had suddenly felt some-
> thing giving way in his arm. He was able to stretch it
> out and now can use it as formerly.[7]

The young man became full of joy and testified about
Jesus the Healer wherever he went. MacMillan regarded
these miraculous healings as God magnifying His name
"by doing His signs among the heathen."

The most remarkable and dramatic demonstration of
MacMillan's authority as a believer resulted in miraculous
healing of his broken leg. Retired pastor Otto Bublat recalls that MacMillan described the incident years later in a
class at the Missionary Training Institute:

> Once on an emergency mission trip where he was
> alone on the rainy, slippery trail, he slipped and
> broke his ankle. . . . His only recourse was the Lord
> since he was alone and about twenty miles from
> even a first aid station. In simple faith, he stepped
> out and began walking those many miles. He got
> home safely, and shortly thereafter had the ankle
> x-rayed. There had been a clean break, but it was
> perfectly healed.[8]

Authority over Excessive Anger

MacMillan recognized from his experience in ministry
that "there is an intimate connection between sinful anger
and the prince of evil, and sustained wrath will surely open
the door to his entrance." In his book *The Authority of the
Believer* he recounted three incidents in which he exercised
spiritual authority over demonically inspired anger. Two
Christian workers, a husband and wife, had been quarrel-
ing. One day as they were yelling at each other, John and

Isabel could not help overhearing their clamor. Quietly but firmly they

> took authority over the spirits of evil who were behind the ostensible cause, and commanded their withdrawal. Almost immediately, the quarreling stopped. As the authority was day by day held and renewed, the spirits were kept in check. Eventually however, the two separated, for they did not seek victory for themselves.

One of the Filipino Bible school students, before he became a worker, possessed a hot temper. "Stirred up by a trivial matter, he utterly lost control of himself, and speedily became almost insane with rage." John, as the principal of the school, stepped into the room next to his and knelt down to pray. He took the authority in the name of Jesus over the spirits of anger. Within a few minutes, the boy calmed down and the spirits that had overcome him were subdued.

MacMillan related that

> similar cases occurred in the Girls' School. On one occasion, after a fight among them, the ringleader was isolated in the office, where she continued shrieking wildly. The writer stepped into the office, sat down, and quietly, and inaudibly exercised the authority of the Lord, commanding the evil spirits to leave the place. The girl instantly ceased, so suddenly that the lady principal asked what had been done to her.[9]

Authority over Fear

In traveling among the islands off the coast of Mindanao, in a native boat, a considerable swell was encountered. His son Buchanan

> began to show fear, which became almost uncontrollable. This was most unusual as he was normally

fond of the water, and was an excellent sailor, having frequently traveled up and down the entire
China coast, where storms are severe. He begged to
be taken ashore; and as the whole affair seemed to
be directed against the progress of the evangelistic
trip, [MacMillan] quietly took the authority of
Christ over the spirits of fear and rebuked them,
though saying nothing openly. In a very few minutes the lad seemed to change completely, and for
the remainder of the journey, lasting several days,
there was no further difficulty. The second night after, while in the center of a wide bay, and about
twelve miles from shore, a heavy squall was encountered, and an outrigger broke. The danger was immi-
nent, but, though the lad was fully aware of it, and
though the waves were washing quite over the boat,
he manifested not the slightest shrinking.[10]

He added that he had observed "other instances of
fear, involving older and experienced missionaries."[11] In
one of those situations, a woman on a boat trip became
highly agitated and began manifesting demonic symptoms. MacMillan quietly exercised authority, binding
the spirits in the name of Jesus Christ. The woman became still and the attack did not return.[12]

Authority over Hindering Spirits

Regarding demonic obstacles to his evangelistic work
in the Philippines, MacMillan wrote:

Here are hindrances to advance in the field work.
Mohammedanism meets us with bigotry and jeal-
ousy; paganism with fear and hatred; ignorance
binds the heathen mind in darkness that seems im-
penetrable. . . . Dissensions rise in the ranks of
brethren, and the Spirit of peace withdraws. Behind
every such situation the presence of the same ma-
lign powers can be assumed. The solution is in their

displacement—we alone are to blame that they continue in power.

The same principle is often applicable in personal evangelism. A soul under conviction has great difficulty in grasping the truth, or in yielding to it. His mind is blinded and bound. A quiet attitude of victory over the opposing spirits has often brought swift release. A Filipino student was suspected of lying, but was resolutely standing by his falsehood. Quietly the position was taken: "In the name of the Lord, I rebuke these lying spirits." Suddenly the student broke down, confessed, and wept his way through to victory.[13]

Authority over Occult Powers

MacMillan was very active in engaging in warfare with evil powers in the Philippines, even more than in China. When George Strohm arrived in the Philippines, he joined John as a partner in deliverance ministry. The animistic peoples of the Philippines frequently manifested occult powers. Speaking of Jesus' encounter with the "Legion" demoniac, MacMillan noted that he knew of one demoniac in the Philippines who claimed that nine hundred demons had entered into him.[14]

One time a spiritist witch doctor was performing a ceremony, chanting in a trancelike mediumistic state and calling on the spirits. A drum in the room began to beat in rhythm without anyone touching it. Then it rose to the ceiling in a state of levitation. MacMillan walked into the room, took authority over the spirits, rebuking them in the name of Jesus Christ. The drum immediately dropped to the floor and ceased pounding.[15] This was a strong demonstration of what today we would call a "power encounter."

MacMillan and George Strohm frequently engaged in exorcism, using the First John 4:1-3 method of testing spirits. This involved questioning the spirit, "Did Jesus Christ come in the flesh?" They elicited many negative verbal responses from demons with accompanying preternatural phenomena. This methodology became one of the trademarks of MacMillan's ministry of discernment and deliverance and will be investigated more fully in later chapters.[16]

MacMillan's reputation for authority over the dark powers became known in the spirit world. More than twenty years later in Nyack, New York, on the other side of the world, a young college girl at the Missionary Training Institute was being attacked by demonic spirits. When MacMillan walked into the room, a spirit spoke to MacMillan through her in a male voice, saying, "I know you from the Philippines." MacMillan had apparently tangled with and defeated that demonic entity some twenty years earlier, and it recognized his authority.[17] It was defeated once again through MacMillan's ministry. Strohm related to Dr. Keith Bailey that MacMillan's ministry of power encounters paved the way for revival among the animistic peoples in the Philippines.[18]

Because MacMillan and George Strohm were so strongly involved in overcoming the spirits of darkness, their wives came under attack in an attempt to distract and dissuade them from the battle. MacMillan would remark later that it seemed like an "infernal fiat" had been decreed to crush them. Isabel was attacked physically, while George Strohm's wife was attacked mentally and emotionally. In March 1928, Mrs. Strohm began suffering from strange hallucinations, imagining herself to be lost. She came under bondage to a spirit of fear, refusing to eat. Through much prayer, she would find relief, but then fall into depression once again. On one occasion, they spent a whole night in prayer. Finally, after three months she was set free from the attacks completely and publicly gave glory to God for her release.

MacMillan had exercised his authority as a believer in greater ways than ever before. He had seen the hand of God at work in amazing manifestations in response to his word of command. His most agonizing times and most intense battle, however, were yet to come.

EIGHT

The Loss of His
Beloved Isabel

I SABEL CONTRACTED DENGUE FEVER and malaria in 1926 and never fully recovered. It left her in a weakened condition and susceptible to other illnesses. Though she rallied again and again, illness occurred as wave after wave. The enemy determined that if he could not get John, he would get his beloved.[1]

MacMillan's journal intimately reveals the struggles they faced during the last year of Isabel's life. In the summer of 1927, Isabel suffered the symptoms of appendicitis. When she was anointed with oil, the pain was relieved instantly and was completely gone by the next day. She remained healthy for a few months, but in the fall she had an unusual skin problem that developed into an abcess on her leg. She was hospitalized, but within a week the abcess healed and the boils disappeared. She was gaining strength daily, when about two weeks later a painful carbuncle emerged on her face and she returned to the hospital for another week.

Isabel recovered for a couple of months until January 1928, when she, John and Buchanan were all prostrated by a serious influenza. John took responsibility himself for their sickness, remarking, "I have in some sense failed—but He restoreth my soul." Earlier in December, when Buchanan was ill, John had discussed with him "concerning conditions, which would be discouraging if one could not see higher than the mist. Through many failures, one will be led to triumph." So often he ended a negative report on a positive note.

During this time, the mission was suffering its own troubles. At the end of January, MacMillan was somewhat discouraged about the progress of the work in the Philippines, lamenting that "the soil is hard." But by the summer of 1928, things seemed to be turning around: prayers were being answered; new missionary reinforcements were in place; the property issues with Mrs. Lund were settled; the Bible Training School was ready to open officially; Mrs. Strohm was recovering from her bout of depression. Isabel, too, was doing well; following her battle with the flu, she gained strength for several months, even traveling and ministering upon occasion.

In early June, however, Isabel became very weak and experienced irregular and rapid heartbeat. On the heels of the final victory over the demonic attack on Mrs. Strohm, Isabel's health plummeted and on June 23 she was hospitalized. Surgery was scheduled for June 25, but she was too weak to undergo the procedure. At a low point, out of his frustration, MacMillan wrote, "Have prayed much for Divine [intervention], but, while grace to the spirit has been afforded, no definite release to the physical condition has been granted. In a sense I feel we have failed."

The next day, however, he reprimanded himself.

> Yesterday, I wrote of failure—but that is not true.
> There is no failure to the soul that is united to God,
> and is living in the power of the age to come.
> Through all conflict, even through seeming defeat,
> we press on. God worketh and I work—but it is not
> I, but Christ Who liveth in me. What the Father is
> doing, I do. Therefore shall be accomplished all that
> He plans.

This became a turning point in the maturing of his walk
with God and his life of faith. Two days later on June 27,
Isabel received the needed surgery. She came near to
death the following day, but after prayer she rallied.

On July 2, the official opening of the Ebenezer Bible
School took place and classes began with George Strohm
acting as principal. In the midst of the struggle for
Isabel's life, MacMillan took great joy in the fact that his
long-laid plans were being fulfilled and declared, "The
spirit is good." After a week of classes, MacMillan reported, "Bible school work continues in encouraging
way. But we need reviving and sanctifying power from
on high for all students."

Though his thoughts must have dwelt much on his wife
and her condition, he still possessed a godly concern for
the welfare of the students. With the property issues now
settled with Mrs. Lund, the mission could proceed with
much needed repairs. The extra costs due to Mrs. Lund's
delays weighed upon his mind, as well as torrential rains.

By July 11 Isabel was improving, but suffering intense
headaches. Five days later she was still making progress,
but experiencing nausea. On the 24th, she appeared to be
much worse again, and MacMillan wrote, "Two or three
times it has appeared as if death was about to claim her,
but the power of God, in answer to prayer, gave delivering

grace. She is exceedingly weak, and living only from day to day."

In the week following, Isabel degenerated into critical condition and John stayed at the hospital with her each night. She made a little progress and was able to retain a small amount of food. In the midst of Isabel's troubles, John took time to conduct a large funeral with "the opportunity of giving the Truth to a good number of Catholics."

John had come to the place of yieldedness to God by praying what some call "the prayer of relinquishment":

> A few nights ago the question of submission to God's will was brought upon my spirit. After a period of careful examination, I was able to say that I am fully in acquiescence with the will of the Lord. I am not standing against Him. But He sent us here on His service; this service we are performing, and He is leading. I am confident that neither her work nor mine is done.

At the same time, he was quite aware that a warfare was raging:

> I am further sure that just as truly as the attack on Mrs. Strohm was demoniacal, so the condition of my wife is a different manifestation of the same fell power. We are, by prayer in Jesus' name, dislodging the spirits that have bound the people of this field. It seems to me that an infernal fiat has gone forth that we must be crushed. But, "rejoice not against me, O mine enemy; though I fall, I shall rise." God is with us and we shall live and triumph.

He had a sense that the enemy was trying to "wear out the saints of the most High" (Daniel 7:25). MacMillan was prepared to face Isabel's death, but he would fight to the end for her life.

How did John reconcile the two seemingly opposing poles of acquiescence to God on the one hand and struggle against Satan on the other? He would explain later:

> As we come to know God better, everything takes on a different aspect to us, and we see God in all that comes. Not that we can accept each incident as from His hand. On the contrary, it may be directly from the enemy, and intended to harm us. But we can believe in His gracious providence, and know that, before it was permitted to come, it had to pass the inspection of His love and perfect wisdom. Thus we can give thanks for evil and for good alike, while at the same time positively resisting the devil, and refusing what comes to us from him.[2]

He did not see a conflict between accepting all that comes as from God and fighting off the enemy at the same time.

On August 5, the mission held its first Communion service in two years. Because of all the dissension, commemorating the Lord's Supper had been laid aside until the church could properly discern the Body of Christ. This was a special service of unity and blessing. The Holy Spirit was moving in conviction upon the people.

By Saturday, August 18, Isabel's state had become precarious again, but John remained hopeful: "The time is determined and will terminate in due season, and it will be not defeat but victory." By Monday, August 21, she had become comatose. On Tuesday John wrote, "This morning at 4 o'clock, she spoke out of an apparent stupor to me, saying, 'Now is your last chance,' meaning that unless I broke the chains she would not last long." Beginning Monday, classes at the Bible school had been suspended, and the students and mission personnel began a continuous prayer vigil. MacMillan wrote, "The battle is hard! But 'thanks be to God who always leadeth to triumph in Christ!' "

On Saturday evening, August 25, a severe earthquake rocked Zamboanga City. That night, instead of praying for Isabel, John and George Strohm led an all-night prayer meeting, burdened for the salvation of ten thousand Philippine souls.[3] John's decision to switch the focus of prayer from Isabel to the lost passionately displays his selflessness. His love for the lost surpassed his real concern for his beloved.

The next afternoon Isabel died with John and twelve-year old Buchanan at her side.[4] The very last entry in his journal recounts:

> This afternoon at 2 o'clock, my wife passed away. Strange that it should be the last record in this book, which contains an account of our wanderings since we left Canada together. It is the anniversary of our wedding day fourteen years ago. The event is one of the mysteries of our Christian experience, but we do not have to solve it. God doeth all things well. What effect it will have on my future movements, I do not know. The financial side appears very uncertain, as the withdrawal of Isabel's allowance will make it impossible to provide for son. The future is in His hands.

The reader can sense his feeling of numbness in his matter-of-fact statement. How sorrowful it must have been to lose his beloved on the very day celebrating the beginning of their life together. One can imagine that Satan attacked him with doubts and questions. Where was God now? Where was this believer's authority he was supposed to be exercising? The same faith and authority which enabled him to stop a fire from spreading, cast out demons, loose the kidnaped, claim protection from a plague, terminate a witch doctor's levitation and walk twenty miles with a just-broken leg, this time was not able to keep his beloved wife from death.

Meaning out of Death

However, her death was not a defeat for MacMillan and the Philippine mission. Rather, it galvanized and united people in prayer even more. Not only was a prayer vigil kept during her last week, but the Bible school students held an all-night prayer vigil in the chapel at Tetuan around her coffin. The morale and fortitude the enemy tried to destroy was actually strengthened. Buchanan remarked, "This seemed to be the beginning of a new era of spiritual life in the mission field, that except for the Subanan work has been singularly unresponsive and discouraging."[5] The loss that resulted in the breaking of John's heart actually became a breakthrough—a breaking of the enemy's stronghold on the peoples of the Philippines.

Following her burial, John expressed the feelings of his loss by writing a poem about her death entitled, "Beside the Grave":

> Island of Mindanao
>   Girt by the moaning sea,
> What was in earth most dear
>   Thou holdest back from me—
> Holdest in dread embrace
>   Under thine earthly crust,
> Citing the age-old law:
>   "Dust shall return to dust."
>
> Proudly thy grasses lift
>   Over the tiny mound
> Their flutt'ring bannerets—
>   Stretching their camp around,
> They guard with jealous care,

Sleeplessly night and day,
Lest through their serried ranks
  Aught should escape away.

O beauteous fronded palm,
  Rising in graceful art
Over the rounded tomb—
  Thou hast a spider's heart:
Deeply thy rootlets twine,
  Wrapping around thy prize,
Binding in meshy web
  The form that silent lies.

Lonely I sit and muse
  O'er the departed years
Fragrant with memories—
  Then thro' the starting tears,
Over the mountains high,
  O'er the savannahs broad,
I see in arching sky
  The covenant of God.

Island of Mindanao,
  Girt by the mighty sea,
Boast not thy league with death,
  Nor triumph over me.
Around this pris'ning cell
  Vainly thou keepest ward;

Thou clutchest but the case,
  The jewel is with the Lord.[6]

In the midst of his sorrow, he recalled the covenant of
God and wrote profoundly of the state of the departed. He
took comfort in his confident hope in the resurrection:

How rich the comfort to our hearts as we remember that—from the promises of the Lord, from the
testimony of His risen body, from the analogies of
the Divine working—the dear face upon which our
last look has seen, it may be, the marring of disease,

> will be returned to us a new, a perfect, a deathless
> beauty. The hope of the resurrection is an integral
> part of the rapture.[7]

Daniel prophesied, "Those who are wise will instruct
many, though for a time they will fall by the sword or be
burned or captured or plundered" (Daniel 11:33, NIV).
Isabel was one of those wise people who had fallen by the
enemy's sword. Jesus' words in John 12:24 became true of
Isabel: "Except a corn of wheat fall into the ground and
die, it abideth alone: but if it die, it bringeth forth much
fruit." In warfare, inevitably there are casualties. Isabel
was a casualty of the turf warfare for the souls of the Philippine peoples.

John never spoke specifically about her death in any of
his writings, but he did make allusions from time to time,
reflecting his understanding and acceptance of her death.
Isabel's death did not keep MacMillan from believing in
healing or exercising the authority of the believer over
principalities and powers. A decade later he wrote,
"Healing thus is by His will in the case of all. . . . Sickness,
or even death itself, may be necessary for the prosperity of
the soul."[8] Reflecting years later his counsel on the mysteries of unanswered prayer he gives a personal commentary:

> Thus, when the child of God, in answer to his cry
> for divine help and for spiritual blessing, finds him-
> self pressed on every side by circumstances that per-
> plex and by foes that oppress, it is his to remember
> that his own God is answering him with "terrible
> things in righteousness" (Psalm 65:5). The enemy
> has been permitted occasion against him that his
> faith and spiritual preparedness may be proved
> upon the field of combat. The opportunity has come
> to "stand" (Eph. 6:13), and to triumph.

> The answer which comes through some "terrible"
> thing, if we are abiding in God, is as truly from Him
> as that which men call a blessing. It may seem other-
> wise: our plans may be disrupted, our friends may
> be puzzled, our faith may be for the moment
> shaken. But its coming is a proof of His confidence
> in us, and an opportunity on our part to trust more
> fully and to glorify Him before the seen and the un-
> seen world.[9]

He had come to understand that from God's perspective, "In nature the farmer is the harvester; but in grace
the Lord puts in His sickle and gathers His ripe saints.
Sometimes we see a saint like Robert Murray McCheyne
of Scotland taken at the age of twenty-eight, but fully
ripe."[10] John recognized that Isabel had arrived to her
fruition of ripeness in God's economy.

He also comprehended that God was doing a work in
him:

> Everything that comes may not seem to be of
> God, but our attitude of thanksgiving towards Him
> must continue, even when we discern that some
> things that have been permitted to touch us are as
> definitely from the enemy as were the afflictions of
> Job. Such things are for our training spiritually, and
> under them it is ours to maintain a heart that dwells
> in praise before the Lord.[11]

Quoting Luke 10:19 on the believer's authority, Mac-
Millan commented, obviously alluding to Isabel,

> This is the normal condition of the ministry of the
> missionary; when trouble is stirred up by the enemy,
> the servant of God has the right to appeal to this
> promise of his Lord. Only when the glory of the
> Lord is better served by resisting "unto blood," it is
> superceded; then it may be that the glory of God is
> promoted by death, rather than by life. But to the

> trusting and obedient soul these things will be plain
> when the time comes.[12]

Many of God's great men of faith have been tested through the fire by the loss of their loved ones. That great apostle of faith, George Mueller, lost a son; the pioneer of faith missions, J. Hudson Taylor, lost four children under the age of ten and his wife at thirty-three years old; C&MA pastor and evangelist F.F. Bosworth lost his son and his wife. These men all continued to walk with a strong faith even after their losses. The healing ministry of Bosworth actually increased after the death of his loved one. The same became true of MacMillan's ministry of the authority of the believer. While he did not understand, he had a sense of the sovereignty and timing of God—bringing closure to an era of his life. He did not know how he would carry on, but he knew that by God's grace he *would* carry on.

Life after Isabel's Death

And carry on he did. MacMillan continued to travel and minister, to evangelize, pray for others who were miraculously healed and exercise power encounters for the glory of God.[13] His hope was not destroyed; his vision had not abated; his authority had not weakened.

Within three weeks after Isabel's death, he resumed his busy routine, focusing on outreach. He continued to speak at Sunday morning and evening chapel services, and traveled with Bible school students to evangelize outlying areas. He noted that there seemed to be a greater openness to the gospel among the Islamic Moros and those of Roman Catholic background.

He also planned evangelistic trips to Jolo, Margosatubig, and Cotobato, areas untouched by the gospel—what we would call today "unreached people groups." In addition, he worked on a project with the American Bible Society to produce an edition of the Gospel of Luke in the Moro dialect.[14]

He wrote articles for *The Alliance Weekly* describing the mission's progress in spreading the gospel in late 1928 and early 1929. He appealed for new missionaries to take up the call, for funds to further the gospel and for intercessors, exhorting, "In this ministry of intercession, you on the hilltop at home can do more than we in the valley facing the foe. Hold up the Rod!"[15]

His sister Bessie wrote in October, inquiring about his loneliness. He responded:

> You speak of the loneliness. Strangely, I have scarcely begun to realize it fully. Perhaps the long absence of Isabel from the house here; perhaps the fact that we have been "strangers and pilgrims" for years, without any certain dwelling place; perhaps the prayers of many friends—probably all of these causes have combined to make the departure an unreality. It was when I returned from Jolo recently, after an absence of two weeks, and found the house in the same confusion in which I left it, for I was forced to leave hurriedly, that the first great sense came. And then it passed away again, and there came the same feeling back that she would step in again shortly. I am kept busy also—there is not much freedom, and this has tended to the same end.[16]

Buchanan continued classes in the boys' school until it closed in March 1929. When John had to be out of town, Buchanan sometimes traveled with him. On other occasions, he stayed with Miss Holsted in Mercedes at the mission house, where he had other friends from school. Both John and Buchanan indicate in their writings that they grew closer to each other during this time.

Father and son took a brief vacation early in 1929. Their scheduled furlough was in the spring of that year and although John recognized that he and Buchanan needed a rest, he struggled with leaving the people in such need.[17] Wisdom finally prevailed, however, and the MacMillan men sailed for America in May, leaving behind many memories.[18]

MacMillan's Legacy in the Philippines

Summarizing his conversation with George Strohm regarding the ministry of John MacMillan, David Rambo wrote, "The . . . years of leadership under MacMillan were as strong as they were brief. He inherited the task of implementing the decisions effected by Jaffray and Williams. Under his leadership, the settlement of the Tetuan property was finalized, and Ebenezer was made a full-fledged training school for pastors."[19] Regarding MacMillan's impact in founding Ebenezer Bible School, Mendoza declared, "Since it opened in 1928 . . . this 'School of the Prophets' has been and will continue to be the heart and hub of the growth of the Alliance throughout the length and breadth of the country."[20]

Before MacMillan left the Philippines, he stood on the coast of the Province of Davao, and "a representative of one of the tribes was pleading with him to come and preach the gospel to his people." Since MacMillan had already made plans to return to America, he was forced to turn down the call. He did not forget the people, however, continuing to pray for them for several years. God answered his prayers by bringing other missionaries to minister to the Mandaya and neighboring tribes. More than ten years later a C&MA missionary reported that "over four thousand are regularly attending services." MacMillan commented:

There are in the homeland many who regret their
inability to go to the foreign field. More and more it
should be realized that distance is no barrier to the
ministry of prayer. A faithful and persistent intercessor in America may accomplish at times more
than an evangelist in a heathen field. Such a prayer
warrior may obtain strength for missionaries both in
body and in spirit, may break down prejudices
against the gospel, may secure the opening of hearts
to the truth, may overcome political hindrances,
may bind the powers of wickedness in the
heavenlies. Advancement on the front lines may be
ensured, and the churches established in the faith,
revival power may be outpoured, and believers
brought to a deep experience of sanctification, if
some one at home will take the time and the energy
to thus obtain promises. The ministry of those actually on the field will be enhanced many-fold by the
cooperation of a real helper together in prayer.[21]

While MacMillan did not use the current terminology
"territorial spirits," there is no doubt he understood the
concept of demonic strongholds over a region. He appealed for intercessors at home "to roll back the powers
of the air, and make it possible to bring the Truth to bear
on these regions where the devil is blocking the way."[22]
The "principalities" of Ephesians 6:12 he regarded as
"satanic princes, angels whose principalities cover the
countries of this world."[23] He had viewed his battle for
Isabel's life as an "infernal fiat" intended to crush them
because they were dislodging the spirits that held the ter-
ritories of the Philippines in darkness.

The revival that for three years MacMillan had been
earnestly battling for and seeking in prayer began toward
the latter part of 1929. In a two-month period about
twenty people sought the Lord for salvation.[24] Then,

during the Christmas season of 1929, three students of
Ebenezer Bible Institute pioneered an evangelistic work
among the Subanun people. Though they initially met
with resistance, by the first day of January 1930, the
break came and the people began to respond to the gospel. In that revival 200 Subanan pagans came to
Christ.[25] By 1938, fifty-eight students were enrolled in
the Bible institute, and over 750 pagans had been converted and baptized in that year.[26]

Another dynamic innovation which might have resulted
from MacMillan's intercession and spiritual warfare involved his friend Frank Laubach. In 1928, after fourteen
years on the field, Laubach left the Philippines in such discouragement that it affected his health. However, after an
extended furlough he returned in December 1929 to a remote pagan area of Mindanao and initiated a work in literacy and evangelism. In 1930 a break came in teaching
the native peoples how to read and write. As a result, he
became world-renowned as a pioneer in the field of literacy.[27]

Is it coincidental that a deeply depressed veteran missionary returns to the field nearly two years later to
make an astonishing discovery which opened wide the
doors of evangelism? MacMillan would no doubt assert
that the spirits that held people in the bondage of ignorance and disheartened Laubach had been dislodged and
bound, freeing him to originate, through the creativity of
the Holy Spirit, a powerful means of spreading the gospel. In later writings, Laubach referred to "binding and
loosing" and "testing the spirits."[28] Since these were two
of MacMillan's major themes, this may be indicative of
an influence on Laubach.

MacMillan's legacy continues into the twenty-first
century. Out of the Philippine mission that he revital-

ized, The Christian and Missionary Alliance has grown to be the largest evangelical denomination in the Philippines today.[29] This is, in part, the outcome of the exercise of the authority of the believer.

NINE

North American Ministry
1929-1934

J OHN AND BUCHANAN ARRIVED in New York City
July 21, 1929, after six years and six months overseas. Before long, John was touring the United States
and Canada, speaking in C&MA churches about his missions work in China and the Philippines, while Buchanan stayed in Toronto with John's sisters. Though
C&MA missionary furloughs are usually only a year
long, MacMillan continued touring through 1931.[1] John
had desired to return to the Philippines after a year, but
the mission board's financial support policy did not provide for a single parent with a child.[2]

God had other plans for John MacMillan, however, and
would use him in a variety of ways in many locations in
North America, broadening his ministry even further.
Contrary to a report that he was in ill health when he returned to North America, he kept up an energetic itinerant ministry and became actively involved in Bible
teaching, preaching, counseling and visitation.

MacMillan demonstrated that he was a man of wise counsel, steeped both in the Word and in experience. While ministering in a city in Canada an elderly man came to him confessing that he had sinned, but had not been able to find assurance of forgiveness for two years. He stated, "I have been baptized with the Holy Spirit and have spoken in tongues, but I cannot find peace of heart."

MacMillan did not cast doubt on his experience with the Holy Spirit, but questioned him on his understanding and acceptance of the Word. "Have you committed the sin against the Holy Spirit?" he asked.

"No," he replied.

MacMillan queried further. "Do you know what that sin is?"

"Yes," he responded.

MacMillan read to him Matthew 12:31, commenting, "The Lord says that all manner of sin and blasphemy will be forgiven, except that against the Holy Spirit. Thus your sin is forgivable. How is forgiveness obtained?"

"By confession," he responded.

Then MacMillan read First John 1:9, and asked him, "Do you believe this word? Have you confessed your sins?" He responded affirmatively to both questions.

"Where, then, is the difficulty," MacMillan asked, "since God's promise is so clear?"

"Well, my sin was of such a nature . . ." the man replied, naming the sin.

"But," MacMillan prodded, "what does God say about it?"

Four times he urged the man to read and claim the promise of the Scripture, and each time the man balked. Finally, he put his hand over his heart, and lamented, "I can't feel it in here."

"Brother," MacMillan responded, "you are looking in the wrong place. For more than two years, you have been taking the testimony of your unbelieving heart against the promise of God. That is a grievous sin. Kneel down, and confess to God your sin of unbelief, and then thank Him for forgiving you when you asked Him."

The elderly gentleman followed his instructions, confessing his sin of unbelief and giving thanks to God. "Suddenly," MacMillan wrote later, "he broke out into a shout and for a few minutes was overcome by deep emotion."

The man stood to his feet, took MacMillan's hand and earnestly cried, "I never saw that before!"

MacMillan counseled, "You have never fully believed God. Always get your feet on His Word; then feelings may come and go, but your assurance is established outside of yourself, on what the . . . God has said." In writing about this incident later, he added, "This principle of faith in God's Word would remove most spiritual difficulties."[3]

As MacMillan traveled around to churches sharing his missionary experiences, he most likely included stories of how God saved, healed and delivered people from the powers of darkness, through the exercise of believer's authority. He also encountered situations which called for exercise of that authority.

In 1930 he visited a pastor and wife in a country district. They were young and devoted, and effectively carried on their ministry. However, the pastor's wife had been suffering for some time from serious heart trouble and was receiving medical treatment. She frequently experienced severe pain which caused fainting spells. Several times the young pastor had come home to find her lying unconscious on the floor.

As MacMillan conversed discerningly with the wife, he discovered that her father had been a spiritist and that she, as a child, had become proficient in the use of the planchette (a device designed to produce automatic writing similar to an Ouija board). MacMillan inquired, "Is it not probable, sister, that your present physical trouble, and your difficulty in receiving healing is due to the past?"

She replied sincerely and seriously, "No, for I was never a medium in the ordinary sense. I simply used the planchette." She related some of the incidents, but felt there was nothing wrong or inappropriate, because she was not seeking to communicate with spirits.

MacMillan admonished, "Nevertheless, in using the planchette, your body had to be surrendered to the evil spirit. There is little question in my mind that the difficulty lies there. Your connection with these powers should be acknowledged and confessed. Then a definite stand, in the authority of the Lord, should be taken, absolutely refusing the further working of evil spirits in your body, which has been purchased by the precious blood."

She did not acknowledge the problem at the time, but about three weeks later MacMillan received a letter from her. After he had left, the truth dawned upon her, and she confessed the sin. Then she and her husband agreed together in prayer, taking authority over the spirits and refusing any further attack of the enemy. Since that time, MacMillan reported, "she has never had another attack of heart trouble, and has been blessed in her service greatly."[4]

During the latter part of 1930 he made a tour of a severely drought-stricken area of Western Canada to encourage churches and to salvage as much of the mission pledges as possible in spite of the financial depression.[5] The situation appeared very grim:

> The majority [of farmers], through the vast areas
> of the Provinces of Manitoba, Saskatchewan, and
> Alberta, have had nothing, or at the best little, to

> send to the market. Hail and drought have been
> widespread; late rain and early snow have made it
> impossible to thresh what the soil has produced.

Spiritually the circumstances seemed no better. "Aggressive work is difficult, and one honors the band of stalwart workers who are bravely facing existing conditions, and carrying on under circumstances that involve real sacrifice." Now a veteran of two Far East mission fields and many trying circumstances, MacMillan observed, "No foreign missionaries are working under greater sacrifices than are some of our western pastors."

On top of all that, he encountered a heavy dose of Western Canadian winter weather: "Heavy snow, accompanied by a fall in temperature to below the zero mark, was preceded and followed by mild rains, which showed up the excellence of the prairie mud, and made motor travelling a joy only to the stout-hearted." He commented sarcastically about being stranded in a snowstorm, "We had the joy of spending one night on the prairie ten miles from anywhere, with a small blizzard blowing and only the shelter of the car."

In spite of all the adverse circumstances, he remained optimistic: "There has been able leadership and far vision, and with reviving conditions the future is bright. The present, then, is a good time to strengthen our stakes that we may be ready for the forward movement." On MacMillan's first visit to Winnipeg, District Superintendent Rev. J.H. Woodward, had just taken charge of a trying situation. When MacMillan returned eight weeks later he reported, "A new spirit of hope was most manifest. Souls were coming to the Lord, the debt was being reduced, individual labor was beautifying the interior of the Tabernacle, and the atmosphere breathed hope and determination."

MacMillan swept through Western Canada, speaking at sixty-three meetings in sixty days, manifesting evidence of his strong health. He gave a positive report of his whirlwind tour: "Souls were brought to the Lord, bodies received healing, about 50 young lives were dedicated, and much gracious blessing was granted by the Lord, for which the praise is due to His Name. One was wonderfully cheered by the earnest spirituality of the many friends met under all conditions. In no part have we met a deeper longing for the Lord, and hearts were blessed outside of our own ranks." Ever the consummate missionary enthusiast, he ended his report with an appeal for workers for the harvest.[6]

When MacMillan engaged in visitation, he sometimes took others with him to assist in ministry, just as he had in the Philippines. In one of the cities of western Canada, he and a young soldier visited an atheist in the hospital and shared the gospel with him. The man expressed a "fierce hatred of God and His Word, and of the message spoken." MacMillan recounts what happened next:

> Then [the soldier], who had been lifted by the power of God from a life of evil, and kept by divine grace for a generation past, intervened with a brief story of his conversion. The atheist was silent; he had not a word to say; his heart was not changed, nor was his mind convinced, but his reasoning failed him. For here before him stood one who could bear a personal testimony of the saving energy of the Almighty.[7]

Also during this time he attended a meeting of Christian men in which a prominent pastor of a large church appealed for Christian ideals in dealing with the terrible drought facing Western Canada. Then a layman got up and spoke, urging the need for a deeper prayer life. MacMillan, himself a layman for many years, later noted the layman's discernment, commenting that he possessed "a clearer conception of spiritual values" than the ministers at the meeting.[8]

While in Western Canada he spoke on the exercise of the authority of the believer, teaching from his own experience that a believer can claim the covenant promises of the Word of God for the spiritual well-being of one's children:

> While conducting meetings in Western Canada, the writer was asked at the close of a service by a mother if he could give her a covenant promise for her son. She said, "He is a Christian, but he is attending medical college, and you know how dangerous that may be." She was pointed to Deuteronomy 30:6, which reads: "The LORD thy God will circumcise thine heart, and the heart of thy seed, to love the LORD thy God with all thine heart, and with all thy soul, that thou mayest live."
>
> It was pointed out that the spiritual Israelite, like ourselves, realized his utter inability to keep the Law, the principal part of which was "Thou shalt love the Lord thy God with all thy heart, and with all thy soul, and with all thy mind." But, as he brought his need to the Lord, he found the provision that God Himself would circumcise his heart to do these very things.
>
> Then, when his thought included his children, and he cried, "Lord, what about my little one," the provision covered that also, "the heart of thy seed." God promised to circumcise his children's hearts, if he himself claimed the covenant and walked after it. The mother was charged, "Hold Him to His Word," and she responded gladly and eagerly, "That I will!"
>
> Let no father or mother, in any place of circumstances, feel that Satan and the flesh must prevail over their children. Such is not God's will.[9]

These principles of the believer's authority, based on covenant relationship with God, which he taught while touring Canada, bore lasting fruit, for this story resulted a few years later:

> In the Province of Saskatchewan, in Western Canada, an earnest Christian farmer covenanted with the Lord to yield a set proportion of all that he received. Much hail fell for several years in that region with damaging effects. One day, when in the field, this man saw the hail sweeping towards his farm. Falling on his knees, he reminded God of the covenant, and committed the matter to His care. The hail came to the end of his farm, then changed its direction and passed on, without damage to any of his crops.[10]

After concluding his speaking tour in 1931, MacMillan served for nine months as acting foreign secretary while A.C. Snead and David Mason were out of the country.[11] Also in 1931, less than ten years after joining the C&MA as a missionary, he was appointed to the organization's board of managers for a three-year term,[12] and later served for two additional terms. Attaining such a position of prominence in the C&MA in such a brief time is testimony to his leadership abilities.

Another incident occurred during his ministry in 1931 which gave MacMillan another opportunity to teach on the authority of the believer:

> Some months ago, after a service in one of our cities, two women came asking an interview. The appearance of one gave an immediate understanding of the situation, which was confirmed by conversation. There had been earnest seeking of deep spiritual experience which was followed by a sudden attack of intense despondency. The attacks persisted, until, after three years, the mind was in complete bondage. All joy had fled, and only a feeble

hold of salvation was retained. Suggestions of suicide were frequent, pressing with an urgency that
was hard to resist.

The following line of approach was taken, after
definitely asserting in prayer the power of the Ascended Lord, and the believer's throne union with
Him. "Sister, this trouble is clearly the oppression of
evil spirits, which have obtained a hold over you in
some manner. These thoughts of self-destruction
are directly prompted by him who is a deceiver and
a murderer. You are a Christian and united with
Christ. This afternoon may be for you, if you will,
the last occasion of the manifestation of satanic
power." In a simple manner, her place of victory and
authority in Christ was shown from the Word. She
was urged to take it audibly before those who were
witnesses (her sister, a friend, and the speaker). After full assertions of her faith and her acceptance of
what Christ had gained and the Father had bestowed, the party kneeled in victorious prayer. As
the group arose, one of the friends remarked: "She
looks different already." There was a life and anima-
tion, most noticeable after the deadness of her previous expression.

A few weeks ago, a letter came: "I feel as if I were
saved all over again." Joy and peace had returned;
the Holy Spirit had come; and soul-saving work had
been granted to her.[13]

This incident, along with the earlier situation of the
pastor's wife in bondage, served as the launching pad for
a series of articles by MacMillan that were destined to
become a classic. Entitled "The Authority of the Believer" and published in *The Alliance Weekly* in early
1932,[14] this eight-part series had a massive impact on
the Christian understanding of the believer's authority
and the nature of spiritual warfare.

Forged out of the fire of MacMillan's experiences in China and the Philippines, as well as his more recent ministry in North America, "The Authority of the Believer" became an instant success. Requests came from all over the world for copies of the material, to which the magazine responded by reprinting the articles in booklet form in 1934. By 1935 *The Alliance Weekly* reported that "the first edition has been blessed to Christians in different parts of the world," and many requests had come for more copies.[15]

Another testimony to the impact of the articles appeared in 1933, in the editorial introduction of the seventh edition of *War on the Saints*, by Jessie Penn-Lewis and Evan Roberts:

> The second type of reader, to whom this book is of immense value is the Christian worker who finds himself or herself faced with cases of spiritual abnormality, of which there seem to be an increasing number in these days of intense satanic activity. To such readers these pages will bring light and guidance, and it is perhaps striking that in recent months a magazine as well informed of Christian work in many lands as *The Alliance Weekly* of America, should feel it necessary to publish some very able articles by the Rev. J.A. MacMillan dealing with demon possession.[16]

The introductory chapter then quotes, summarizes and paraphrases sections of the MacMillan articles. It must have been gratifying to MacMillan to have his work cited in introduction to a work by Jessie Penn-Lewis, who had influenced his theology and practice of spiritual authority.

Pastoral and Writing Ministries

MacMillan showed great insight into the spiritual conflict behind many church disputes, as illustrated by his response to a pastor who complained to him, "There are about four different troubles going on all the time among my people. As soon as I get one straightened out, the devil has another ready to take its place." MacMillan replied,

> Brother, you are right in your diagnosis of the source of your troubles, but you are wrong in your method of meeting them. What you are looking at are the coils of the old serpent through your congregation, and, as you straighten out one kink, you may be sure that another will appear. Leave the coils alone, and go for the head; put your foot on that in the authority of the Lord; recognize the active agency of the enemy and conquer him; the coils will straighten out of themselves if he is dealt with.[17]

Another example of MacMillan's discernment in the area of church problems occurred in 1932, when he served for nine months as pastor of the recently established Alliance branch in Truro, Nova Scotia. Canadian C&MA historian Lindsay Reynolds observed that MacMillan had "put his finger on the historic problem" which plagued the attempted planting and sustaining of a church in Truro.[18] MacMillan reported, "Truro is over-churched and over-missioned. Indeed, I have never been in a town of this size with so many places of worship." He went on to explain that "the churches were highly competitive and suspicious of each other, so that goodwill and cooperation were almost impossible." His admonitions were prophetic, for the church closed after six years of struggling ministry under nine pastors.[19]

From October 1932 to May 1934, MacMillan served as assistant superintendent of the Eastern and Central Canadian Districts under Rev. J.D. Williams, who had appointed him to the Philippines several years earlier.[20] While serving in Truro, he had more time for writing, and produced three articles for publication in *The Alliance Weekly*, as well as two poems.[21] Between 1932 and 1934 he also served as interim pastor at St. John, New Brunswick; London, Ontario; Windsor, Ontario; and Winnipeg, Manitoba.[22] In 1933 he took on the commitment as editor of *The Full Gospel Adult Quarterly*, preparing his first lessons for the 1934 quarterly, a responsibility he continued to fulfill right up to his death twenty-three years later.[23]

MacMillan was constantly alert to opportunities to share the gospel. He continued to be especially fond of sharing with Jewish people the Messiahship of Jesus, with his good grasp of Hebrew and the Old Testament. He wrote of his ministry to Jews, "We have visited many Jews in many stores and homes, and have been received with kindness, while the Christian message has been listened to with eagerness in some cases."[24]

In 1934, he conversed with a Hebrew man who was "under deep conviction of sin, and hungry for deliverance. In answer to questions he divulged the fact that he believed that Jesus Christ was the Son of God, though as yet he had not connected Him with the Messiah of Israel." Though the man "knew little of his own Hebrew Scriptures, he was persuaded through reading Charles Dickens articles on 'The Life of Our Lord' published in daily newspapers."[25]

While pastoring in Winnipeg, Manitoba, in 1934, he witnessed to another Jewish man:

> Speaking to a Jew in the city of Winnipeg, who was under conviction of his need, he cried out twice in the street of his soul, stretching his hands upward: "O God, save me." Then, suddenly remembering his race, he asked, "Does this mean that I must tell this to my people?" Realizing that it meant just that, he declared, several times, "I'm not con-

verted." We answered, "Brother, no one can convert
you. Conversion is your own act of turn to God. But
if you will turn to the Lord, and accept Him as your
Saviour, He will regenerate, you, giving you a new
heart to love and obey Him." But, in fear of the consequences, he refused to take the step. We never
saw him again alive; a few days later he was found
hanging in his cellar. What had impelled him to
self-destruction, we do not know, save that there is
an ever-present enemy deceiving the souls of men.[26]

Also while serving in Winnipeg in 1934, he wrote a
seven-part series of articles for *The Alliance Weekly* entitled
"The Spirit-Filled Christian."[27] The content presented a
sound, balanced teaching on sanctification, the baptism in
the Spirit, the Spirit-filled life, spiritual discernment, and
the gifts and manifestations of the Spirit. As a frequent
contributor to *The Alliance Weekly* and editor of *The Full
Gospel Adult Sunday School Quarterly*, his name was becoming well-known and established in C&MA circles, and his
teaching through writing was becoming authoritative and
popular. His writing skills, sound teaching, printing background and leadership qualities all combined together to
prepare him for an even broader scope of ministry as an
editor and college professor, to which he was called in the
summer of 1934.

MacMillan as Writer and Editor

MACMILLAN HAD DEVELOPED INTO a proficient writer, equipping him for a even broader career as a magazine editor and Sunday school curriculum writer. His experience in the printing business, his breadth of reading and study, his personal journaling, and his wife Isabel's editorial capacities all contributed to his budding writing skills.

He began writing for *The Alliance Weekly* in 1928, reporting on the mission work of the C&MA in the Philippines. When he returned to North America, he continued to cover Philippine developments for the magazine, but also began writing biblical exposition and Christian living articles. His series on "The Authority of the Believer" in 1932 and "The Spirit-Filled Christian" in 1934 distinguished him as an author of spiritual insight, erudite in the Scriptures.

As a result, he was entrusted with the task of presenting weekly exposition of Scripture through *The Full Gospel*

Adult Sunday School Quarterly, produced by the C&MA publishing house, which he began compiling in 1933. The quarterly consisted of "Daily Readings, Lesson Text, Bible History, Lesson Outline, Lesson Encyclopedia, Practical Points, Lesson Questions, and Suggestions for Further Study, as well as a scriptural and devotional exposition of each lesson."[1]

The lessons also frequently included a feature called "Gleanings," which contained insights from the Greek or Hebrew text. MacMillan had accumulated extensive information about Scripture, hermeneutical principles, and Hebrew and Greek exegesis. Through his Old Testament studies and contacts with Jewish people, he became familiar with Jewish culture and customs. He also made use of a vast array of translations, commentaries and reference materials.[2]

His interesting and informative expositions, combined with practical applications, made the Sunday school materials popular. In an editorial comment, C&MA publication secretary David J. Fant observed,

> The quarterly which has shown the most rapid increase in circulation among all our Sunday School literature is our *Adult Quarterly*. Its phenomenal growth doubtless may be attributed to its author, Rev. J.A. MacMillan, whose editorials in *The Alliance Weekly* have proved to be such a blessing to our readers.[3]

The material was so well received that it was also produced for the *Home Bible Study Quarterly*.[4] MacMillan continued to write the weekly lessons until his death over twenty-two years later.[5]

A prolific and productive author, MacMillan was soon given even more writing responsibility. The position of associate editor of *The Alliance Weekly* was created in 1934 to free the editor, Alliance president Harry Shuman, from day-to-day responsibilities so that he could fulfill other duties of his office, including frequent travel.[6] With all his writing experience, theological insight, business expertise and leadership capacity, MacMillan was a natural for the job. He was also appointed a part-time lecturer at the Missionary Training Institute in Nyack, New York.

Leaving his pastorate in Winnipeg, he relocated in New York; eventually he became a naturalized American citizen. His first articles as a member of the editorial staff of *The Alliance Weekly* appeared on June 9, 1934. Predictably, his first editorial, entitled "The Conflict of Truth and Error," advanced the theme of spiritual warfare.[7]

For the next sixteen years, MacMillan would become the chief weekly editorial writer for *The Alliance Weekly*. Dr. Shuman's role, according to his own admission, was primarily in an advisory capacity, giving direction and approval for the overall policies and content of the periodical, only occasionally injecting an editorial or an article.[8]

In his editorial capacity, MacMillan received many letters requesting counsel, especially regarding spiritual, emotional and physical distresses, which he often discerned to be due to oppression from Satan.[9] He sometimes addressed such questions in his editorials and answered many a troubled questioner with a personal letter. He even had a short-lived column in the magazine entitled "The Inquirer's Corner," in which he answered theological and Christian living questions posed to him by readers.[10] Upon MacMillan's retirement as associate editor in 1950, Shuman remarked, "Through his extensive correspondence with subscribers he has had a very rich ministry in prayer and personal counsel among those in spiritual need."[11]

For a man who had reached what today is considered retirement age, MacMillan showed no signs of slowing down. His mental capacity appeared to increase as he got older and he seemed to have boundless energy into his eighties. Students and colleagues attributed this to maintaining divine health and healing through his exercise of the authority of the believer.[12]

In addition to his other writing duties, MacMillan capitalized on his voracious reading habits by producing an occasional book review.[13] He also wrote a Nyack correspondence course entitled *Christian Missions* in 1938, no doubt based on the missions course he taught at Nyack.[14] In 1940 he assisted other Alliance leaders in compiling a catechism entitled "Questions and Answers for Young Disciples."[15] In 1942 Charles Finney's *Christ Our Sanctification* was republished by Christian Publications in cooperation with the Finney Sesquicentennial Memorial Conference. MacMillan's fondness for Finney is shown in the preface he penned for this new edition.[16] For all his proliferation of writing, it is amazing to consider that he was not a skilled typist, but pecked away year after year on a manual typewriter, using only his two index fingers.[17]

His popular articles on believer's authority in 1932 were followed up by a sequel in 1936 entitled "The Authority of the Intercessor."[18] This too was so well received that it was published and spread abroad in tract form. In 1940 he wrote yet another article entitled "The Authority of the Rod."[19] These two articles were later combined together with "The Authority of the Believer" to form a book under the original title.

MacMillan's next major publishing success began as a five-part series of articles in *The Alliance Weekly* in 1948 entitled "Modern Demon Possession."[20] The series was his response to the many requests to put his teachings and experiences on spiritual warfare and exorcism into writing. Compiled from his Nyack lecture notes,[21] this popular article series was also republished in book form and was frequently cited by scholars.[22] In 1980, Keith Bailey, then managing editor of Christian Publications, received additional lecture materials from a former student of MacMillan's, added them to the book and reissued it under the title of *Encounter with Darkness*.[23] In 1997 Christian Publications combined *Authority of the Believer* and *Encounter with Darkness* into a single volume.

MacMillan's business acumen was demonstrated in the steady growth of *The Alliance Weekly*. Circulation increased from 8,500 in 1933 to 48,000 in 1944.[24] In 1937 it was stated of *The Alliance Weekly*, "The paper is the best in all its honored history."[25] Even with a postwar decline in circulation, the magazine continued to be rated highly, especially the editorials. The editor of another Christian journal remarked, "We thank you for your excellent magazine which we thoroughly read each week with deep appreciation. We consider it one of the most beautifully edited magazines of our generation."[26] *The Alliance Weekly* continued to receive letters of commendation and inquiry worldwide, "from different sections of Asia, Africa, Europe and Latin America."[27]

While he probably consulted with Dr. Shuman and other Alliance leaders, MacMillan was chiefly responsible for the selection of authors and content. The *Weekly* not only included articles by current and past C&MA leaders, but also by a variety of writers, many of them MacMillan's favorites: Jessie Penn-Lewis, Carrie Judd Montgomery, D.M. Panton, George H. Pember, Charles Spurgeon, Charles Finney, Andrew Murray, A.J. Gordon, F.B. Meyer and many other noted Christian leaders. MacMillan fre-

quently featured articles by A.W. Tozer, an articulate pastor and author, who would later become the magazine's
editor in 1950.

In 1937, the golden anniversary of the C&MA, *The Alliance Weekly* featured many historical and biographical stories about A.B. Simpson and the early Alliance, as well as
articles by Simpson. Kenneth MacKenzie, a long-time
friend and colleague of Simpson, contributed a ten-part
series entitled "My Memories of A.B. Simpson."[28]
MacMillan reported, "Much that has never been published from his pen appears in the regular issues of *The Alliance Weekly*."[29]

Also in 1937, MacMillan published a chapter from
Penn-Lewis' publication *Prayer and Evangelism* entitled,
"How to Pray for Missionaries." The excerpt featured
biblical teaching on binding and loosing for advancing
the kingdom of God on the mission field. The selection
was so vital to MacMillan that he reissued the article in
the *Weekly* again in 1941.[30]

After fourteen years of leadership on *The Alliance
Weekly*, MacMillan was able to make the following statement about the magazine:

> The test of a religious journal is the extent and na-
> ture of its ministry to its readers and to the body
> which it represents. For over six decades *The Alliance
> Weekly* has maintained a high standard of sound doc-
> trine and of spiritual teaching. It has sought to com-
> ment helpfully upon world and national issues from a
> scriptural and prophetic standpoint, but has carefully
> refrained from politically controversial matters.[31]

During his years as associate editor of *The Alliance
Weekly* and adjunct professor at Nyack College,
MacMillan also actively served the Alliance in other ca-
pacities. Elected three times to the board of managers,

he served with A.W. Tozer during his last term.[32] He was elected as a member of the foreign department in 1941 for a term and also served on the committee on location and arrangements for Annual Council.[33]

Content and Themes of MacMillan's Writing

In his Bible studies and editorials MacMillan demonstrated a broad range of knowledge and research from a wide variety of resources. The *Adult Quarterly* lessons were on books of the Bible or were topical studies of scriptural doctrines or biblical characters. Each year's studies usually covered both the Old and New Testaments, with one lesson each quarter directed toward a temperance emphasis. MacMillan also periodically made mention of archeological discoveries which affirmed the historical accuracy of the Bible against modernist views.[34]

The content of his lessons ranged from theological issues to practical Christian living. He did not shy away from controversy, but addressed such topics as Calvinism and Arminianism, prophecy and the end times, racial prejudice, inerrancy of Scripture, liberal ("modernist") theology, modes of baptism, etc. Many of these same themes were common in his editorials.

MacMillan wrote editorials on many facets of the Christian life. Two popular ones were entitled "The Unhurried Christian" and "The Unworried Christian."[35] A Midwestern business executive was so impressed with these articles that he duplicated portions of them and handed them out to others.[36]

MacMillan "had understanding of the times" (1 Chronicles 12:32), frequently writing about a wide variety of social, moral and political issues. He wrote much against communism, Nazism, fascism and other totalitarian systems, frequently applying prophetic Scriptures to them. In 1938 he called the Nazi regime a "goat nation," declaring it will be under the judgment of the tribunal of heaven. After reading Hitler's *Mein Kampf*, he challenged its philosophy in his editorials.[37]

As war threatened to rage all around the world, MacMillan strongly declared that there is no such thing as a Christian soldier any more than a Christian nation. He agreed that some soldiers "have borne a noble witness for Christ," but he warned against associating Christian service with military service, because "the soldier is enlisted for the purpose of war, and war is essentially the trade of killing men. . . . The wars of Israel cannot serve as an analogy for the Christian of today."[38]

And yet he was no pacifist, either; his own son served in World War II, though in a noncombatant role. True peace would come to the world, he insisted, only through divine intervention:

> Pacifism will not cure the raging of the nations nor the vain imaginings of the peoples. Should any government cast away its armaments and depend upon divine intervention to protect it, as is suggested by some religious leaders, it would speedily be overwhelmed by the conscienceless enemies which surround it, and which covet certain of its territories or riches. . . . Christ in person is the only solution for the unrest and injustice of earth.[39]

He held no postmillennial optimism about consummating the kingdom of God on earth: "Nor may we look for a 'Christian world order' evolving from the chaotic conditions of old-world society. The only permanent world order will be set up by the Son of God at His coming."[40] He displayed insight into governmental affairs: "The attainment of the Presidential office is never in itself a guarantee that the head of the government may be other than an un-usually successful student of the art of pleasing the peo-ple."[41] He also supported the government's right to exercise capital punishment, defending it from Scripture.[42]

MacMillan also spoke prophetically to the North Amer-ican Church. In the 1940s Islam and Eastern mysticism exerted little influence and were considered no great threat to Christianity, yet he predicted the growing entice-ment of these "doctrines of demons," declaring, "These things are both a challenge and a warning to the Christian Church."[43] Today, less than fifty years later, what Mac-Millan foresaw has come to pass; militant Islamic funda-mentalism plagues the entire world and Eastern mysticism pervades American culture through New Age philosophy.

A man who "understood the times," MacMillan fre-quently related Scripture to contemporary circumstances and made repeated references to prophetic passages of Scripture, particularly those in Daniel.[44] On the other hand, he also cautioned against undue speculation and jumping to conclusions. He recognized that talk of form-ing a Jewish state and building a temple could lead to ful-fillment of prophecy, but warned to leave fulfillment in God's sovereign hands. He agreed that Mussolini could end up being the Antichrist, but also saw signs that did not seem to fit or fulfill the biblical pattern.[45]

Unlike some Christians of his time, he was no Zionist:

> The Jews have no right to Palestine by inheri-tance. That right was long ago nullified by conquest. The nation's sole claim to *Eretz Israel* (the Land of Israel) rests upon the divine covenant with Abra-ham (Gen. 15:18ff.), and, since Calvary, the whole people have been out of covenant with God. When once more they are restored to His favor, the terms of the covenant will again become operative.[46]

Still, he had a deep love for the Jewish people and often wrote on Jewish themes—heritage, history, culture and their restoration today. He appealed to Christians to pray for the Jews.[47]

MacMillan also promoted social justice in many editorials, decrying prejudice against Jews, African-Americans and other racial and ethnic groups, years before it was acceptable to do so,[48] and received letters of criticism for his stand.[49] Other cultural and social issues he addressed included gambling, drugs, alcohol, tobacco, crime, divorce, immodest dress, movies and theater.[50] "The movie," he asserted, "should be reformed, or it should go. It is based wholly on financial profit, and has little consideration of the social or spiritual welfare of its patrons, young and old."[51] Over fifty years later, his critique is all the more relevant.

MacMillan had great concern for the home and family, giving counsel for godly parenting in the raising of children.[52] He tackled the problem of juvenile delinquency[53] and condemned emerging support for euthanasia.[54] These problems are even more prevalent today, and MacMillan's counsel is just as timely.

Advertised as presenting "editorials that interpret the great spiritual movements in this fast-changing world,"[55] *The Alliance Weekly* under MacMillan countered divergent religious teachings such as Islam and Roman Catholicism,[56] beliefs he had confronted while a missionary in the Philippines. He also noticed the rise of a prophetic doctrine that was developing into a cult in his day: British-Israelism, the attempt to identify Anglo-Saxons with the lost tribes of Israel. (Such cultic groups as Herbert W. Armstrong's Worldwide Church of God would arise out of this teaching.) In response he wrote a series of articles entitled "British-Israelism—A Latter-Time Heresy."[57]

His editorials addressed many of the other religious "isms" of the times—Unitarianism, religious liberalism ("modernism") and the social gospel.[58] He commented on Einstein's atheism.[59] He was even critical of fundamentalism: "Brethren, even our so-called fundamentalism very often presents little that attracts, and being devoid of spiritual power, has nothing that will touch the springs of the inner life or bring under conviction the conscience."[60] Nevertheless, at the same time, he considered himself a fundamentalist:

> We, as Fundamentalists, accept and glory in the offense of the cross; we rest and rejoice in redemption through His blood; we are content to find in Christ crucified the power of God and the wisdom of God; and we join with the Apostle of salvation by faith in crying: "God forbid that I should glory, save in the cross of our Lord Jesus Christ, by whom the world is crucified unto me, and I unto the world."[61]

The term "evangelical" was not in vogue at that time. Today he would be classified as an evangelical, because he did not advocate separatism, as many later fundamentalists did in opposition to evangelicals. For instance, while he wrote strongly and frequently in opposition to Roman Catholic teachings and practice, he frowned upon the intolerance of some fundamentalists toward Roman Catholic people in public or private life:

> There is a tendency to identify the individual with the system to which he belongs, and to regard both with the suspicion which has come down from past years of persecution. Let us rather be enlarged in our sympathies, and practice toward all men a Christly courtesy and a generous fellowship which shall ward off hatred, and win others to our Christ.[62]

MacMillan periodically wrote to the C&MA constituency concerning the Alliance message and ministry. He was especially concerned about the creeping disease of historical drift:

> We would err seriously in substituting a stately modernism for the heart religion of the past. Sentiment has a real part in the setting forth of our relationship to God. The church from which emotionalism has vanished is already moribund. When "amens" and "hallelujahs" are no longer heard in Alliance assemblies, we may write "Ichabod" over our doors, for the glory of the Holy One has departed. And the same is true of the old-time phraseology.[63]

MacMillan was fond of using typology, especially regarding the tabernacle,[64] but he avoided strange and unusual interpretations or forced exegesis. Recurrent in his Sunday school lessons and editorials were illustrations from John Bunyan's *Pilgrim's Progress*.[65]

The themes of spiritual authority, binding and loosing, demons and spiritual warfare, "doctrines of demons," deception and discernment appeared again and again in both his editorials and Sunday school lessons. MacMillan was ahead of his time, advancing such concepts as "praying geographically," which could have been a forerunner of the sometimes questioned contemporary concepts of spiritual mapping and breaking the strongholds of territorial spirits.[66]

One of his favorite concepts (commonly interlaced among diverse themes) was expressed in the terms "spiritual energy," "divine energy" or "energizing by the Spirit." In "The Authority of the Intercessor" he stated, "The solution of every spiritual problem is to be found in the working of the divine energy."[67] He contrasted the

Spirit-energized life with "fleshly energy" or even "demon-inspired energy" or "satanic energy."[68]

MacMillan wrote often about the inner life and sanctification. The influence of Simpson's writings is evident in his frequent use of hyphenated terms when discussing the self-life (self-exaltation, self-pleasing, self-seeking, self-glory, etc.). He commonly referred to the "three-fold" composition of man—body, soul and spirit—often drawing typological comparison with the three dimensions of the tabernacle: outer court, Holy Place and Holy of Holies.

Whether discussing prophecy, praise, prayer, joy, faith or any number of other topics, MacMillan often illustrated his points with personal experience. Some illustrations were repeated in various forms and contexts through the years in the quarterlies. The humility of the man is shown in the fact that he almost always wrote these anecdotes in the third person. Sometimes he even disguised personal illustrations by making it sound like he was talking about someone else.[69]

MacMillan was the kind of person who studied with the newspaper in one hand and the Bible in the other. He often referred to secular newspapers and magazines such as *Reader's Digest*, *British Weekly*, *New York Times* and *New York Herald-Tribune*.[70] He also consulted several Christian periodicals including *Moody Monthly*, *The Dawn* (edited by D.M. Panton), *The Evangelical Christian* (edited by fellow Toronto native G.V. Bingham), *The Overcomer* (founded by Jessie Penn-Lewis) and *China's Millions*.[71]

MacMillan loved old Scottish and Anglo-Saxon jokes and stories; examples of such stories are sprinkled abundantly throughout his editorials and Sunday school lessons.[72] He wrote and published several poems in *The Alliance Weekly*, including "Rapture!," "The Grace of

Love," "Heart Rest," "The Tides of Life" and "A New Year
Meditation."[73]

"Heart Rest" addresses one of the themes he periodically wrote about in his editorials:

> O precious, precious Fountain
>   How gloriously free
> Thy satisfying waters
>   Are springing up in me!
> The "Promise of the Father"
>   Abides within my breast,
> "A well of Living Water,"
>   The Spirit's blessed rest.
>
> What need of earthly fountains
>   When, from His Throne below,
> There gusheth forth a River
>   Of soul-refreshing flow?
> And while the Throne endureth,
>   And while our need remains,
> That River never faileth,
>   But aye its strength sustains.
>
> Earth's rivulets are tasteless,
>   Nor meet the soul's deep need;
> Earth's pleasures are deceitful,
>   To deeper thirst they lead;
> Earth's love is ever changeful—
>   Our souls we cannot fill
> When from Heaven's mighty River
>   We turn to earth's weak rill.
>
> Yet to those streams insipid
>   Our fickle hearts supine
> Often return, forgetful
>   Of richer Love Divine;
> Then He, whose grace stupendous
>   Redeemed us from our loss,
> His pierced hands outstretching,
>   Recalls us to the Cross.

Jesus, Thyself the Giver
  Of Heav'nly grace most free;
Jesus, Thyself the River,
  Life's waters flow in Thee;
By Thy blest banks abiding,
  Each restless soul below
May slake its thirst forever
  And perfect Heart Rest know.[74]

Though little of MacMillan's work is currently in print, there is no doubt that his sixteen years as associate editor of *The Alliance Weekly* and more than twenty-two years as author of the quarterlies had a great effect upon his readers, helping to shape the spiritual life of The Christian and Missionary Alliance for more than two decades. Many of his writings are worthy of being republished for the spiritual benefit of Christians today.

ELEVEN

Alice Sherwood—
A Second Divine Match

A FTER FOURTEEN YEARS OF marriage, John resumed bachelorhood once again—a lifestyle
well-suited for a ministry of itinerant preaching
and interim pastorates. By 1934 Buchanan, who lived
much of the time with his aunts while John was traveling,
had graduated from high school and enrolled in a Toronto
college. With his son through school, John was free to accept the call to New York. He had become readjusted to
single life once again, though he must have been lonely at
times, yearning for the type of companionship he had enjoyed with Isabel. Little did he know that God was preparing a second "divine match."

Alice Sherwood, a 1926 graduate of the Missionary
Training Institute, was born in September of 1900 in up-
state New York and raised in the Ballston Spa area. After
graduation she became a secretary at the C&MA national
headquarters for foreign secretary A.C. Snead, and later
for treasurer David Mason.[1] John became acquainted with

Alice while visiting headquarters sometime during his administrative and itinerant work with the Alliance, perhaps shortly after he returned from the Philippines.

Alice occasionally wrote poems that were published in *The Alliance Weekly*. This was one of the many things she had in common with John, who himself had a flair for poetry. One such poem, written from her heart apparently out of some painful life experience unknown to us, was entitled "He Asks Us to Believe." Published in *The Alliance Weekly* in 1932, it may have struck a sympathetic chord with John's own heartrending experience of losing Isabel. Like John, Alice demonstrated a godly maturity through her fiery trial:

> He asks us to believe;
>> We may not see
>> How God can gracious be
>> And let His children know
>> Heartbreaking woe,
>> But He is kind,
>> And some day we shall find,
>> In heaven's glory-light,
>>> The way was right His wisdom would achieve.
>
> Perhaps our Saviour knows
>> That pain we need
>> Before we fully heed
>> His tender, loving voice.
>> We rejoice
>> That He has planned
>> For us to understand
>> Some day. But now He cares,
>> In love He shares
>>> Our strange and unknown woes.
>
> Oh may we trust Him still!
>> His loving heart
>> Bids every fear depart,

And over all our way,
If we obey,
His joy and peace
And blessing never cease,
Until our hearts will say,
Each passing day,
    "We long to do Thy will."[2]

It is obvious from her writing that she was a woman fully surrendered to God, matured through trial and desiring to serve and please Him with all her heart—the kind of a woman who would be spiritually compatible with a man like John MacMillan.

When John moved to New York in 1934 they worked together regularly at the C&MA headquarters and over the next two years developed a close friendship. Even though Alice was twenty-six years his junior, they enjoyed one another's company. Alice's hair had whitened prematurely, and John, not knowing her age, one day teasingly prodded her, "Miss Sherwood, just how old are you?" Alice's revelation that she was only thirty-six did not deter John, now sixty-two, from proposing marriage shortly thereafter.[3]

Initially, Buchanan was not happy about this romance; though now a young man, the memory of his mother was still painfully fresh. But he eventually accepted Alice, and they had a warm relationship through the years.

On September 3, 1936, John MacMillan and Alice Sherwood were united in marriage in her hometown of Ballston Spa, New York.[4] Alice left her job at the C&MA offices, and they settled in Nyack on South Boulevard, across the street from the college. It was also in 1936 that Alice wrote the hymn "My Lord Will Come Some Day" which was published in the C&MA hymnal *Hymns of the Christian Life*.

Alice was very hospitable and gracious, opening their home to students in need and those in spiritual distress. Jane MacMillan recalled that her step-mother-in-law was good-hearted and that "her world revolved around her husband." She was "a gracious hostess with the gift of hospitality," entertaining many guests in their home. For four years, Jay Smith, a Nyack student disabled by polio, lived in their home. She was affectionately known as "Gammy" to her friends and her step-grandchildren who loved her dearly.

Alice was an able helpmate, supporting John in prayer and intercession. She often accompanied him on out-of-town speaking engagements and assisted him in his ministries of counseling and deliverance.[5] In his book *Encounter with Darkness* MacMillan describes in great detail an extensive ministry of deliverance over several weeks in 1947, in which Alice, along with others, assisted him. The warfare became intense, at one point continuing for seven consecutive nights.[6] On another occasion in 1951, a series of exorcism sessions on behalf of a Nyack student lasted at least three months and involved more than 170 demons.[7] During part of that time John and Alice kept the demonized woman in their home, caring for and ministering to her without any fear of evil attack. Rev. Jerry McGarvey, a Nyack student who assisted MacMillan in his ministry of deliverance in the early 1950s, recalls, "His wife was very much like him in her quietness and complete acceptance of her authority over evil spirits. She worked with him, but always behind the 'scenes,' mostly by praying while he and others cast out the spirits."[8]

During the last six months of his life, when he became severely ill, John needed constant care. Alice stayed close by, lovingly nursing John through his final days. She was assisted by other Nyack students taking turns.[9]

After John's death in 1956, Alice returned to secretarial work, employed for many years by McGinley Insurance writing insurance policies. She continued to open her home to students and others who needed a place to stay. She also had an upstairs apartment available. For a period of time, Becky, the daughter of A.W. Tozer, and her husband lived in the apartment.

A member of Simpson Memorial Church in Nyack for more than twenty-five years,[10] Alice came out of retirement from secretarial work to volunteer for her pastor, Maurice R. Irwin, typing his sermons for distribution to the congregation. Several of them were published later in *The Alliance Witness* and one series was published by Christian Publications as a book entitled *Eternally Named*.[11]

Alice died at the age of eighty, on September 11, 1980, in Valley Cottage, New York, after several months in a nursing home.[12] Her funeral service, conducted by Simpson Church minister Rev. Neal Clarke, fittingly concluded with the singing of her own hymn, "My Lord Will Come Some Day":

> When dark the night and burdens press,
>   When steep and rough the way,
> This hope o'erfloods my soul with joy;
>   My Lord will come some day.
> I listen for His blessed voice,
>   I seek to watch and pray;
> I trust His precious promise true,
>   My Lord will come some day.
>
> At early dawn I watch for Him,
>   I watch for Him at noon;
> My heart sings o'er the sweet refrain,
>   "My Lord is coming soon."
>
> As evening shadows gather 'round
>   And darken all the sky,

I lift my head, I cry with joy,
   "His coming draweth nigh."

Refrain:
Some day, some day,
   My Lord will come some day.
Through His wondrous grace
   I shall see His face;
My Lord will come some day.[13]

MacMillan as Professor

CONCURRENTLY WITH HIS WORK as associate editor of *The Alliance Weekly*, MacMillan taught classes at the Missionary Training Institute in Nyack, a responsibility he fulfilled for nineteen years, from 1934 to 1953. While today his lack of formal education would disqualify him from most academic teaching, his life experience and extensive study uniquely authorized him to train young men and women for missionary and pastoral ministry.

He was admired by his students as a stable, astute man of God. Some of them affectionately called him "Dr. Mac," conveying on him an "honorary doctorate" to show their respect for his breadth and depth of knowledge. Forty years later, former students still refer to him as "Dr. MacMillan."[1]

O.H. Bublat, who studied under MacMillan, was impressed by his professor's humility: "He was one of the few people I have known over the years who exhibited the quality of meekness. He was a living demonstration of a

meek and quiet spirit."[2] He was so meek and unassuming
that when talking about himself he would never say "I,"
but rather "*we* went to the store" or "*one* went to the store."
This affectation won him the nickname of "Mr. We."[3]

Jay Smith, a student who lived with the MacMillans,
described him as having "an imposing and commanding
demeanor" but also a "gentle and humble . . . spirit."[4]
Students who sat in his lectures had to listen closely, as
he spoke softly and deliberately.[5]

Charles Gifford, who studied at Nyack in the late
1930s, remembered MacMillan as stable and solid, re-
maining unflappable under pressure: "Niagara Falls could
flow upwards and it wouldn't upset MacMillan."[6] In the
school's 1943 yearbook it was said of him, "Deliberately
and purposefully he lays out truth worth gathering up. His
pedagogical principles include humor . . . very, very dry,
unique, and almost inexhaustible!"[7]

Several students have memories of MacMillan on the
platform of the chapel along with John Cable, E.R.
Dunbar, Harold Freligh and other Alliance notables of the
time. Other colleagues of MacMillan were South American missionary V. Raymond Edman, who later assumed
the presidency of Wheaton College, and Kenneth Mac-
Kenzie, Episcopal minister and close friend of A.B.
Simpson, who displayed a distinguished demeanor with
his clerical collar and beard.[8] To the students, these leaders were more than just professors; they were mentors,
men of maturity they could get to know personally and
from whom they could glean wisdom.

Jerry McGarvey, missionary to Africa, recalls, "My first
impression of Mr. MacMillan was accompanied by awe.
First, because I knew he had been a missionary (which I
planned to be) and then secondly his quiet, strong manner
which literally emitted authority."[9] The baptism or filling

of the Spirit and sanctification were strong themes of MacMillan's teaching. Though he never talked about his own experience, Cliff Westergren remembered that it was such a natural part of his life that it flowed through his teaching and conversation, not so much "as a theological teaching, but as a personal reality."[10]

Throughout these years MacMillan taught courses on Christ in the Bible, Acts, missions, biblical counseling, Alliance distinctives and demonology.[11] He spiced his courses with practical application.[12] Being a man of prayer, he made the C&MA prayer directory a required text for his class on Alliance missions,[13] encouraging his students to pray through the directory geographically, interceding for specific locations and missionaries around the world.[14]

MacMillan assigned students to write on topics like the state of the lost according to Romans 1. "As I studied this passage," Jerry McGarvey recalls, "I was nothing less than astounded at how clearly and logically and irrefutably it put forth the fact that man is indeed lost."[15] Regarding his course on Acts, Jay Smith remarked, "He lectured with a fervency on the missionary journeys of St. Paul as though he were the Apostle reporting on those journeys."[16]

In his classes he shared many of his experiences in China and the Philippines.[17] Richard Barker (Nyack, 1951-1954) declared that MacMillan's "stories of confrontation with the spirit world rivaled the Book of Acts."[18] John Nevius (1947-1950) recalled that MacMillan once told about praying for a person in the Philippines who was pronounced dead but was restored to life.[19]

The Authority of the Believer was a required textbook in MacMillan's "Principles of Missions" course, which included training in exercising spiritual authority and cast-

ing out demons.[20] In on-the-job training, he had students
assist him in exorcisms; several who were gifted in this area
ministered to demonically afflicted students during a revival at Nyack in 1950.[21] After several students assisted
him in a particularly notable case of deliverance, he insti-
tuted a course in 1951 on demonology and spiritual warfare. This put MacMillan on the cutting edge, for such
courses were virtually unknown at Christian educational
institutions until at least the 1970s or 1980s.

MacMillan was the stereotypical "absent-minded professor." One time, while he was preparing a chapel message, his wife Alice reminded him, "You spoke on that
before," so he changed his topic. In the midst of the message, however, he lost his train of thought and went back
to speaking about his original topic.[22] On another occasion, F. Paul Henry recounts,

> After he had announced his subject, he suddenly
> stopped and looked blank for a few seconds. Then
> he said, "I have completely forgotten what I had in-
> tended to preach about. It must be that God has
> some other truth in mind." He then prayed and
> asked God to give him the message that He had for
> us. He then proceeded to preach from another
> text.[23]

In personality MacMillan was described by students as
kind, polite, quiet and gentle. With the dignity of a true
gentleman, he never offended others and kept his appoint-
ments strictly.[24] John and Alice were warm and friendly
toward students, inviting them into their home, sometimes even letting them stay for a period of time when
there was a need.[25] He was not dynamic in his teaching
style and could even be considered a boring speaker, yet
some students testified that they listened "with rapt atten-

tion."[26] Ross Ingraham said that he spoke with "monotone voice, but riveting."[27]

MacMillan never took attendance in class. Instead, he would say, "You are your own roll-takers. And don't think that you can get away with it, because when Spiritual Emphasis Week comes, you will be convicted by the Holy Spirit." Invariably a few students would come to him at that time and confess that they had skipped class.[28] He always made an effort to help a student pass a course and did not seem overly strict in his grading. On one occasion, he jokingly announced to the students that he would throw their papers in the air, and the order in which they came down would determine their grades.[29]

MacMillan possessed a number of other notable idiosyncrasies. He almost always wore a gray suit and had a preference for bow ties. When he taught, he held both lapels on his suit with his hands. He had a fountain pen which was flat on one end, which he would stand pointed upward as an unconscious gesture while lecturing. He would also put the fingers of his two hands together tip-to-tip when he was deliberating about something. One student remembered him as "articulate in his speech, always pronouncing the 't' in the words 'apostles' and 'epistles.' " Another student, Don Kenyon, recalled, "He had a repertoire of songs which he taught the kids to sing."[30]

MacMillan exercised great insight in the spiritual counsel he gave to young people. A student from another theological college came to inquire of MacMillan concerning the Holy Spirit. As he proceeded to give a biblical exposition on the Holy Spirit, the student responded, "My professors do not teach this way."

MacMillan simply asked, "What does the Bible say?" The student admitted that the Scripture clearly contradicted what he had been taught.

By the leading of the Spirit, MacMillan pointed him to
Second John 9: "Whosoever transgresseth, and abideth
not in the doctrine of Christ hath not God." Then he
asked, "If a man has not God, where is he?"

The student "instantly and heatedly replied,
'Dr._____ (naming a nationally known modernist) is
not lost.' "

MacMillan responded, "We have not discussed him in
any way, but if you think the shoe fits him, put it on
him."[31]

Another example of his wise counsel concerned the
thorny issue of Calvinism versus Arminianism. Though
steeped in Reformed theology, MacMillan did not take a
definitive position, but was practical in his approach to
theology. Once, while discussing the nature of salvation in
one of his Bible classes, he was asked a question about
eternal security. He responded,

> In His Word, God has outlined to us His ap-
> pointed method of salvation, through faith in His
> Son. He has also indicated the path in which the
> saved one should walk, saying, "This is the way;
> walk ye in it" (Isaiah 30:21). All of the divine prom-
> ises are given to us when in the way of faith and obe-
> dience. If we go aside out of that way, there is no
> promise that applies to us. Theologians may specu-
> late about the condition of the soul, but the only
> place of security is when walking in the way of holi-
> ness.[32]

One highlight of MacMillan's tenure at Nyack occurred
in the fall of 1940, when revival visited the school. He
called it "the greatest outpouring of the Holy Spirit at
Nyack since 1906."[33] MacMillan described the 1940 spiritual awakening in terms reminiscent of the Welsh revival:

When the Rev. H.E. Nelson arrived to conduct the revival services, he exclaimed at the opening of his first message: "The revival we longed for is already here." It was true. On the campus the presence and power of the Holy Spirit was so real all hearts were melted in contrition before God. How easy it was to pray! How easy to seek the Lord! How precious the victories won! Students were broken in spirit and burst out in confession during the meetings held in the auditorium; others found peace on bended knee in the silence of their own rooms, while the burdens of others were lifted in the small prayer groups that gathered spontaneously in a score of places on the campus.

The Holy Spirit was recognized as the Divine Leader. He had control of both minister and those to whom he ministered, and was allowed to move upon all hearts as He willed. Sometimes the speaker did not have opportunity to give his message. On one occasion, before the close of the opening hymn, the altar was filled with seekers, weeping and crying out to God in confession of sin and agony of soul. Then their weeping would be turned into paeans of praise, as they pressed through to victory and stood up to testify. In a four-hour service on the Friday night, the leader only had opportunity to give a ten-minute message at the close, the remainder of the time being spent in prayer and praise. All who testified to meeting God were given a word of comfort or caution by Brother Nelson, who was granted a special anointing for this ministry. . . . "This is that" for which we have sought as a Society, with strong cryings and tears. It is a heaven-born, God-sent Holy Ghost revival. . . . It came because of believing prayer; because the Alumni and friends of the Institute were concerned and prayed; because the Faculty, Staff, and Student Body set themselves

to seek God in the darkness of the early morning
hours and far into the night, refusing to be satisfied
until God made good His promise, "If my people,
which are called by my name, shall humble themselves, and pray, and seek my face, and turn from
their wicked way; then will I hear from heaven and
will forgive their sins, and will heal their land."[34]

Nine weeks later the movement of the Spirit was still
going on and MacMillan reported on it in *The Alliance
Weekly* under the title "Nyack Revival Continues."[35] Following midsemester examinations and a half night of
prayer after a Friday night missionary meeting,

revival fires blazed forth again. The congregation was
moved by the presence and power of the Holy Ghost
as with contrition of heart they went to their knees in
prayer. . . . After seasons of prayer and testimony . . .
earnest prayer [was] offered that God would give vision and passion, men and means, to develop the borders of our Society. . . . The result of revival fire on
the Nyack hillside is the passionate desire of faculty
and student body to reach all with the gospel message. During the last three weeks nearly 400 students
were out in practical Christian work. Jails, hospitals,
missions, Sunday Schools, churches, and literally
hundreds of homes were visited. . . . At one service
ten confessed Christ as their Savior, and twelve were
brought back to the Lord. [Others] had the joy of seeing five souls saved in house-to-house visitation, and
at one hospital a Catholic boy and a Jewish boy testified with joy: "Jesus has come into our hearts, too!"[36]

A Crowning Achievement

Near the end of MacMillan's ministry as professor and
mentor at the Missionary Training Institute, the students
of Nyack honored him by a dedication in the 1950 yearbook, *The Missionarian*. Featuring a full-page portrait of

MacMillan, the yearbook included a letter from the Class of 1950 expressing their deep respect and gratitude:

> As a token of our appreciation for your faithful teaching ministry, your wise counsel, and your spirit of devotion to the Saviour, we take great pleasure in dedicating to you the thirteenth volume of the MISSIONARIAN. . . .
>
> Future Nyack alumni, as well as those of previous years, will long remember Mr. MacMillan—a man of God, gracious, and humble. This remembrance will continue to be a challenge to us who once sunken in miry clay are now cleansed by Jesus' precious blood—a challenge to abandon ourselves in the Potter's hand, that we too might be vessels from which He shall pour out His rivers of Living Water.[37]

MacMillan as Speaker and Evangelist

URING THE LAST TWENTY years of his life, MacMillan served as a guest speaker at many churches and conferences. He was a speaker at the annual missionary convention at the Gospel Tabernacle in New York City (the congregation founded by A.B. Simpson) in 1937 and 1941.[1] Even though some did not consider MacMillan a dynamic speaker, the report came back from the Camp Hebron Convention of the New England District in 1941, "Rev. J. A. MacMillan stirred his listeners with fresh lessons from the Scriptures."[2] His delivery may have been unadorned, but the content of his teaching was inspiring.

MacMillan also ministered through healing. He taught students how to pray for themselves for health and healing, by laying their hands daily on the parts of the body afflicted.[3] "In one instance," MacMillan reported,

A lady, who had been pronounced incurable from cancer, was visited in the hospital. After conversation she was told that God was able to meet her need for healing. "I know He is," she replied, "if it is His will." It was pointed out that the Word reveals it to be His will to meet His people thus, unless there is something between them and Him, and that if such an obstacle exists, it may be removed. About two weeks later that truth was revealed to her heart, and she sought the Lord and was healed.[4]

"We greatly respected his prayer life," said Richard Barker, a former student. "It was a thrill during a college day of prayer to listen as he named the physical or spiritual need of one after the other and then in quiet faith asked, 'Heal him; heal her; provide what this one needs, Lord. Thank you.' "[5] Barker said that his calm boldness was not brazen, nor was there any straining, but it was simply confidence that the Lord would respond.

John Stirzaker, who was later a C&MA pastor and district superintendent, had a personal experience with MacMillan's healing ministry. While he was a married student at the Missionary Training Institute from 1938-1941, his young son became severely ill and could not eat. MacMillan came and prayed for the boy. He was healed immediately and then got up and ate a full meal.[6]

During all his years of ministry as editor and professor at Nyack, MacMillan was actively engaged in evangelism, a practice he had developed early in life. In his editorials and Sunday school lessons he encouraged believers to invite other people to church, just as he and his family had done years ago in Toronto.[7] During his speaking engagements, MacMillan frequently gave evangelistic invitations.

On one such occasion MacMillan was kneeling at an altar with a young farmer, attempting to lead him to salvation. The man bemoaned his condition, saying, "I cannot repent." MacMillan replied, "I am not asking you to repent, but to believe on Jesus." He explained,

> The Lord Jesus deals with the humble heart, and if a man will truly accept Him, it will not be long before his heart is filled with deep consciousness of his sin and need, and he comes to the place of real repentance. The fact that the young man said he could not repent showed that he was regarding repentance as an emotional feeling rather than a forsaking of sin.[8]

MacMillan recognized that if a person truly believes and confesses that faith, genuine repentance will follow regardless of whether he has an emotional experience or not.

In another service a man about fifty years old came to the altar desiring salvation, but had difficulty understanding the truths of the gospel. Reading John 5:24 to him, MacMillan asked, "You have heard the Word of the Lord?"

"Yes."

"And you believe on Him?"

"Yes."

"Now what have you received?"

The man looked puzzled and MacMillan repeated the Scripture and his questions. All of a sudden it dawned on him: "Why! I have eternal life!"[9] Through John's patience and simplicity of presentation, he was able to guide these seekers into spiritual insight and new life in Christ.

MacMillan occasionally picked up hitchhikers, a much safer practice then than today, and witnessed to them. In 1946 he picked up a man on the highway, and in the course of conversation found out he was a member of a church. John asked him if he was saved, and the man responded, "I don't know what you mean."[10] As MacMillan so often discovered, many church members do not really understand what it means to be born again.

Early in 1949, MacMillan picked up a another hitch-hiker, an eighteen year-old West Point cadet, and shared the gospel with him. The young man "claimed that he was too young to accept Christ and surrender his life to Him." MacMillan, then in his late seventies, was frustrated that he was unable to convince him of his need of Christ. As a result, he challenged young people to share their faith, ex-plaining that this cadet needed "a young man to deal with him, one who personally knows the Saviour and the real-ity of His saving power and enabling grace and satisfying love. For Jesus is the Ideal of young manhood."[11]

MacMillan loved to share the gospel with everyone he met, young or old, rich or poor. In 1946 he conversed with a wealthy farmer, who remarked, "I am nearly eighty years of age. I have been successful and have built up a comfort-able fortune. But now, just at the time when it would be of the most benefit to me, I must leave it. There is not much satisfaction in life and what we gain in it." John pointed out his need of the new birth and "the better things that await those who have their hope set on the things that are eternal."[12]

MacMillan especially had a passion for sharing the good news of Jesus as Messiah with Jewish people. He noted that less than a generation earlier, "the mention of the name of Christ would produce a contemptuous reaction from any to whom it was spoken," but that attitudes had changed: "We have visited many Jews in many stores and homes, and have been received with kindness, while the Christian message has been listened to with eagerness in some cases."[13] One conversation he had with a Jewish per-son demonstrated MacMillan's ability to get to the heart of the matter:

> A Jew once said to [MacMillan], when confronted
> by the words of the prophets: "The thing is impossi-
> ble." He was answered, "It is impossible with man,
> but with God all things are possible. Your trouble is
> that you do not believe your own prophets." For
> faith has no difficulty in accepting God's revelation
> concerning the birth of His well-beloved and
> only-begotten Son.[14]

MacMillan's easygoing style of evangelism became a
model for others to follow and many sought his advice on
sharing their faith. In an Eastern town where he was ministering two young women approached him about witnessing. One confessed, "I know I ought to speak to others
whom I meet. But I just can't seem to do it, and I get into
awful bondage." MacMillan, out of his own experience,
answered, "The Lord never brings us into bondage; that is
the work of the enemy. Moreover, the Lord does not ex-
pect you to speak to everybody you meet. But, if you will
commit your way to Him, He will lead you to people and
bring others to you. Just trust Him for your service, as you
do for your salvation and your sanctification." A few
weeks later the woman wrote John, testifying that she was
experiencing a "new fellowship with the Saviour and a
great delight in confessing Him."[15]

MacMillan as Counselor

Counseling soon became a major area of ministry for
MacMillan. Anita Bailey, who worked with him as managing editor of *The Alliance Weekly* for seven years, recalled
that people came to him frequently for spiritual guidance
and always received a kind word and a helping hand.[16]
Many of the letters he received as editor also asked for
spiritual and personal counsel.[17] Pastors, missionaries and
lay people alike sought him out for advice.[18]

Many who came to him suffered from emotional distress. Though active in spiritual warfare, MacMillan recognized that not all emotional problems were demonic in origin. He even used the assistance of a medical doctor in certain counseling situations.[19]

MacMillan combined sound doctrine with practical psychology, so that his advice often included principles such as taking personal responsibility for one's actions and attitudes. One man who came to him was at one time a prominent preacher, but had slipped into physical and mental depression. He complained, "I don't think that God has treated me fairly."

MacMillan suggested to him that "his inward attitude held tightly shut the very door which the Lord sought to open, a door which might prove to him a way of liberation if he would enter it in submission and faith." Yet the minister did not respond. God wanted to bless him but he could not receive it. MacMillan concluded, "Men are individually responsible for the doors that open and close before them."[20]

A woman lamented to MacMillan, "I failed God, and He has left me." Still another man said, "I cannot get any light at all; the darkness is more than I can bear." To each of them he gave the same counsel: "That is not God's way; you have believed a lie about Him and His love and wisdom." MacMillan noted that "each one, as the realization came that they were under spiritual deception, took a fresh hold of the Lord's goodness and truth, and their joy and confidence returned."[21]

This is an example of what we would call today a "truth encounter," based on John 8:32, "And ye shall know the truth, and the truth shall make you free." He appeared to use a two-pronged approach in counseling such persons. First he would seek to bring a fresh illumination of who God is and what He is like, correcting bad theology. Then he would guide the troubled soul to a self-revelation of who he or she is in Christ, helping the person understand the privileges, inheritance and authority of the believer.

This is akin to the cognitive approach of psychology, which aims to change the way a person thinks in order to change behavior. MacMillan, though, never expressed his approach in psychological terms, but saw it from a biblical perspective, possibly pointing to such Scriptures as Proverbs 23:7: "For as he thinketh in his heart, so is he," and Romans 12:2, "But be ye transformed by the renewing of your mind."

MacMillan's ministry experience prepared him well to give wise counsel to those in the midst of church and personality conflicts:

> A lady, in another church, came to the writer some years ago with the complaint that she was the object of such an [slanderous] attack. She wished to defend herself, and asked if it would not be advisable to openly denounce her persecutors. The counsel given her was: "Sister, the scriptural way is clear. 'Commit thy way unto the LORD; trust also in him; and he shall bring it to pass. And he shall bring forth the righteousness as the noonday' (Ps. 37:5, 6). Leave your cause entirely in His hands, as He asks. If you put forth your hand to defend yourself, He will withdraw His, and let you fight the battle in your own way." She took the advice, and remained silent before God, with the result that very quickly the talking ceased, her honor was vindicated, and she was promoted to a ministry in the congregation that gave much opportunity of helpful service to others. Best of all, she had learned a secret of the Lord that will never fail.[22]

This was the very way in which he dealt with the unethical handling of his affairs with Armac Press after he went to China and the way in which he had handled Mrs. Lund when she had verbally attacked him in the Philippines. In both cases, he committed the injustice to the Lord, and the Lord vindicated him and resolved the problems in both situations.

At another time, a young lady came to MacMillan concerned about her weak prayer life. "Her complaint was that she said the same things each time she engaged in prayer and very quickly exhausted all the ideas she had." He advised her that the Bible is "the best textbook," and demonstrated to her from Scripture "how men of old cried to God and how their petitions were embodied in the pages of Scripture." He especially recommended to her Psalm 119:

> Here we find a spiritual heart expressing his longing for communion with God, and telling out his love, confessing his sin and weakness, pleading for help and guidance. By studying this Psalm we can understand the nature of spiritual desire, and how the renewed heart craves holiness and likeness to God. Using the same petitions we will find our prayer vocabulary enlarged and enriched.[23]

Again, decades ahead of contemporary teaching on the subject, MacMillan counseled her to pray the Scriptures, a practice which was so much a part of his own life.

On another occasion, John was asked to visit a woman in a mental hospital. While praying with her, he discerned the presence of demonic activity, took authority over the spirits, and her mind was dramatically healed.[24] He possessed the unique discernment to perceive when a problem was merely psychological in nature, or when the powers of darkness were involved. The tendency today is

either categorically to deny demonic activity, or indiscrim-
inately to blame all problems on demons. MacMillan was
able to maintain a balance between the two extremes.

He also counseled with people overcome with addictive habits, obtaining remarkable results. MacMillan believed that the secret to victory was supernatural:

> The influx of divine life, sweeping through the
> spirit of the redeemed drunkard, removes the very
> desire for drink. . . . A young man who had been
> held in the thrall of intoxicants and tobacco . . . told
> how overnight his body had been so changed that,
> not only had all desire to partake of either of these
> things passed away, but he could not even touch
> them without repulsion.[25]

On another occasion he ministered to a young woman
who had inadvertently become addicted to narcotic medication. She was set free from the bondage, and avoided
any further contact with the medication.[26] His method
was a forerunner to such ministries as Teen Challenge
which have applied the supernatural power of the gospel
to those bound by chemical dependence and abuse.

Predating modern teaching on "generational sin" by decades, MacMillan warned of the consequences of sin being
visited upon succeeding generations, on the basis of Exodus 20:5. While counseling a man in prison, he noted that
his propensity for binge drinking was inherited from his
father's appetite for liquor. He called it "an inexorable law
of return and of increase," explaining with a poetic flair,

> Nor does it end with himself; the drunkard trans-
> mits a poisoned frame to his offspring; the loose
> woman has a daughter who is hurrying in the ways
> of shame. Our sins do not die with ourselves; they
> scatter themselves over the society about us like the
> winged seeds of the thistle and the dandelion, im-

possible to catch, settling down in choice places to
reproduce their kind.[27]

He adds that such a "principle of heredity" can result in
"sometimes a weakened body, always a tendency to
worldliness and departure from God."[28] However, he
notes, "Grace is shown in that the curse runs out in the
third and fourth generation, unless persisted in."[29] Commenting on MacMillan's teaching, chaplain Jay Smith
says,

> Breaking family curses was not a concept articu-
> lated in those words in the 1950s; but John felt
> strongly that the demonic hold on some had its roots
> in family history, in spiritism, occult, drugs, etc., and
> referenced the Old Testament Scripture that speaks
> to the iniquity of the fathers being visited on the chil-
> dren.[30]

MacMillan was later called on to visit the same man in
the hospital when he was suffering from *delirium tremens*.
MacMillan pointed out to him that his root problem was
not his appetite for liquor, which God could take away in
an instant, but "what He seeks is the surrender of your
life to Him. If you will do that, He will give you the victory."[31] He did not allow counselees to excuse their sin or
blame it on their parents, but emphasized their personal
responsibility, as well as their ability to break free from
the bondage with Christ's help.

MacMillan also recognized a connection between
wholeness and holiness, pointing out how such habits
can weigh down a Christian's life:

> [MacMillan] visited a young professing Christian
> in the hospital. Beside the bed lay a packet of ciga-
> rettes. No reference was made to them until the
> Word of God had been read and prayer offered.
> Then attention was casually drawn to them, when

> the young man bridled up and said sharply, "There's
> no harm in that." The answer was made: "Perhaps
> not. But such things are what the Bible calls a *weight*.
> They hinder us from making progress in the Chris-
> tian life. And it is essential for us to lay aside all that
> holds us back from the highest that God offers."[32]

MacMillan's approach was not to condemn, but to call
a person higher and deeper in the things of God. He contended that when someone becomes wholly committed
to God and to righteous living, God enables the person
to rise above temptation and overcome bondage.

MacMillan found that people in bondage to addictions were often also deeply in bondage to demonic spirits as well.

> Thus an inordinate desire for tobacco, or for li-
> quor, or for sensuality, may be a sign of the indwell-
> ing of such a spirit. A young woman, who suffered
> from drug addiction, when delivered from the
> demon power, found herself free from the power
> also of narcotics. Another, suffering from homosex-
> uality, in like manner was delivered from possession
> and her immoral tendencies at the same time.[33]

MacMillan's counseling through the years ministered
broadly to a wide diversity of people and problems. Even
as late as 1954, *The Alliance Weekly* reported that
MacMillan, now eighty years old, continued to provide
counsel for many people.[34] Until just a few months before
his death, John MacMillan continued to minister energeti-
cally and effectively to all who came to him with a need,
demonstrating the wisdom of a sage and the stamina of
youth.

FOURTEEN

MacMillan's Ministry of Spiritual Warfare

MACMILLAN GAINED A REPUTATION for his ministry of spiritual warfare, especially in what we know today as "deliverance ministry" or "exorcism," the expulsion of demons. As early as 1940 one of his students quipped, "If a demon confronted J.A. MacMillan, I feel sorry for the demon."[1] Several years later, Nyack president Thomas Moseley introduced him as "a man before whom demons tremble."[2]

MacMillan never went out looking for demons to bind and expel, but "the powers of darkness," as he frequently called them, would often show up. "John felt it [deliverance ministry] grew out of necessity that was 'laid upon him,' " former student Jay Smith explains. "Wherever he ministered there seemed to be individuals who were in need of deliverance from spiritual bondage."[3]

For more than thirty years, MacMillan actively engaged in combating attacks of the powers of darkness of every type on every level, whether false guilt and con-

demnation, depression, oppression, demonically induced illnesses, deception, obsession or possession. He
recognized that not all emotional illnesses were demonic, yet he also recognized that not all emotional illnesses were merely psychological.

He possessed a rare gift to discern the presence and activity of demonic spirits, when others could not. In fact,
"Some thought he was off," T. Robert Brewer said.[4] "He
was not always understood for his convictions," Jay Smith
explains. "In the '50s, deliverance ministry was not always
accepted in evangelical circles or in the Alliance. [It was]
accepted as a possible 'foreign field' phenomena, but there
could not be a need in cultured United States."[5] John
Ellenberger, a professor at Alliance Theological Seminary
and a former missionary, affirmed that "the C&MA was
on the forefront of dealing with the demonic because of
MacMillan."[6]

Many students at the Missionary Training Institute had
come out of mainline churches and were totally ignorant
of spiritual warfare. According to Cliff Westergren, who as
a student had worked with him, MacMillan engaged in
spiritual warfare in behalf of dozens of students who had
been caught in the web of cults and spiritism, some of
them for years.[7]

Through the years MacMillan made occasional mention in his writings of his encounters with these powers. In
1940, for instance, he reported, "The writer has seen a
woman immediately after the demon left her almost stran-
gled by the effort of the unclean spirit, but the recovery
was quick."[8] He mentioned "another class of sufferers"
which are not rendered unconscious by the spirits. Their
experience of the presence of the enemy is usually that of
deep mental or physical depression. A young man would
complain of manifestations to his mind; at another time,

he felt terrible pressure on his head and ears; at still another time, his body would start jerking uncontrollably. A young woman suffered from fear, from manifestations, from a strong desire for psychiatry. These symptoms, apparently proceeding from demon power, were addressed as demons, called by name, and commanded to leave. There was no further trouble from these sources.[9]

While MacMillan agreed that counseling and therapy could benefit in some cases of emotional illness,[10] he believed that "depression is often the direct result of the impact of spirits of evil upon the mind."[11] He argued that "many cases could be quoted," and cited one example which would be adequate to illustrate his point:

> A lady, about fifty years of age, was brought in a most deplorable state of nervous weakness. She was dealt with first of all regarding her spiritual condition, and led to the Lord. Then it was pointed out to her that her condition was quite unnatural, that her nervous state was unnecessary, that it was due to pressure of the enemy upon her mind, and that she could with the help of the Lord assert her will, and throw off the power assailing her. In an hour she was master of herself, and has remained so for several years. The ladies who brought her were astounded, and declared it to be a miracle.[12]

MacMillan also enumerated several other demonically inspired emotional illnesses, such as severe depression due to condemnation from deep sin:

> Suggestion to the mind that the unpardonable sin has been committed is repeatedly the cause of mental depression. It can be pointed out to the patient that, if that sin had been actually committed, there would be no conscience of it, because the Holy Spirit would have withdrawn. When every other cause for depression has been explored, the teaching

that it is the work of the enemy frequently clears up the situation. If the sufferer is rightly instructed on how to oppose and overcome the enemy, relief quickly comes.[13]

Sometimes it takes the form of pseudo-guilt, or overbearing guilt about a lesser sin:

A deaconess in a prominent church was seized with the conviction that she ought to confess some slight fault. At a prayer meeting of the members accordingly she rose and stated her failure openly. But at the next gathering the same pressure was on her mind, and she again confessed. Thereafter, at every meeting, there was a similar feeling of conviction; she did not confess, and the rebuke in her mind grew to such proportions that she was in agony of soul. When it was pointed out to her that the conviction was not of God, but the act of an accusing spirit, there was quick relief, with following complete liberty.[14]

Unreasonable fear is another frequent harassment induced by the powers of darkness. MacMillan gives this example:

A lady sitting in a chair in her kitchen heard a voice telling her that she was shortly to die. A sudden fear gripped her mind, which quickly covered nearly every aspect of life. She stated that if she went down into the cellar, fear would possess her so that her heart would pound severely. A missionary among the Mohammedan people told how a spirit of fear came upon him until he would lay [sic] awake at night listening for murderers to come. These might seem to be natural, but they so overcame the individuals that their life and work was [sic] hindered. An understanding of the cause of the trouble cleared away the dread. But in a thousand forms, this trouble is repeated, causing much distress and agony of mind.[15]

In addition, MacMillan maintained,

> A surprising number are met with whose ministry
> is disturbed by false guidance. They are not sure
> that the inward suggestions which come to them are
> of God, but they cannot determine what is right, or
> what they ought to do. This indecision becomes a
> real burden to them, and a decided hindrance in
> their service.[16]

MacMillan ministered to many such afflicted people
through what Neil Anderson today calls a "truth encounter."[17] In other words, rather than expelling demons
through overt commands, MacMillan helped these
counselees to recognize the truths of Scripture and to
speak words of authority and faith based upon the Scriptures, often by exercising the authority of binding and
loosing. Demons then have to flee, and the person is set
free.

Anderson similarly describes a "truth encounter" as
"the necessity to take every thought captive in obedience
to Christ (see 2 Corinthians 10:5) and to think upon
that which is true (see Philippians 4:8)."[18] Anderson advocates making "faith declarations" by "announcing and
renouncing," his terms for binding and loosing.[19] While
MacMillan's terminology and methodology is not as developed and elaborate as Anderson's, decades earlier
MacMillan was practicing a similar concept.

In actuality, both Anderson and MacMillan may take
their cue from Jessie Penn-Lewis, who advocated "the
place of truth in deliverance,"[20] rather than expulsion of
demons. While today a debate exists between whether
to use truth encounter or power encounter, MacMillan
implemented both in his ministry.[21] It would appear that
MacMillan would engage truth encounter methodology
unless he discerned the need for a power encounter.

In 1947 an Alliance pastor asked MacMillan to help a woman who was afflicted. Accompanied by his wife Alice, he joined a group of Christian friends who had gathered to pray for her. They did not discern at first that she was under the power of demons, but it soon became evident. MacMillan described how she became afflicted:

> A few years previously, following the death of her mother, she had sought the services of a Spiritist medium, believing that she could thus come into touch with the departed loved one. The person in question was a sincere Christian, but very poorly instructed in the Word of God. She had no conception that in thus tampering with necromancy she was breaking God's direct commands, and also opening herself to the danger of spirit attack in some form.
>
> The medium quickly recognized that her visitor was specially open to psychic impressions. Before long she asked her to unite with her in certain trance experiences; and later sought her cooperation in her spiritistic seances, inducing her to surrender herself to the will of the spirits. Some time afterward, the woman found herself in serious trouble through the control exercised over her. But her efforts to obtain relief were thwarted both by the opposition of the medium and the active working of the demon powers to which she had yielded. In this condition several years passed before she sought the aid of the pastor above mentioned and made a full confession of her actions. There was still no realization of the sin, merely the desire to be free from the control exercised over her life.[22]

When MacMillan arrived on the scene, the woman had become unconscious. MacMillan discerned that this was an occasion to test for the presence of demons. He recited in detail the process of her deliverance:

Though the individual was in a coma, the scriptural test was at once put to the indwelling demon, "Thou evil spirit, has Jesus Christ come in the flesh?" (I John 4:3). Instantly there came a response in the form of a bitter "No." The spirit being thus identified, another question was presented, "Spirit, what is your name?" Refusal to tell followed, but under the power of continued prayer, the name was eventually given.

However, there quickly came the consciousness that the demon was not alone, but one of a company. All that night, from about eight o'clock until seven the following morning, the battle continued. In that time eighteen separate demons left the body of their victim, each one identifying himself before he left by uttering his name. Most of the names given were those of spiritual states, such as "Fear," "Death," etc. But these were varied by others, as "Chief," "Mug," "Legion," one calling himself the "Chief Servant of Lucifer."

When morning came the patient seemed revived and normal, and it was thought by some that the work was done. Four days later, however, a hurried call came again, and a visit revealed the woman in the same condition. That night four more spirits revealed themselves and departed. For perhaps three weeks a measure of relief continued, and then the trouble recurred. The question arose as to whether other spirits had gained entrance, but this did not seem to be the case; rather there were those which had not revealed themselves. At intervals covering a period of two months fresh manifestations occurred, and these were dealt with as they appeared. In all, seven entire nights were thus spent.

The sufferer was throughout this time unable to take hold of the Lord for herself. Intense fear possessed her mind. At times, during the seasons when

definite effort was being exerted by prayer and authority for the casting out of the evil spirits, she
would come briefly out of the coma in which her
senses were bound. To reply to exhortations to utter
the name of Jesus, or to give praise to God, she would
attempt to do so, but immediately the spirits would
seize her, and use her hands in a fierce endeavor to
strangle herself. Two brethren were constantly on the
alert to hold her hands. At other times she would try
to bite those about her, as a dog might do.

The trouble was seen towards the end of the long
struggle to be attended by a sexual mania. One
demon, calling himself by the name of "Internal Mas-
culinity Cacoethes," seemed to be the source of this
uncleanness. He remained alone, after perhaps thirty
other demons had been expelled. Having gained a
hold in the sensual part of the being, it seemed almost impossible to dislodge him. But God's Word
gives unquestionable authority to His faithful people.
"Ye are of God, little children," says the Beloved Disciple, after his instructions regarding the presence
and deceitfulness of the agents of the evil one, "and
have overcome them, because greater is he that is in
you, than he that is in the world."

The end came at last. One demon, as mentioned
above, had held the fort defiantly, giving, whenever
asked, the name mentioned above. On the last night
the powers of evil seemed to fill the room. The patient, awakening from her coma, cried out in fear that
spirits were coming at her first from one side and
then from the other. These unseen beings were rebuked in the name of Jesus, and seemed to withdraw.
The quoting of passages from the Bible were resented
by the indwelling demon with cries of "No! No!"

Finally a pastor said to the demon, "You are
beaten," which he acknowledged, but refused to go.
The spirit then said, "I will go out tomorrow." The re-

ply was, "No, you will go out now." He spoke again,
"I'm going out," and then, through the lips of the patient, "I'm outside now." At once the question was
asked, "Why do you lie to us?" bringing the reply,
"Because I am going to kill her before I go." Shortly
after, in a sad voice, the spirit said, "I must find a new
home," and suddenly came out through the mouth,
the woman nearly strangling. But, immediately she
began to praise God with complete freedom, and has
so continued. Attempts were made by the spirits to
regain possession, but steadfast resistance has given
full relief.[23]

This story illustrates one particular feature which was
a trademark of MacMillan's deliverance ministry, which
he had practiced since his days of missionary work in the
Philippines: the use of First John 4:1-3 in testing the
spirits. Toccoa Falls College professor Gerald McGraw
summarized MacMillan's approach:

Mr. MacMillan's deliverance methodology, as I observed it, was a very simple 3-step Testing-the-Spirits
method. When a demon came into manifestation, he
would ask, "What is your name?" When he had received the demon's response, Mr. MacMillan would
ask, "Did Jesus Christ come in the flesh?" After he received "No" for a reply, then the demon was commanded by name to leave . . . in the name of Jesus
Christ.[24]

He found this methodology to be both biblically based
and practical.

This incident appears to have been his most extensive
and problematic deliverance to that point. In 1947
MacMillan had written, probably shortly after this incident,

[The] Christian life is not a being "carried to the
skies on flowery beds of ease"—it is a wrestling with

"principalities and powers, the world rulers of this darkness, the spiritual hosts of wickedness in the heavenlies." There is never any "discharge in this warfare": on the contrary, the believer's advancement in spiritual capacity is rewarded with an intensifying of the struggle.[25]

MacMillan's sunset years were not spent on "flowery beds of ease," but in spiritual warfare. His advancement in spiritual capacity was indeed rewarded with a more intense struggle than he had ever faced. At the age of seventy-seven, four years after writing this statement, his greatest battle with the powers of darkness would take place.

The Dramatic 1951 Exorcism

In 1951, while he was still teaching at Nyack, a female student was overcome by demonic powers. This case of demonization, notes retired Nyack professor Don Kenyon, "affected the whole school—faculty, students, as well as men from headquarters who had homes on the 'Hillside.' "[26] MacMillan describes the case in his book, *Encounter with Darkness*:

> The subject [was] a woman of about thirty-five. In her early childhood she had been cared for by her grandmother, who was a devotee of Christian Science, and who also was interested in a number of the heterodox cults which flood America. As the child learned to read—she had a very precocious mind—she was used by the grandmother to read to her their literature. In this way her mind was prepared to receive demon working. For it is a most serious and solemn fact that, just as the Word of God is charged with heavenly power, so the writings of these cults convey to their readers a power that is diabolic.
>
> The woman was converted when nineteen years of age, but did not go deeply into spiritual things for a

number of years; in fact, not until she had begun to
attend a Bible school. Then she began to seriously
follow the Lord, and was baptized. After this event,
the spirits began to seriously trouble her. She had begun to help in the kitchen of the school where she was
attending; suddenly, while working, she fell unconscious to the floor. This occurred a second time,
whereupon she was taken to the hospital room.
There the school doctor visited her, and, as her actions were somewhat violent, decided that it would
be best to commit her to the State Hospital. A student who was interested in her asked the doctor if he
would allow the writer to first see her, which was
granted. She was partly unconscious, and a challenge
being given to the demon, the response came from
her lips in a decided "No." The demon was then commanded to name himself, to which he responded
with the word, "Cults." When this was followed by
casting out of the spirits, the first group that left her
called themselves by the names of well-known cults,
surprising some of those present. At intervals, groups
of demons were expelled, the number totalling 171.[27]

Many of the demons had infested the woman when she
had also worked at a publication house where occultic
books had been printed.[28] According to Paul Valentine,
she was a brilliant young lady, serving as a teaching assistant for a professor. This woman's boyfriend detected a
problem. When they were studying together and he was
reading Scripture, she reacted to verses mentioning the
blood. They went to MacMillan for help.[29]

MacMillan was apparently not involved in the initial
encounter, and did not lead every session of the deliverance ministry, but he orchestrated the plan for ministering to her through other Nyack professors. President
Moseley and his wife, having dealt with demons in Ti-

bet, were involved with the case, but they mostly stayed in the background and let MacMillan take the lead, spelled by others.[30]

The student was kept in a room in the dispensary located in Simpson Hall, in the women's wing of the dormitory. Intercessory prayer and ministry times were scheduled around the clock. Students were assigned to be with her at all times, especially since she had become suicidal. They also observed and assisted during the exorcistic procedures.[31] MacMillan was again ahead of his time. He gave students on-the-job training in the ministry of deliverance. As a freshman, John Ellenberger was not permitted to participate, though his older sister was involved as a prayer partner for those sessions. He recalled that some sessions lasted late into the night and he could hear the cries and wailing.[32] This deliverance actually took about three months to accomplish. "It never seemed to be 'quick and easy,' for the demons would stubbornly refuse to cooperate and would hide over and over again."[33]

At this time there was also trouble in the school—immorality and money being stolen. President Moseley started to pray. During one chapel service, some students passed out. One large young man fell backward, then ran off into the woods and others had to tackle him.[34]

Valentine recalled on one occasion the woman was praying what seemed to be a beautiful prayer. He was sitting near professor Peter Wiseman, who was standing, holding his fists on a chair, squinting and praying, "O God, O God," then he discerned, "there is something wrong here," and rebuked a spirit of deception.[35] At one point, "Someone held a Bible over her and the demons cried out, 'Take it away; I'm defeated by it.' "[36] Jerry McGarvey, one of the students assisting, relates one of the earlier incidents in the months-long deliverance:

One day, after a frustrating time of trying to get the demons to manifest itself/themselves, the student was lying there quietly talking to some of us, when the door opened and Mr. MacMillan walked in. It was the first time he had been able to come. As he approached her bed, suddenly her eyes became enlarged. She turned to look up at Mr. MacMillan, and a voice (not hers, for it was a male voice) said, 'I know you; I know you from the Philippines.' And with that, it started her trembling until her body had to be held down. That was indeed impressive, but was NOT what impressed me the most. Mr. MacMillan stood over her, his hands folded in front of him, and quietly, but firmly commanded the demon to cease talking and come out of her. And it did.

This was such a contrast to some of the yelling and arguing others had done in order to cast them out. I don't remember in detail all that happened after that, but I do know that several demons were cast out in this same quiet, authoritative manner.[37]

Valentine remembers that MacMillan was deliberate, direct, "a take-charge man." With his hands he would make as if wrapping and tying something and at the same time declare, "I bind you, Satan." Valentine also observed that her lips would be bleeding badly from biting them and she could not talk, but a voice would come from her midsection.[38] According to Howard Emary, some of the spirits screamed, "We will keep her," and tried to choke her throat. Voices spoke out in a low guttural tone, "We hate you. You are covered by the blood."[39] When MacMillan was reading from Scripture about the blood of Jesus, her eyes lifted and became like marbles. One skeptical student who scoffed looked into her eyes and passed out. MacMillan taught students how to pray and plead the blood according to Revelation 12:11.[40]

One Sunday at a table in the school dining hall, Valentine was sitting with her. Her eyes turned like black marbles and her knuckles turned white from squeezing a glass. She had an impulse to break it. She was taken for more ministry of deliverance and was set free from a demon of murder. She commented later to Valentine, "Paul, all I could see was your neck sliced open with blood pouring out." At times, Valentine recalled, you could almost feel the oppression like a mist coming out of a vaporizer.[41] On another occasion, Emary recounted that a spirit of destruction was identified. MacMillan counseled, "Let's be quiet." Then they prayed and sang. All of the sudden, the woman sat up, and the demon yelled, "Jesus Christ conquers me," and it instantly came out.[42]

Ross Ingraham recalled that MacMillan's hands and voice would shake.[43] This occasion appeared to be a manifestation of the power of God as he exercised authority over the dark powers. At one point, when he commanded a demon to reveal its name, it responded with a garbled sound that MacMillan could not understand. Then he commanded it to spell out its name, and it responded by spelling out "P-A-I-N."[44]

On one occasion police officers came to investigate. According to one student who wished to remain anonymous, when they saw the bizarre manifestation of a demon being expelled, they became "bug-eyed" and hurriedly left in their cruiser. Paul Valentine, who was present on that occasion, also confirmed this.[45]

MacMillan corresponded with Mrs. Lulu Gordon Cheesman, who herself had been involved in effective deliverance ministry, regarding the latter part of this ordeal, writing a lengthy and detailed account:

June 13, 1951

Dear Mrs. Cheesman:

There has been further development in the case mentioned in my last letter—you will be interested. Commencement was near at the school, and knowledge of the case had spread rapidly. It was decreed that the student must be delivered by a certain date or else must be removed from the buildings and the campus by that time. She came to my home crying bitterly, and as there seemed no other place, we took her in. Then the storm broke.

I have never seen anything like it nor have I heard of any similar experience. A number of students gave aid most willingly, and helped through the periods of convulsions which were at times most severe. On Wednesday, June 6th, the enemy attacked during united prayer about 5:00 P.M., the conflict lasting until the following afternoon without abatement. Demon after demon came out. The first group made various threats to kill her, and attacks of suffocation came which seemed as if the threat would be fulfilled. One demon seemed to be the master spirit, calling himself "Negro Trainer." He was the most powerful I have seen, and several strong men (G.I. students) had difficulty in controlling her.

During the attack just mentioned, this demon revealed himself, and after a hard struggle seemed to go. There followed a multitude of lesser spirits, who seemed connected with experiences she had undergone while employed in relief work in a mountain district. They narrated the most foul stories and talked with hilarity which made it most difficult to silence or control them. Eventually they were expelled. Then suddenly Negro Trainer appeared with a scornful "Ha! Ha! Ha! You thought I was gone, but here I am again." After a long struggle he seemed to go.

On Saturday noon without warning another attack came. She had barely time to cry out when the power seized her. A young man and a nurse were at hand, and I was at the scene in a few moments. Her struggles were intense, but quickly other helpers were at hand. Then began a struggle which lasted unbroken for eighteen hours, until 6:00 A.M. Sunday morning.

Again the attempt was made to suffocate her, the tongue sinking into the throat and respiration ceasing. A challenge as to the coming of Christ in the flesh would bring the tongue back, or commands to the demon to release it. Even the nurses feared for her life and often artificial respiration had to be used, but grace prevailed. Later on towards daylight a sudden attack of hysteria came in which she loudly wept, protesting that she was weary and unable to continue.

I saw it as a deception, though some of the helpers felt that I was wrong and that her physical state should be considered. But suddenly, as we continued to pray, the demon gave a great shout and released her. Immediately she became normal, protesting that she wished to be delivered at any cost.

During this time the demon had taunted us and sneered at us. He said, not like the others that he would kill her, but that he wanted her life and that if she would not be his servant he would take her when he left. When conscious she steadfastly stood with us, defying the demon and claiming victory through the blood of Christ. Through her wide-open eyes he looked at us with a look of the greatest terror. Gradually he weakened until his voice could hardly be heard. Again and again he appeared to leave with a gasp, until finally we could contact him no more. But he, or some other, is still within.

Since Sunday morning there has been no evidence of demon presence until yesterday. About noon I drove the nurse to the hospital, being away about ten minutes. During that time a sudden discouragement came upon her and she called for help, but when I came back this disappeared. The young man who was with her is most capable in handling the case. Just now he is reading to her the prayer tract you sent, and she is repeating it after him.

Each evening a group gathers for prayer that the deliverance may be complete. Today the power seemed to be building up within her, but it appears to be held in check. When the enemy is in control her face swells and the chest and abdomen seem also to enlarge. This is according to the old-time teaching of the *obh*, as mentioned by Pember and others. Perhaps we have learned more from this case than at any other time in the past. But we are heartily wearied of it, and pray for full deliverance. However, we feel that there is but one demon left—the total thus far reaching 171. He hides himself but must soon yield.[46]

A follow-up note to Mrs. Cheesman from MacMillan records the account of the final and complete victory:

This young woman was entirely set free with no further trouble whatever. She took hold of your prayer tract, Mrs. Cheesman, with zeal and eagerness, and it was in reality the key to her deliverance. At first she repeated it after those who read it to her, and, as soon as she was able, she used it for herself to ward off attacks and found it fully effective.[47]

Though it was a long and torturous process, the woman was gloriously delivered and returned to school the following school term. Students commented that, comparing her pictures in the yearbook, her countenance had changed. Through all of the victorious expulsion of the numerous evil spirits, MacMillan always depended on the work of the Holy Spirit, claiming "the power is all God, not me."[48]

The confrontation did not end in confusion, but in a re-
sounding victory. Howard Emary's impression of
MacMillan's impact speaks for the vast majority of the
students: "What power in the name and blood of Christ!
The Enemy must retreat."[49]

FIFTEEN

The Sunset Days

JUST BEFORE HIS RETIREMENT from the editorship of *The Alliance Weekly* in 1950, MacMillan wrote, "There is never a point at which a Christian body can rest and say, 'I will settle down here.' "[1]

MacMillan took his own advice—he did not settle down. After leaving the magazine, he continued to teach at the Missionary Training Institute and to speak in churches and minister to people through prayer, counseling and spiritual warfare. Former Nyack President Rexford Boda recalls him preaching a series of meetings in Ithaca, New York, while Boda was a teenager.[2] In 1954 MacMillan participated in a funeral service for a pastor's wife by reading her favorite Scriptures.[3]

The November 24, 1954, issue of *The Alliance Weekly* carried a final article by MacMillan, entitled "Thankfulness and Thanksgiving." In the editorial comments introducing the article, it was said of him, "Offically retired, Mr. MacMillan is kept busy [at the age of eighty-one!]

counseling people from far and near who know him
through his writing and teaching."[4] He continued to write
for the adult quarterly to the end of his life.[5]

Jay Smith, a polio-sticken student who lived with the
MacMillans from 1952 to 1956, became close to John,
whom he affectionately called "Da." He related an incident of their care for him: "An incident took place while I
was there when I fell and injured my foot. It swelled and
discolored. John and Alice prayed for me, and John faithfully massaged my foot over a two-day period until the
swelling and discoloration was gone and I was able again
to walk with my braces and crutches."[6] Of John's devotional life, Smith recalled that he "rose early to spend time
in prayer and reading the Word. Daily, during the week
after the evening meal and Sunday after the noon meal,
the meal ended with Bible reading and prayer."[7]

Later Spiritual Warfare Ministry

During the 1950s, MacMillan continued to write and
teach about, and even engage in, spiritual warfare. As a result of the exorcism on the Nyack campus in 1951,
MacMillan initiated a course in the next school year on
demonology and spiritual warfare—possibly the first of its
kind in Christian higher education. In the *Sunday School
Quarterlies* he continued to write about the importance of
discernment and overcoming the principalities and powers.[8] In an article in the August 1953 issue of *Herald of His
Coming*, Lulu Cheesman publicized MacMillan's ongoing
deliverance ministry: "J.A. MacMillan, formerly a missionary in the Orient, then Associate Editor of *The Alliance
Weekly*, is now being used by the Lord in spiritual warfare,
casting out many demons in the Name of the Lord and the
power in His shed blood."[9]

Also in the early 1950s, MacMillan received a request for help from Keith Bailey, a young missionary to Native Americans. Bailey (later a vice president of the C&MA), had encountered many demonic spirits among the people he worked with in Minnesota.[10] Years earlier he had come across *The Authority of the Believer* and had begun to practice MacMillan's principles, but still considered himself inexperienced in confronting occultic powers.

Over a period of two years, by phone and letter, MacMillan mentored Bailey in the ministry of deliverance. Bailey said that MacMillan "was practical in approach" and counseled, "Do not let the thing control you—you be in control." Among the other advice he gave was not to get worn down in the struggle, but to get rest; to carry out the exorcism over several sessions rather than marathon sessions; and to maintain one's regular routine, not letting the deliverance dominate one's time and energy. According to Bailey, MacMillan's counsel was frequently sought by others as well during this time.[11]

In 1952 Jay Smith asked MacMillan for help concerning a friend who had been raised in a non-Christian home, was saved and came to Nyack as a student. He harbored a prideful desire to become a great preacher, but also struggled with unbelief and doubt, and began seeking the gift of tongues to give him assurance of his spiritual experience.[12] In describing what appears to be the same situation, Jerry McGarvey explained what happened next:

> He became overly obsessed with "speaking in tongues." As I understand it, by his own testimony, he said a voice came to him as he was crying out in desperation to be filled with the Spirit and said, "I am Tongues, may I come in?" The student agreed and he began to speak loudly in another tongue. I was far

away from him in the dorm but I awoke immediately,
sensing the feeling of demon influence and power.[13]

The student had been a friend of Jay's, but he began to
respond coolly toward him. John suggested Jay invite
him for dinner. It was the custom in the MacMillan
home after dinner to pray and read the Scriptures. During this devotional time, the student fell off his chair in
an unconscious state. John responded, "I think we have a
problem here."

He applied the First John 4:3 test, asking, "Did Jesus
Christ come in the flesh?" Initially there was no response,
but then he began to thrash violently. Jay tried to hold
him down, but the student flipped him, even though Jay
weighed fifty pounds more. When John commanded the
spirits to stop, the young man calmed down, regained consciousness and was set free.[14] MacMillan records his account of this incident in *Encounter with Darkness*:

> A young man of twenty-two years of age . . . had
> been very desirous of the gift of tongues. Though
> warned of the serious danger of concentrating upon
> any gift, rather than on the Giver, he persisted in
> seeking with intensity. Finally, he obtained what he
> sought. So confident was he that the experience was
> of the Lord, that he considered he now had suffi-
> cient light to carry him forward without the Word
> of God; the personal revelation was all-satisfying.
> Then came suddenly the understanding that his
> tongues were not genuine. The effect was a most bit-
> ter disillusionment. He came to the writer's house,
> and while attempting to pray became unconscious.
> The test revealed the presence of demons, one of
> whom gave the name of "False Tongues." Deliver-
> ance came after a somewhat protracted struggle,
> and he is now free in spirit and mind and body. He

has learned to abide in the Lord, and is recognized
as a helper of others.[15]

McGarvey noted, "I'm of the opinion that it was the
discernment of Mr. MacMillan that brought this session
to a quick conclusion."[16] Smith remarks that at that time
he discussed the attack extensively with John. To his
knowledge, it was the only case of counterfeit tongues
that MacMillan had personally seen, although he had
written of the possibility of such spurious manifestations
years earlier.[17]

Not all of MacMillan's endeavors in exorcism were
successful. Some cases took "exhausting days and nights
of prayer and fasting."[18] "It never seemed to be 'quick
and easy,' for the demons would stubbornly refuse to cooperate and would hide over and over again."[19] There
were times in which "he questioned why it took so long
at times to see deliverance and would diligently search
the Scriptures for an answer."[20] Smith recalls, "I was
present at times when demons would play cat and mouse
and not answer. But they could not hide indefinitely,
but had to respond to the authority of the name of Jesus
and to His shed blood."[21]

Smith related that at one point a strong thought came
into his mind, "If you will give yourself to me, I will
make you walk." An oppressive spirit had come upon
him when he gave no heed to the thought. He talked
with John about the deceptive impression and subsequent attack. He discerned that it was due to spiritual
warfare they had engaged in the past ten days, in which a
young man had not been fully delivered. He prayed with
Jay and the oppression lifted.[22] MacMillan recognized
the need for ongoing protection from the enemy, and
went around the dormitories praying for protection and

cleansing them of any lingering powers of darkness whenever he engaged in exorcism on campus.[23]

MacMillan was very compassionate, trying to go and help all who were oppressed to be set free from the powers of darkness. In another exorcism in which Smith participated a woman from Long Island whose mother had died became involved in spiritism. She began seeking to communicate with her dead mother through a medium. Before long she became suicidal.

Jay and another student, Ralph Lindsay (who had assisted in the 1951 deliverance), traveled with John to Long Island to minister to her. Once they arrived, although she had asked for MacMillan's help, she just stared and would not speak to him. Under the influence of a spirit, she engaged in automatic writing, inscribing a perfect circle on a piece of paper. In spite of their efforts, she did not want to give up talking to her dead mother, so they were not able to set her free.

She kept repeating that she wanted to be "a Jesus girl." MacMillan noted that though she claimed to be a "Jesus girl" she did not mention the name of Christ. He surmised that she had been infested with a false "Jesus spirit" (2 Corinthians 11:4).[24] He began to perceive that some people were never completely set free because they were not totally yielded to the Lord and were holding on to something that displeased Him—a foothold for the powers of darkness.

After this incident, John, now in his eighties, commented to Jay, "I am not sure I am called to go all over the country trying to deliver them."[25] It seemed the Lord was telling him that his ministry of spiritual warfare was winding down. For more than thirty years he had battled the forces of evil. Though he wanted to help everyone, he realized he could not, and that some would not be willing to do what was necessary to become free. Through all the struggles, however, Keith Bailey said, "He understood the nature of demons and their manifestations, and maintained deep confidence in the victory of Christ."[26] McGraw agreed that his ministry of deliverance was "courageous, authoritative, bold."[27]

Finishing the Course

In December 1955, John and Alice were walking up the hillside to the Nyack campus to attend a concert, when John slipped and fell on the ice. In his typical habit, however, of exercising faith and authority for physical strength, he got back up and attended the concert. Soon after, though, his health began to deteriorate rapidly. Upon examining him, the doctors discovered that he had cancer of the spine, a condition that caused him constant pain.[28]

Students took turns assisting Alice in taking care of him. Harry Arnold, a student who had chiropractic training, gave him periodic massages.[29] Rexford Boda, Cliff Westergren and others helped to care for MacMillan during his final months of life. Westergren recalled:

> I remember his gratitude for our personal concern and love, and he never forgot to express this to us. He was a spiritual giant, and his acceptance of us made us want to be there. I remember his anticipation of wanting to see Christ personally, and he spoke often of First John 3:2: "Beloved, now are we the sons of God, and it doth not yet appear what we shall be: but we know that, when he shall appear, we shall be like him; for we shall see him as he is."
>
> His greatest delight was in having the Word of God read to him. It was like he revived as he lay on his bed in pain. I remember his patience in suffering. He never complained or gave the impression he

felt sorry for himself. I loved to talk with him. It took away the fear of death.[30]

Regina Jagst (Fischer), then a freshman at Nyack, recounts her memorable experience of caring for John:

> I remember hearing from one of my floor-mates that volunteers were needed for several hours of late evening, early night watches with a former professor who was living in a small house on campus not too far from our dorm (Christy Hall). He was very ill, in the last stages of cancer. I don't remember what motivated me to volunteer, it just seemed something that I felt I wanted to do since I had some experience in the care of the ill and always seem to be drawn to caring for children or the elderly.
>
> Although Prof. MacMillan's body was extremely weak and wracked with constant pain, his mind was clear. His waxy, white face seemed to be always set in a smile and he greatly enjoyed the company of us volunteers. He showed sincere interest in my life as a student, in my family and history in my plans for the future and my walk with the Lord. At one time I must have mentioned my financial struggles to the MacMillans because at a time when I needed money the most an envelope with a 10 dollar bill was left in my mailbox. This unanimous [sic] gift was a direct answer to my prayer and to this day I am sure that the MacMillans were God's agents in His answer, as they so lovingly shared with me from what little they had. $10.00 may not seem much these days, but at that time it took care of a very great and urgent need. (The minimum wage was raised to $.75 while I was at Nyack.) Prof. MacMillan also shared with me some of his life on campus and on the mission field and I always looked forward to my visits in that quiet little home, a real haven of peace and rest just glowing with love. I'll never forget the feeling of

warmth, welcome and comfort which enveloped me each time I entered the MacMillan's home.

But the thing that impressed me most about Prof. MacMillan was his real and constant joy in His Savior, even in his deepest pain. Moving him, turning him over, getting him to sit up was excruciatingly painful for him. Still, instead of crying out in pain which would have been the natural thing for him to do as I have seen even other dear, loving Christian people do, Prof. MacMillan cried out over and over again: "Hallelujah, Praise the Lord, Oh praise the Lord with me." This praising of the Lord in his pain came very natural for him and I'm sure he did not learn it during his illness but had practiced it all along in all circumstances of his life.[31]

His friend and colleague Harold Freligh remarked, "Affliction did not stifle his song. On one occasion, when his pastor was calling on him, Mr. MacMillan said he was ready to go any time the Lord called him, and then remarked dryly that the Lord had missed a number of good opportunities."[32]

Experiencing Isabel's death decades earlier helped to prepare him for his own. Some may wonder why John, who had exercised authority over illness many times over the years, was not able to exercise that authority at this time. The answer may be found in an experience Robert Jaffray had shared with him years earlier about A.B. Simpson. In retelling the story, MacMillan shows his mature understanding and attitude on old age and death:

Dr. R.A. Jaffray told the writer of one of the closing days of our beloved Founder. Dr. Jaffray and two or three others were by the bedside of the weakening body of the great leader. A season of prayer ensued, in which one or more began to "take" promises of physical life for the departing chieftain. Then

his voice quietly interrupted, "Boys, I'm afraid I
can't go that far with you now." He was waiting for
the adoption, and realizing that the manifestation
of the sons of God lay still beyond his mortal reach.
Praise God, each day brings it nearer for the Church
and for the world.[33]

On the morning of May 15, 1956, John ate breakfast
with Alice and Jay, then sat in his favorite brown swivel
rocker. He was chatting with Buchanan, who had dropped
by the house after breakfast. Then he stopped talking, and
his head bowed, and his eyes closed. He had gone peacefully into the presence of his Master. Dr. McKaig, pastor
of Simpson Memorial Church and long-time friend of
John, came by to visit the family. They experienced a
"deep sense of loss and a vacuum."[34] His grandson, Alan,
felt that a light had gone out of his own life.

Harold Freligh, MacMillan's Nyack faculty colleague
and partner in his deliverance ministry, wrote the obituary in *The Alliance Weekly* entitled "A Prince in Israel:
John A. MacMillan." He showed unbounded admiration
for his friend's spiritual life:

> Prayer was one of the greatest expressions of Mr.
> MacMillan's Christian conduct. He was in touch
> with the Throne. He knew the authority of Jesus'
> name, and saw demons cringe and depart. He waged
> conquests in heavenly places that bound the power
> of Satan and set captives free. Praise was also an ac-
> companying characteristic.[35]

MacMillan's passion for China and his love for the
people continued to his dying day. Smith recalls, "He
died with the conviction that the bamboo curtain would
some day come down and China would again be open to
the gospel. He daily petitioned God for China."[36]

Freligh notes that just four days before his death, John "was at his typewriter preparing the lessons" for the *Adult Sunday School Quarterly*. John left the following words in the typewriter:

> Think how Christ watches over us and longs to enrich us with all the treasures of His grace. "All that I have is thine," saith He. How He would array us and beautify us with heavenly gifts; in place of our ill-temper and selfishness He would give us gentleness, patience, forgiveness, love. To do this in us, He has given us Himself in all the shame and agony of the cross. Now in His high glory He "makes all things to work together for our good."[37]

Freligh observed, "It is a fitting word that speaks for itself and for him and for his Lord."[38] They are appropriate last words for a man of God such as John MacMillan, one whom others described as a saint. He had fought a good fight, finished his course and kept the faith, proving the truth of the words of the psalmist, "Precious in the sight of the LORD is the death of his saints" (Psalm 116:15).

SIXTEEN

Twentieth-Century Impact

AROLD FRELIGH ENDED HIS obituary of John
MacMillan with these words of eulogy, "Of
MacMillan it can be appropriately said,
'Blessed are the dead which die in the Lord . . . their works
do follow them.' "[1] This statement certainly became prophetically true of MacMillan. His works have followed
him with great impact in the latter half of the twentieth
century, even greater than in his lifetime.

Macmillan's Continuing Impact on The Christian and Missionary Alliance

MacMillan's impact on The Christian and Missionary
Alliance began with his emerging ministry of leadership
and exercise of the authority of the believer in China.
His ministry burgeoned in the Philippines as he saved
the floundering C&MA mission. He provided wise leadership and pastoral insight through his Canadian ministry from 1929 to 1934.

During his sixteen years as associate editor of *The Alliance Weekly* and twenty-three years as writer of adult cur-

riculum, he quietly but powerfully shaped the theology and ministry of the C&MA through his editorials and Sunday school lessons, through his choice of articles for the magazine by other writers, through his correspondence and counsel. His editorials, especially, reflected a concern to avoid historical drift as a movement and continue to maintain the philosophy and emphases of A.B. Simpson and the early C&MA. As a member of the board of managers for three terms, he was influential in shaping the policies and programs of the C&MA.

MacMillan also made a lasting impression upon the C&MA through the lives and ministries of the dozens and perhaps hundreds of students he touched with his teaching, ministry and example. Many of those who came under his tutorship became notable leaders in the Alliance, including Louis L. King, who later became a C&MA president; Rexford Boda and Thomas Bailey, who both advanced to become presidents of Nyack College; and Robert Niklaus, who rose to become a historian and director of communications for the denomination.

Keith Bailey, as mentioned earlier, who encountered demonic forces while a young missionary to Native Americans, considered MacMillan his mentor in the deliverance ministry. Bailey himself has engaged in deliverance ministry for more than fifty years, and has served as a C&MA district superintendent and vice president. A highly sought-after speaker and author of several books, he recently published the book *Strange Gods*, which traces the rise of spiritism in America.

Jay Smith says of the four years he lived with the MacMillans, "I considered that I received two educations: one at Nyack College, and the other, while being mentored by John and Alice. They shared my concerns, prayed for me, counseled me, and took me in as a member of the family." Smith overcame his disability to go on to a career as a hospital chaplain, ordained by the C&MA.

Jerry McGarvey became a career missionary with the C&MA to Burkina Faso, West Africa. He writes that MacMillan "made a big impression on my life and I used his booklet *The Authority of the Believer* in one of my courses in our Bible school in Burkina Faso." *The Authority of the Believer* was used on the mission field in a number of other locations and was translated into several languages as well.

Several of MacMillan's students learned firsthand how to discern the presence of evil spirits and cast out demons. John Stirzaker served in pastoral ministry, eventually becoming a district superintendent in the C&MA. He engaged in exorcism on a number of occasions throughout his ministry, utilizing the principles MacMillan had taught. Paul Valentine became a C&MA pastor, planting four churches in Canada. On several occasions, he was involved in the ministry of exorcism. Currently, Valentine serves as a minister-at-large for the C&MA. He regards MacMillan as his "example and role model," recalling "marvelous lessons I learned which helped in ministry." He especially noted MacMillan's emphasis on the ministry of the Holy Spirit and the authority of the Word of God. He asserted that of his whole education, the most important part was participating in the deliverance of the college student and seeing her set free by the power of Christ.

John Ellenberger, who took a course on missions from MacMillan, himself became a missionary to Irian Jaya, Indonesia. He currently serves as professor of missions at Alliance Theological Seminary. He was involved in deliverance ministry in Indonesia, and for the past twelve years has engaged in exorcism in the United States, using MacMillan's principles. He has recently taught a course on "Theology of Power Encounter" at the Manhattan campus of Nyack College.

Dr. Gerald McGraw practices perhaps the most extensive deliverance ministry based on MacMillan's teaching and practice. He continued his education and became a professor at Toccoa Falls College. He writes of Mac-Millan's influence:

> Mr. MacMillan's work on *The Authority of the Believer* is a priceless gem that can transform a Christian's entire outlook toward ministry against the powers of darkness. It can also raise one's expectations to see how our personal lives can enjoy victory over the powers of evil. . . .
>
> I have taught courses in Power Encounter in colleges and seminaries 24 times in the past 10 years. I always speak of MacMillan's fine grasp of the believer's position of authority in Christ, calling attention to his works and the policeman illustration. I usually either require students to read some of *The Authority of the Believer* or else one of the other works that retell it. . . .
>
> Without doubt, the greatest influence of John MacMillan on my life has been his courageous, authoritative, bold ministry of casting demons out of troubled people. Although I did not seriously launch into such work until I had gotten further education and had spent about 15 years in full-time Christian work, yet I never forgot his unique contribution and was therefore much more ready when the Lord thrust a troubled person in my path.

John MacMillan launched a host of students into a wide variety of ministries, equipping and preparing them to prevail over the powers of darkness. He modeled godly character and a life of prayer. These citations are but a handful of the dozens, perhaps hundreds, in the C&MA who have been impacted by his ministry.[2]

MacMillan's Impact on Evangelical Christianity

MacMillan's first and almost immediate impact on the evangelical world came just a year after the publication of his series of articles on "The Authority of the Believer" in *The Alliance Weekly* in 1932. When the seventh edition of *War on the Saints* by Jessie Penn-Lewis and Evan Roberts was published in 1933, it included in its introduction an endorsement of and a lengthy quote from MacMillan's articles.[3] Shortly after this, the articles were published in booklet form.

By 1935, the booklet was in its second printing, due to an overwhelming response, according to David J. Fant, director of publications for the C&MA. "The first edition has been blessed to Christians in different parts of the world, as witnessed by their letters of appreciation and gratitude."[4] The British deeper life periodical *The Overcomer*, founded by Jessie Penn-Lewis and edited by J. B. Metcalfe, also published MacMillan's articles in the 1930s.[5]

A sequel article, "The Authority of the Intercessor," was also produced in booklet form, and later published by another evangelical organization.[6] Eventually it was added to *The Authority of the Believer* and produced by Christian Publications in book form.

MacMillan's 1948 series of articles in *The Alliance Weekly* on demon possession and deliverance ministry were compiled in a small book entitled *Modern Demon Possession*. At a later time Keith Bailey added to it some of MacMillan's lecture notes and republished it under the title of *Encounter with Darkness*. In 1997 Christian

Publications published *The Authority of the Believer* and *Encounter with Darkness* into a single volume. These writings have been referenced again and again through the years by ministers and theologians alike.

MacMillan's Influence through *Herald of His Coming*

Herald of His Coming, a popular interdenominational evangelical newspaper in the 1940s and 50s, featured articles by many evangelical leaders, including deeper life writers such as A.B. Simpson, A.W. Tozer, A.T. Pierson and Oswald J. Smith. In July 1948, the editor of the monthly journal wrote regarding *The Authority of the Believer*, "This is so far as I know the very best presentation of the great subject of the believer's place and power with the Lord Jesus to be found anywhere."[7] In 1952 the magazine reprinted MacMillan's sequel booklet, *The Authority of the Intercessor*.[8] Also in the same year, Lulu Cheesman wrote in *Herald of His Coming* of her correspondence with MacMillan regarding the Bible institute student who had been infested with demons.[9]

In another article in the August 1953 issue entitled "Oppression, Obsession and Possession," Cheesman commented, "J.A. MacMillan, formerly a missionary in the Orient, then Associate Editor of *The Alliance Weekly*, is now being used by the Lord in spiritual warfare, casting out many demons in the Name of the Lord and the power in His shed blood."[10] Her title is an obvious takeoff on MacMillan's 1948 article series, "Modern Demon Possession," in which he distinguishes the same three categories of demonic influence.

In 1954 *The Authority of the Believer* was reprinted in full in *Herald of His Coming*.[11] In 1956 in the same periodical an advertisement appeared inviting readers to send for a copy of *The Authority of the Believer*.[12] The journal became one of the most extensive disseminators of MacMillan's teachings in the mid-twentieth-century evangelical community.

The Foundation for Billheimer's Teaching

Even more significant is the influence of MacMillan on Paul Billheimer, a Bible college president and radio preacher in the Wesleyan holiness tradition. In a radio message entitled "Deliverance from the Hands of Our Enemies," which was printed in *Herald of His Coming* in 1952, Billheimer echoed MacMillan's themes, though he did not mention MacMillan by name.

In his radio message, Billheimer declared that, on the basis of Ephesians 1, believers are "made sharers potentially of the authority which is His. They are made to sit with Him. That is, they share His throne."[13] The influence of *The Authority of the Believer* is evident from the fact that this is a virtual quote of MacMillan's words. It is all the more significant that Billheimer acknowledged that he had only recently come to this understanding of believer's authority.[14]

On another occasion Billheimer spoke of binding and loosing, asserting that "man was made to have dominion over the works of God's hands," themes also reminiscent of MacMillan.[15] Also the same year Billheimer published one of his radio addresses entitled "The Technique of Spiritual Warfare," in which he expanded upon Mac-Millan's theme of the authority of the believer. This message would later be republished in 1982 by Bethany House as part of his book *Destined to Overcome*.[16] He became a leading holiness proponent of the overcoming Christian life.

Additional influence from MacMillan can be observed in Billheimer's more recent book, *Destined for the Throne*. Though he still makes no reference to MacMillan, he does mention some of the same themes of the authority of the believer based on Ephesians 1:20-22 (taught by MacMillan in his chapters entitled "Christ's Gift of Authority" and "The Legal Basis for the Authority of the Church").[17] Other MacMillan-like themes can be found throughout the book. There is little question that Billheimer's popular book *Destined for the Throne* is based on and birthed out of MacMillan's principles.

For example, a central theme of Billheimer's writings—that the believer's life on earth is a training ground for rulership in heaven—was originally voiced by MacMillan in *The Authority of the Believer*.[18] Through the years he continued to expand upon this concept in *The Alliance Weekly*.[19] One of his most succinct expressions of this theme is in a 1949 quarterly: "When, in the appointed time, the powers of evil are cast down (Revelation 12:9; cf. Ephesians 6:12), the saints will occupy their places [in the heavenlies] and assume the authority possessed by them. The saints are now being trained by the long discipline of life for this wonderful ministry."[20] Three years later Billheimer began teaching in corresponding fashion: "God's object in originating his prayer program was to *give us training for overcoming* in preparation for rulership."[21]

Often, Billheimer developed MacMillan's concepts, applying them specifically to prayer warfare. In 1939 MacMillan wrote, "Adversity is God's laboratory."[22] More than four decades later, Billheimer wrote in *Destined for the Throne*, "This world is a laboratory in which those destined for the throne are learning, by actual practice in the prayer closet, how to overcome Satan and his hierarchy."[23]

These are just a few examples of numerous parallels which can be found between Billheimer and MacMillan. MacMillan's teachings clearly predate and furnish the foundation of thought upon which Billheimer built. When a person thus reads Billheimer, he is reading a magnification of what MacMillan originally presented in germinal form—and no doubt, MacMillan would add his "Amen!"

Other Influences on Evangelical Leaders

Also in the early 1950s, F.J. Huegel, missionary to Mexico and long-time friend of Billheimer, also taught on the authority of the believer in his 1955 book *Forever Triumphant*.[24] Like Billheimer, Huegel built upon MacMillan's principles based on Ephesians 1 and Luke 10:19, but did not mention him by name.[25] Huegel's books have become classics in their own right in holiness circles.

Moody Press also gave a nod of acknowledgement to MacMillan in 1960 when they published a portion of his *Modern Demon Possession* in *Demon Experiences in Many Lands*. The book is a compilation of the experiences of many missionaries dealing with demonic forces.[26]

The most widespread referencing of MacMillan's material by an evangelical, however, occurs in the writings of Merrill F. Unger, one-time Foursquare Church minister who became a professor at Dallas Theological Seminary. Unger graduated from the Missionary Training Institute at Nyack in 1934, the semester before MacMillan joined the faculty, but his writings reveal his familiarity with MacMillan and his popular classic.

In his books *What Demons Can Do to Saints* and *Demons in the World Today*, Unger included a total of twelve references to MacMillan.[27] In addition, he included the lengthy, previously unpublished letter written by

MacMillan to Lulu Cheesman, describing the significant
and difficult case of exorcism which took place in 1951 at
Nyack.[28] Unger probably read about the incident in *Herald of His Coming* and contacted Cheesman for further information. It is apparent that Unger, himself a scholar,
regards MacMillan as an authority on dealing with demonic forces.

John Ellenberger, professor of missions at Alliance
Theological Seminary, says that the deliverance ministry
of Ernest Rockstad was derived out of MacMillan's ministry and teaching—in particular, the use of the First
John 4:1-3 method of testing spirits. Rockstad became a
mentor to Ed Murphy, a missionary and professor who
recently authored *Handbook of Spiritual Warfare*, the
most comprehensive study on the subject to date.[29]

A Prairie Bible Institute professor in Canada, Archie
Ruark, is another leader who extensively used the First
John 4:1-3 procedure for testing spirits as early as 1946.[30]
He was ordained with the C&MA, but never served in Alliance ministries.[31] Ruark was a student at Prairie Bible Institute in Western Canada in the early 1930s, the same
time MacMillan was itinerating throughout Western Canada and teaching on the authority of the believer, so it is
conceivable that he learned the technique from MacMillan.

In 1969, J. Dwight Pentecost, a colleague of Unger's at
Dallas Theological Seminary, wrote *Your Adversary, the
Devil*, in which he included a chapter entitled "The Believer's Authority over Satan."[32] Written as a popular
evangelical treatment of the topic of Satan and spiritual
warfare, it does not reference MacMillan—or any other
sources, for that matter. And yet, Pentecost seemed to be
familiar with MacMillan's material, since he commented
on the same Scriptures as MacMillan, such as Ephesians

1:19-23, 2:1-10 and Colossians 2:15.[33] Mark Bubeck, on the other hand, in his 1975 book *The Adversary*, quotes from *The Authority of the Believer* and freely recommends it as "one of the finest expositions on the subject and basis of the believer's authority that I have ever read."[34]

Episcopal Church leaders have also recognized the work of John MacMillan. Episcopalian John Richards, in his book on exorcism entitled *But Deliver Us from Evil*, cited *Modern Demon Possession* in his bibliography.[35] More recently, Samuel Wilson, an ordained C&MA minister and former missionary, now a professor of missions and evangelism at Trinity Episcopal School for Ministry, made reference in his article "Evangelism and Spiritual Warfare" to MacMillan's *Encounter with Darkness*, calling it "an old but reasonably sound exposition of the power given to believers by our identification with Christ."[36]

Other contemporary evangelical scholarship has also recognized MacMillan's principles. An illustration from *The Authority of the Believer*, in which a policeman's authority to stop a car in the name of the law is compared to the believer's authority in the name of Jesus, has been borrowed by a number of authors. Baptist pastor C.S. Lovett, in his 1967 book *Dealing with the Devil*, used the analogy, but made no reference to its source.[37] Timothy Warner's 1990 book, *Spiritual Warfare: Victory over the Dark Powers of Our World*, cited the illustration and gave MacMillan proper credit.[38] Ed Murphy, in both the 1993 and 1996 editions of his monumental volume *Handbook for Spiritual Warfare*, also uses the policeman illustration, changing the car to a truck, but does not cite MacMillan.[39] By this time, perhaps, the illustration had been so widely circulated that the original source had become forgotten.

Murphy frequently cites Unger, who frequently cited MacMillan.[40] This shows MacMillan's indirect influence on the foundation of Murphy's thinking through Unger. Fuller Theological Seminary professor Charles Kraft includes a chapter on the authority of the believer in his book *Defeating the Dark Angels*,[41] but again like Murphy, does not cite MacMillan, though he makes several references to Unger.[42] Unger's book had become the foundational scholarly work on spiritual warfare and demonology upon which other academic study was built—and Unger's theology was influenced in part by MacMillan.

Wayne Grudem, professor of theology at Trinity Evangelical Divinity School, recently published his extensive *Systematic Theology*. In his chapter, "Satan and Demons," he discusses the concept of the authority of the believer and deals with questions regarding demonization of Christians.[43] While he does not cite MacMillan by name in his discussion, he does list *The Authority of the Believer* and *The Authority of the Intercessor* in his bibliography at the end of the chapter.[44]

Richard J. Foster, a Quaker author and professor, in his recent book *Prayer: Finding the Heart's True Home*, includes a chapter entitled "Authoritative Prayer," in which he discusses the authority of the believer according to Ephesians 1:20-22 and 2:6.[45] Again, he does not mention MacMillan as the source, but it has become so common a teaching throughout evangelicalism that it is not surprising. It is clear that MacMillan's works and concepts have been cited as standard fare in scholarly books and bibliographies, and have been highly regarded by evangelical leaders and academics from a variety of backgrounds.

Pentecostals, charismatics and the modern faith movement have also made extensive use of MacMillan's writings and concepts, but have sometimes adopted teachings and practices of which MacMillan would not approve.[46]

The Authority of the Believer

MacMillan's Most Important Doctrine

MACMILLAN WAS NOT THE first to teach principles on the authority of the believer, but he was apparently the first to combine many of those principles together into one treatise and to expand upon them, thus becoming the seminal writer on the concept.[1] The notion of the authority of the believer arises originally out of the Reformation doctrine of the priesthood of the believer. A.J. Gordon notes that Swiss healing movement leader Dorothy Trudel realized the authority of the believer, declaring that it is the believer's privilege to be kings and priests of God.[2]

The Keswick and Higher Life movements picked up the theme with their emphasis on Covenant theology and the privileges and inheritance of the saints through the Covenant. In 1885 Andrew Murray was teaching that believers have authority: "Church of the living God! Your calling is higher and holier than you know! God wants to rule the world through your members. He wants you to be His kings and priests. Your prayers can bestow and withhold the blessings of heaven."[3] He quoted famed Scottish preacher and hymn writer Horatius Bonar, saying, "God is seeking kings. Not out of the ranks of angels. Fallen man must furnish Him with the rulers of His universe. Human hand must wield the scepter, human hands must wear the crown."[4]

In 1895, as interim successor to Charles Spurgeon, A.T. Pierson taught, "Obedience to Him means command over others; in proportion as we are subject to Him, even the demons are subject to us in His name."[5] Pierson also taught "the authority of faith": "This we regard as the central, vital heart of this great lesson on Faith. The Master of all girds the servant with His own power and entrusts him with authority to command. Faith claims not only blessing but power to bless."[6]

MacMillan's concept of the believer's authority was also taught in germinal form by A.B. Simpson in an article entitled "The Authority of Faith":

> The word "power" should be frequently translated "authority," in the New Testament. "Behold, I give unto you authority," Christ says, "to tread on serpents and scorpions, and over all the power of the enemy; and nothing shall by any means hurt you."
>
> He did not promise the disciples power first, but the authority first; and as they used the authority, the power would be made manifest, and the results would follow.
>
> Faith steps out to act with the authority of God's Word, seeing no sign of the promised power, but believing and acting as if it were real. As it speaks the word of authority and command, and puts its foot without fear upon the head of its conquered foes, lo, their power is disarmed, and all the forces of the heavenly world are there to make the victory complete.

This was the secret of Christ's power that He spake with authority, prayed with authority, commanded with authority, and the power followed. The reason we do not see more power is because we do not claim the authority Christ has given us. The adversary has no power over us if we do not fear him, but the moment we acknowledge his power, he becomes all that we believe him to be. He is only a braggart if we will dare to defy him, but our unbelief clothes him with an omnipotence he does not rightly possess. God has given us the right to claim deliverance over all his attacks, but we must step out and put our foot upon his neck as Joshua taught the children of Israel to put their feet upon the necks of the conquered Canaanites, and faith will find our adversaries as weak as we believe them to be. Let us claim the authority and the victory of faith for all that Christ has purchased and promised for our bodies, our spirits, or His work.[7]

Further, Simpson wrote: "'I give you authority.' This is the policeman's badge which makes him mightier than a whole crowd of ruffians because, standing upon his rights, the whole power of the state is behind him. . . . Are we using the authority of the name of Jesus and the faith of God?"[8] Simpson taught on the basis of Christ's delegated authority that the church has authority to act as Christ's law enforcement officer, as a legal authority as a representative of the government of the King:

There is a fine force in Luke 10:19, "I have given you authority to trample on snakes and scorpions and to overcome all the power of the enemy" [NIV]. It is not power that He gives us. We do not have the power. He has the power. But He gives us authority to act as if we had the power, and then He backs it up with His power. It is like the officer of the law stepping out before a mob and acting in the name of

the government. His single word is stronger than a
thousand men because he has authority, and all the
power of the government is behind him. So faith
steps out in the name of heaven and expects God to
stand by it.[9]

This would appear to be a source for a similar policeman analogy of spiritual authority used by MacMillan in
The Authority of the Believer. There he changes it from a
mob to bustling traffic stopped by a policeman at a busy
intersection, and further expounds upon the idea.[10]

At a China Inland Mission conference in 1897 Jessie
Penn-Lewis taught on the believer's position in Christ
according to Ephesians 1 and 2:

The Cross is the gate into this heavenly sphere, so
that if the Holy Spirit reveals to us that when we are
submerged into the death of Christ, we are loosed
from the claims of sin, the flesh, and the devil, He
will as certainly impart to us the life of the Risen
Lord. He will lift us in real experience into our place
in Him, seated with Him in the heavens far above all
principalities and powers . . . far above the powers of
darkness.[11]

Further she says, "The soul hidden with Christ in God
has authority over all the power of the enemy, for he
shares in the victory of Christ. In Him he has power to
tread on serpents and scorpions, and power to deliver
and loose others from the bonds of the evil one."[12] Later,
in 1912 she and Evan Roberts included a short section
on the believer's authority in their book *War on the
Saints*.[13]

Also about 1897, A.B. Simpson began teaching the believer's position in Christ according to Ephesians 1:

He "raised us up with Christ and seated us" (Ephesians 2:6, NIV) with Him in the heavenlies. This is

> much more than resurrection. It is ascension. It is
> taking the place of accomplished victory and con-
> ceded right, and sitting down in an attitude of com-
> pleted repose, from henceforth expecting with Him
> until all our enemies be made our footstool. . . . It is
> throne life. It is dwelling with Christ on high, your
> head in the heaven even while your feet still walk the
> paths of the lower world of sense and time. This is our
> high privilege.[14]

Whether he was influenced by Penn-Lewis, or vice versa, we cannot be sure, but apparently they all came to the same basic insight, either through the Holy Spirit independent of one another or perhaps through interchange of ideas. MacMillan's book *The Authority of the Believer* is a more thorough exposition of the position of the believer according to Ephesians 1 and 2, expanding on the germinal thought of both Penn-Lewis and Simpson. Alluding to Simpson's exposition of Ephesians entitled *The Higher Christian Life*, MacMillan wrote, "The Epistle to the Ephesians is the manual of the higher life. In a fuller degree perhaps than any of the others it leads the believer up to the heights of fellowship, of authority, and of victory."[15]

Throne Power

This concept of throne life described by Simpson is one of the foundational principles of MacMillan's understanding of the authority of the believer. MacMillan declared that the believer can assert "in prayer the power of the Ascended Lord, and the believer's throne union with Him."[16] Again he writes, "Where in faith the obedient saint claims his throne-rights in Christ, and boldly asserts his authority, the powers of the air will recognize and obey."[17] Commenting on Exodus 17, he writes,

> The rod [of Moses] symbolizes the authority of
> God committed to human hands. By it the holder is

made a co-ruler with his Lord, sharing His throne-power and reigning with Him. . . . So today, every consecrated hand that lifts the rod of the authority of the Lord against the unseen powers of darkness is directing the throne-power of Christ against Satan and his hosts in a battle that will last until "the going down of the sun."[18]

The theme of throne life permeated the Keswick, Higher Life and overcomer movements. In 1888, George B. Peck, a friend of A.J. Gordon and Simpson, wrote his book *Throne-Life*, or *The Highest Christian Life*, in which he wrote concerning "throne-power," or the "command of faith."[19] Also in the late 1800s George D. Watson wrote on "Steps to the Throne."[20] In 1906, Jessie Penn-Lewis wrote a booklet entitled *Throne Life of Victory* which was hailed as "God's answer to powers of darkness."[21] As was mentioned in chapter 2, MacMillan developed his concept most directly from George D. Watson's book *Bridehood Saints*.

The Basis for the Believer's Authority

MacMillan adopted the various ideas regarding the believer's privileges and authority and synthesized and expanded upon those thoughts for a more comprehensive conceptualization. His understanding of the authority of the believer is based upon these principles of the priesthood and the inheritance of the believer. MacMillan mentions several grounds of the claim to the believer's authority:

1. He is a spiritual Israelite and thus inherits the authority and glory of Israel.[22]
2. He is a child of the King. The authority of the believer is grounded on recognizing that we are children of the King and acting accordingly:

Sons and daughters of the Most High, it should be ours in every place to manifest the amiability and politeness of the Father's house. We are members of a kingly family, and in our walk and conversation there will be, if we live much in the King's presence, that true courtliness which becomes His children.[23]

These he calls "family privileges."[24] On this basis, "He will clothe with His own authority, so that spirits of evil will acknowledge the command of the child of God."[25]

3. He is in covenant relationship with God:

Compassing us on every side are His covenant promises covering every situation of life, every unforeseen exigency which we must face, every subtle snare or fierce assault of the enemy. These promises are His will for us, the gracious heritage which we have entered, the sphere in which all spiritual blessings can be appropriated and become our very own. It is the way of glory here below as we tread it in the faith of the victory of Calvary.[26]

4. He abides under the shadow of the Almighty:

In this supreme ministry of the son of God for lost men there was secured for those who believe Him and abide in Him a sharing in the fulness which He received as Son of man (Col. 2:9), and which makes them partakers of His authority and sharers in His kingdom. Before such overcomers the hosts of hell give way, and the utmost energy of the unseen world cannot harm them as they dwell "in the secret place of the Most High," and "abide under the shadow of the Almighty." . . . In the case of every obedient believer who today fulfils the conditions, God stands waiting to show him His victory.[27]

5. Christ has regained man's dominion over the earth:

> He became the Representative of His redeemed
> ones before the throne, holding in trust for them the
> dominion which men had forfeited through disobe-
> dience, and He had regained on their behalf.[28]

6. All things are under the Church as His Body:

> "[He] hath put all things under his feet." The feet
> are members of the Body. How wonderful to think
> that the least and lowest members of the Body of
> the Lord, those who in a sense are the very soles of
> the feet, are far above all the mighty forces.[29]

7. The Church is seated in the heavenly places in Christ:

> It is His people's privilege and duty to take shelter
> in the heavenlies where alone they may breathe the
> unpolluted air of divine love.[30]

Arenas of the Believer's Authority

Authority of Claiming Divine Protection

MacMillan believed that believers who walk closely to
God can claim divine protection, just as he did when fire
threatened to spread to his house:

> The children of the Lord have not been exempt
> from accident, and some have suffered severely. Do
> we all fully realize that the element of chance does
> not exist for the believer? And is it equally clear that
> the malignity of the enemy is never absent from the
> environment of those who confess the name of Christ
> and who carry the message of salvation? True it is
> that the angel of the Lord encamps round about them
> that fear Him, with a view to their deliverance. But
> the child of God is personally responsible for the defi-
> nite claiming of such protection, and also for abiding
> within the circumscribed limits wherein it is effective.

THE AUTHORITY OF THE BELIEVER

> Faith is the channel along which the grace of God
> flows, consequently, there is the necessity for main-
> taining a constantly victorious spirit over all the wiles
> and the attacks of the enemy. . . . More and more,
> therefore, it is vital that every true servant of God
> learn the secret of dwelling "in the secret place of the
> Most High," thereby in all the going out and coming
> of life, experiencing the security of those who "abide
> under the shadow of Shaddai."[31]

Covenant Right to Claim Family Salvation

MacMillan declared, "Every child born to a Christian
family can be claimed for God with full assurance."[32]
However, family salvation is not automatic, for "salvation is not hereditary, but a covenant of grace provides
for the salvation of the children of believers. The believer
must claim the covenant and abide in it; and when he
does so, its working will be found to be effectual."[33]

Authority over Creation

MacMillan discerned that the forces of nature sometimes were directed by demonic powers to wreak havoc on
mankind. As with Jesus rebuking the storm on the sea
(Matthew 8:23-27), MacMillan believed that believers
can speak to the powers of the darkness "who were behind
the fierce disturbance of nature."[34] He also held that believers can exercise authority over animals. He tells the
story of a saloon keeper loosing a ferocious dog on a group
of Women's Christian Temperance Union protesters:

> In spite of appeals from his more merciful cus-
> tomers, the beast was sent through the door upon
> the kneeling women. Savagely it rushed toward the
> one who was praying. But, as it reached her, it
> paused suddenly and began to tremble. Quietly the
> woman laid her hand on its head, and it crouched by
> her side, subdued by a Higher Power. Thenceforth it

accompanied the women as a protector and friend. They had taken refuge under the wings of the Almighty, and He did not fail them.

In like manner, to the uttermost parts of the earth, the shadow of our God extends. Our intercessions draw it over those of our fellow workers as, in their journeying from point to point, they also incur the rage and the assaults of the enemy. It is a privilege to share in this ministry of prayer.[35]

Authority to Open Locked Doors to Evangelism and Missions

From his experiences in China and the Philippines, MacMillan recognized that Satan often impedes the advance of the gospel and must be rebuked:

> The enemy has been preternaturally active; he has shut the doors of the lands against the Church's efforts; he presses on her heels as she goes forward. It is a time for those, who know the experience of sitting in heavenly places with the risen Lord, to hold the rod of His authority over the blocked roads before His people that all hindrances may be removed, that the way to the last tribes may be opened and the last individuals of the people for His name may be called out.[36]

Authority to Declare God's Purposes to Principalities and Powers

The Apostle Paul declared, "His intent was that now, through the church, the manifold wisdom of God should be made known to the rulers and authorities in the heavenly realms, according to his eternal purpose which he accomplished in Christ Jesus our Lord" (Ephesians 3:10-11, NIV). MacMillan understood this to mean, "The Church is to be God's instrument in declaring to these rebellious, and now usurping powers, the divine purpose, and in ad-

ministering their principalities after they have been un-
seated and cast down."[37] He explains further,

> "Authority" moreover is God's constant offer to
> His children in every department of spiritual life. . . .
> To such as yield themselves in full obedience and
> faith, the mysteries of the kingdom are opened; they
> are made to share the throne of the risen Lord; prin-
> cipalities and powers are put under their feet; and
> there is granted an ever-increasing knowledge of the
> purpose of the ages which the Father has purposed
> in His dear Son.[38]

With that increasing knowledge of the purposes of
God, believers also share in the government of God over
the powers of heaven and earth:

> It is the believer's privilege to realize that there is
> nothing that affects his fellows which is not of real
> moment to himself. Prayer becomes to him an out-
> let for his sympathetic reactions. As he follows the
> urges of his spirit, and takes to the throne every-
> thing that touches his heart, he becomes a partner
> with his Lord in the government of the universe. His
> intercessions become channels along which the di-
> vine power is enabled to flow for the alleviation of
> suffering, the extension of the gospel, and the con-
> trol of the activities of the rulers of mankind. At his
> word the unseen principalities and powers are re-
> strained, wars are hindered or delayed, calamities
> are averted, and national and individual blessings
> are bestowed. He may think himself but an infini-
> tesimal factor in all this, but it is the divine purpose
> that the people of the Lord shall be associated with
> Him in His administration.[39]

Authority to Avert War

As just cited, MacMillan believed that the believer's
authority can control world events. This belief he inher-

ited from the Overcomer Movement in which Jessie Penn-Lewis and others were involved.[40] He declared, "Devastating wars might at times be held back if the Church of Christ realized its authority and privilege."[41] Further, he averred, "The boldness of faith can meet the territorial greed and the arrogant ambition of the invader and turn him back in the name of the Lord of hosts."[42] He cited examples:

> Even in world matters where war seemed inevitable, there have been times in recent years, when groups of instructed believers, united with one accord against the working of the powers of the air in some great crisis, have seen the problem gradually clear up without coming to the worst. Christians are far from realizing the extent and the reality of their union with Christ in His great task of world authority.[43]

He appealed to the Church to band together to attempt to thwart Satan's efforts, rather than to resort to human effort to solve what ultimately are spiritual and supernatural problems. Hence, he disagreed with Bonhoeffer's approach to get rid of Hitler.[44]

Authority over Depression

Spiritual and mental depression, MacMillan averred, must be met with authority, as he did with Mrs. Strohm in the Philippines:

> It is this authority of Christ that must be exercised by the believer, or, in case of his absolute inability, by some instructed soul on his behalf. There are few ministries of the church that are becoming more urgent than that of releasing from spiritual bondage the increasing multitude of children of God who suffer from the attacks of deceiving spirits,

or perhaps from nervous complaints that result
from unrecognized working of the enemy.[45]

Authority to Claim Health and Healing

MacMillan believed that healing is a privilege for the
Christian as a provision of the atonement, and needs to be
affirmed actively and strenuously: "We should claim this
gracious relationship to the fullest degree for our own flesh
and bones, and refuse the sicknesses that seek to fasten
upon our physical frames."[46] He believed that illness and
calamity are often the doing of the forces of Satan and are
not to be accepted submissively as the will of God:

> It is ours to take hold jointly with the Spirit—for
> as He takes hold with us we must also cooperate
> with Him—against the things and the forces which
> assail our individual lives with a faithful and firm re-
> fusal of their right to control our bodies or our cir-
> cumstances. Too often the Christian passively
> accepts whatever comes to him as being the will of
> the Lord, yielding without resistance at times to the
> wiles of the enemy himself. True faith in conflict is a
> steadfast and earnest will for victory. . . . That "God
> hath spoken" is the ground upon which every for-
> ward step in the spiritual life must be taken.[47]

Authority to Bind and Loose

"It is the believer's right to bind and loose in the name
of Him who has appointed him," MacMillan declared.[48]
He understood Matthew 18:16-20 to refer to two kinds of
binding and loosing: the authority of the assembly in discipline and the authority of united intercession to overcome demonic powers.[49] This concept was not unique to
MacMillan, but had been actively taught and practiced in
evangelical and holiness circles for decades, with increasing understanding. For instance, one of MacMillan's spiri-

tual mentors, Andrew Murray, in his classic book *With Christ in the School of Prayer*, had prayed, "Grant especially, blessed Lord, that your Church may believe that it is by the power of united prayer that she can bind and loose in heaven, cast out Satan, save souls, remove mountains, and hasten the coming of the Kingdom."[50] Carrie Judd Montgomery and Jessie Penn-Lewis had popularized the concept in their writings by 1921.[51] As mentioned in previous chapters, MacMillan reprinted in *The Alliance Weekly* a portion of Penn-Lewis' booklet entitled "How to Pray for Missionaries," which discussed the practice of binding and loosing.[52]

Authority over Territorial Spirits

Though he did not use the contemporary terminology of "territorial spirits," he understood that principalities and powers had established strongholds in certain geographical locations. Penn-Lewis had hinted at the concept as early as 1897 at a China Inland Mission conference in London, declaring on the basis of Daniel 10 that there are " 'principalities' who rule over various lands."[53] MacMillan's friend and senior missionary statesman Robert Jaffray discerned a "prince of darkness" over a specific geographical area.[54] From his own experiences, MacMillan developed the theological concept further. Some personality trait weaknesses that are usually considered characteristic of a certain nationality or ethnic group, MacMillan suggests, are "quite as likely to be a working of that undercurrent of Satanic force."[55] He posited the atheism of Russia and the unexplainable submissiveness of its people as due to an occult power, what he calls a "hellish counterfeit."[56] For most heathen religions, MacMillan explained, "Every god is confined to definite territorial limits, outside of which his influence does not extend."[57]

Islam, however, he called "our most stubborn foe," because it conceives of a "universal consciousness" and "worldwide conquest" that "emanates from supernatural and demoniacal power."[58] From his many encounters with Muslims he believed, "Mohammedanism is the supreme fortress of Satan, and no permanent breach in its walls has ever been made."[59] Nevertheless, he called for intercessors "to roll back the powers of the air, and make it possible to bring the Truth to bear on these regions where the devil is blocking the way."[60]

Though not nearly so sophisticated a strategy as presented today, nonetheless, MacMillan taught and practiced what he called "praying geographically":

> There is among the saints of the Most High a chosen group—perhaps larger than we think—whose divinely appointed ministry is that of the prayer closet. There, on their knees with a world map before them, its members individually and methodically pray out the problems of the advance of the kingdom. They precede missionaries into areas where Christ has not been named; they observe them as they attack firmly placed barriers, breaking down by the high explosive of authoritative prayer the Satanic opposition that continues to impede the forward progress of the gospel. Because the working of the Spirit of God is everywhere, working through some mysterious law, dependent on intercession, these unseen workers are the real pioneers of Christian missions. Unknown to themselves their word in the heavenlies is mighty through God to the overthrowing of principalities and powers. National boundaries are melting down before the faith and fervor of their supplications.[61]

This type of ministry is not for everyone, but only for "men and women whose lives are yielded to God," for

"True geographic prayer ministry needs close abiding in God."[62] Those who engage in this kind of ministry need to exercise spiritual discernment. They are to be "watchers," who have their heart and mind "trained in spiritual observation" and "can discern constant shifting of the lines of combat, which is not obvious to others." He warns that "it is also a service of peculiar peril to those involved. For the enemy strikes with malignant vigor and keen knowledge at every opportunity."[63]

He spoke out of the authority of his own experience, having done battle in the Philippines. In spite of the dangers, he envisioned a greater authority and victory over these strongholds:

> As we continue to abide closely in Him, our prayers for the advancement of the kingdom will become less and less the uttering of petitions, and will increasingly manifest the exercise of a spiritual authority that recognizes no national boundaries, but fearlessly binds the forces of darkness in any part of the world.[64]

Authority to Speak to the Mountain

MacMillan understood the exercise of spiritual authority to be not merely prayer: "While prayer precedes the exercise of authority, it does not take its place."[65] The exercise of authority, then, involves the "command of faith":

> The command of faith is the divine means of removing [mountains] out of the way: "Ye shall say to this mountain, Be thou removed and be thou cast into the sea; and it shall obey you." The question involved is not that of an imposing faith, but that of an all-sufficient Name. . . . As he speaks to the mountain in the name of Christ, he puts his hand on

the dynamic force that controls the universe. Heavenly energy is released, and his behest is obeyed.[66]

We are not merely to pray to God about our problems; we are to speak an authoritative word in the name of Jesus to our problems. He asserts further,

> It is a good exercise to "*say*" aloud to our difficulties, as we kneel in prayer, "Be thou removed." The *saying*, if in faith in the name of the Lord, will cause a stirring at the roots; and as we keep stedfastly holding to God and *saying*, the time will come when the tree which has been opposing, or the mountain which has been hindering, will quietly move into the sea of oblivion.[67]

This concept MacMillan clearly gleaned from A.T. Pierson, interim successor to Charles Spurgeon. Expounding on Mark 11:22-24 and its parallel passages in Luke 17:5-6 and Matthew 17:20-21, Pierson comments,

> The coincidence is too remarkable to be either accidental or unimportant. In all these cases it is not "pray" but "say," not the word of petition but of direction, not a suppliant but as of a sovereign.
>
> This we regard as the central, vital heart of this great lesson on Faith. The Master of all girds the servant with His own power and intrusts him with authority to command. Faith claims not only blessing but power to bless. This lesson is at first sight so astounding as to seem incredible—it passes all understanding, and faith itself staggers at such promises.
>
> Let us reverently seek to take in the marvelous thought. Faith in God so unites to God that it passes beyond the privilege of asking to the power of commanding.[68]

Commanding God—Isaiah 45:11

Springing out of the authority to speak a word of commanding faith, the most controversial of MacMillan's concepts is that of "commanding God." The idea is based primarily on a prophecy of Isaiah: "Thus saith the LORD, the Holy One of Israel, and his Maker, Ask me of things to come concerning my sons, and concerning the work of my hands command ye me" (Isaiah 45:11). MacMillan comments on this passage of Scripture:

> So unreasonable to the natural mind seems the proposition of Jehovah to His people (Isaiah 45:11) that they should "command" Him concerning the work of His hands, that various alternative readings of the passage have been made with the intent of toning down the apparent extravagance of the divine offer. Men are slow to believe that the Almighty really means exactly what He says. They think it a thing incredible that He would share with human hands the throttle of divine power. Nor have they the spiritual understanding to comprehend the purpose of the Father to bring those who have been redeemed with the precious blood of His dear Son into living and practical cooperation with that Son in the administration of His kingdom.[69]

MacMillan is correct that there are a wide variety of interpretations attempting to explain the verse. There is no consensus on how to interpret it. It is like the Jewish saying that when four rabbis get together to discuss a passage, they come up with five opinions! Matthew Henry gives three different interpretations, apparently preferring the imperative interpretation ("Command Me"), but leaving room for the other possibilities.[70] The more recent exegetes and expositors tend to emend the passage, proposing textual changes of a character or two, or a different word division, etc., to make the clause more palatable.[71] Some translators soften the word by changing it to "ask" rather than "command," but the word clearly means command, not ask. In fact, it is in the piel conjugation in Hebrew, which is more intensive.[72]

George Rawlinson (one of MacMillan's sources) in *The Pulpit Commentary* translates it as an imperative, explaining it in this way:

> First learn of Me what in My designs is to be the course of human events, and then (if necessary) give Me directions concerning My sons (Israel), who are the work of My hands; but do not presume to give Me directions while you are still in utter ignorance of My design. In any case remember who I am—the Maker of heaven and earth, the Creator of man, One accustomed to give directions to the angelic host.[73]

Albert Barnes interprets,

> This verse is designed . . . especially to show them, that instead of complaining of his designs, or of finding fault with his sovereignty, it was their privilege to inquire respecting his dealings, and events. . . . The word "command" is here to be taken rather as indicating the privilege of his people to present their desires in the language of fervent and respectful petition, and that God here indicates that he would, so to speak, allow them to direct him; that he would hear their prayers, and would conform the events of his administration to their wishes and their welfare. This is the most obvious interpretation.[74]

Charles Spurgeon declares,

> You are yourself a decree. . . . Our prayers are God's decrees in another shape. . . . Do not say, "How can my prayers affect the decrees of God?" They cannot, except to the degree that your prayers are decrees, and that as they come out, every prayer that is inspired of the Holy Ghost in your soul is as omnipotent and eternal as that decree which said, "Let there

be light: and there was light" (Gen. 1:3). . . . The ear
of God shall listen, and the hand of God shall yield to
your will. God bids you cry, "Thy will be done," and
your will shall be done. When you can plead His
promise, then your will is His will.[75]

Spurgeon's friend A.T. Pierson commented on this
Scripture as well, asserting:

Faith in God so unites to God that it passes beyond the privilege of asking to the power of commanding. This language of Christ is not that of a
request, however bold, but of a *fiat*. . . . And so—
marvelous fact! The child of God, laying hold by
faith of the Power of the Omnipotent One, issues
his fiat. . . . Obey the Law of the Power and the
Power obeys you. Conform to the Laws and modes
of the Spirit's operations, and in the work of God's
hands you may command the Spirit's Power.[76]

A.B. Simpson likewise follows in the footsteps of
Spurgeon and Pierson: "In the name of Jesus we are to not
only ask, but claim and pass in the orders of faith to the
bank of heaven." Then he refers to John 15:7, saying "as
one has translated it, 'Ye shall ask what ye command and
it shall be done unto you.' "[77] He calls this "the confidence
of prayer." So the idea is not original with MacMillan, but
has substantial evangelical exposition behind it.
MacMillan has drawn on earlier teaching, especially that
of Pierson and Simpson, and expanded upon it.

It is important to understand that these godly leaders
are *not* teaching that man is now sovereign and God is
not. Rather, when a believer is in such intimate communion with God in the secret place of the Most High, he
knows beyond a shadow of a doubt the will of God, and
can speak with confidence for God to carry it out.[78]
MacMillan expresses it this way:

> To them [the authoritative intercessors] the
> Word of God has become a battle chart on which is
> detailed the plan of campaign of the host of the
> Lord. They realize that they have been appointed by
> Him for the oversight of certain sections of the ad-
> vance, and they have humbly accepted His commis-
> sion. Deeply conscious of their own personal
> unworthiness and insufficiency, they yet believe
> God's statement concerning their identification
> with Christ in His throne power. . . . Their closet be-
> comes a council chamber from which spiritual com-
> mands go forth concerning matters widely varied in
> character and separated in place. As they speak the
> word of command, God obeys. His delight is in such
> co-working.[79]

This is a far cry from what one modern faith leader
claims, "Now this is a shocker! But God has to be given
permission to work in this earth realm on behalf of man.
. . . Yes! You are in control! So if man has control, who no
longer has it? God. . . ."[80] MacMillan, as well as Simpson,
Pierson and Spurgeon, would strongly repudiate such an
idea.

The Scope of the Believer's Authority

Who can exercise the authority of the believer? And to
what extent can it be exercised? Penn-Lewis and Evan
Roberts contended that "the authority of Christ a
Conquerer over the evil hosts of Satan is not inherent in
the believer, but is laid hold of by him through the power
of the Holy Spirit, and is borne witness to by Him only in
response to faith."[81] Though MacMillan highly respected
Penn-Lewis and was strongly influenced by her teaching,
on this rare occasion he took exception to her view on this
issue.

He begins his treatise on the authority of the believer by asserting that it is *not* "the property only of a few elect souls. On the contrary, it is the possession of every true child of God. It is one of the 'all things' received in Christ. Its reception dates from the soul's contact with Calvary."[82] He further declares: "The weakest and the most unlettered saint is able by the cross and its conquest of the powers of hell to drive the fiercest 'bulls of Bashan' (Psa. 22:12) in headlong flight."[83]

However, he does acknowledge that "the authority of His name could never be efficacious in the mouth of an unspiritual disciple."[84] It is a "consecrated hand" that directs the throne power of Christ.[85] Further, he believed that along with the baptism with the Spirit comes "a supreme confidence in the wisdom and omnipotence of the Lord of the harvest, and an inward assurance of the sharing of His authority over all the power of the enemy arrayed against us in the warfare to which we have been called."[86]

Contrary to some in the modern faith movement who have picked up and modified his concepts, MacMillan did not believe that Jesus Christ transferred all authority to believers: "In the world's long history, one Man only, with the unmeasured unction of the Holy Ghost upon Him, has been able to say, 'All authority hath been given unto me in heaven and in earth.' "[87] He states rather that this delegated authority is only potentially and partially the believer's now, and that believers will be "co-regents with Himself in the millennial reign."[88]

In all of our exercise of authority and faith, MacMillan asserts the need for humility:

> So Jesus says, when you as servants have done all those things which are commanded you; when you have uprooted trees, removed mountains, healed

the sick, led multitudes to salvation—remember
that you are still servants of God. What you have
done is simply what He has endued you with power
to do, and what you have engaged to do for Him.
You have not done aught of yourselves—all has
been of His working.[89]

The authority is "potential," that is positional, with
the necessity of working it out in life. It is not automatic,
nor is it complete in this life. Yet MacMillan believed
that the Church has not yet reached the limit of exercising its authority on earth:

Christ is at the right hand of God, the very seat of
all authority, and united with Him are His believing
saints. To them is given to share His authority even
here and now, to the limit of their faith and their
spiritual comprehension. But such is the blinding
power of the enemy that few indeed have any conception of the gracious purpose of God in this regard. . . . Herein lies much of the weakness of the
Church.[90]

His commentary on the Church in the 1940s could
well be applied to the Church today:

A united, instructed and praying church could control the power of the air. But the church is not united,
neither is it instructed in the matters of heavenly warfare. Nor yet is it a praying church. A little flock of intercessors bears the burden of supplication for "kings
and for all that are in authority."[91]

This is but a brief summary and synthesis of
MacMillan's teaching on the authority of the believer.
Limitations of this study do not permit a thorough analy-
sis. Nonetheless, it can be concluded that while there are
limits to what the Church can accomplish in this age,
MacMillan attests that it has not yet reached the potential

that God has intended for exercising the believer's authority. His teaching also corrects some contemporary faith misconceptions of the doctrine. MacMillan's teaching on the authority of the believer is comprised of sound exegesis of Scripture and creative compilation and expansion of the teachings of respected classic holiness leaders, especially A.B. Simpson, A.T. Pierson, Jessie Penn-Lewis, Andrew Murray and George Watson. As a result, his insights are a sound model for contemporary belief and practice.

Epilogue
Macmillan's Family Legacy

JOHN MACMILLAN BELIEVED STRONGLY in the importance of family life. Referring to Psalm 127:3, he commented, "The little ones are looked on as a heritage of the Lord, and it is the first purpose of the parents that they shall know and honor Him with all their hearts."[1] Though the MacMillans had only one child, Buchanan, he indeed was a heritage from the Lord and through him the MacMillan legacy continued. John and Isabel raised him up in his early years "in the nurture and admonition of the Lord and taught the way of prayer and the instruction of Scriptures."[2] On behalf of Buchanan they prayed Manoah's petition regarding Samson, "How shall we order the child and how shall we do unto him?"[3]

Buchanan was very close to his mother.

> Although she died when I was twelve, her memory and influence remain one of the great things in my life. . . . My mother was of a naturally happy disposi-

> tion. She frequently sang at her work about the
> house. Although she had little musical training and
> could only play imperfectly, I recall when a piano
> came into our home, undoubtedly with the hope that
> I would eventually learn to play it. She did her part to
> interest me in many things. . . . She frequently read to
> me, as did my father on occasion, and endeavored to
> arouse my interest in many things—nature, music,
> etc. She was indefatigable in my spiritual training.

His father taught him the Scriptures, trained him in the
Westminster Catechism, romped with him, took him on
walks through the nearby ravine down to the waterfront.
Buchanan recounts, "He attempted with somewhat indif-
ferent success to teach me the Shorter Catechism—my
span of attention must have tried his patience with its
brevity at such times—but he was wonderfully patient."

The love and instruction they gave to Buchanan in his
early years prepared him for the separation that was to follow. Though it was agonizing for him and Isabel to leave
Buchanan at the mission boarding school in Chefoo, they
regarded their role as stewards of the Lord: "Our children
are not our own. . . . In a deeper sense, the children of the
Christian belong to the Lord. . . . He claims them for His
own. And the true attitude of every parent is that of
Hannah concerning the boy Samuel: 'As long as he liveth,
he shall be lent to the Lord.' " [4]

His pain in adjusting to the Mission school and being
separated from his parents was indicative of his sensitive
nature. His tender spirit no doubt contributed to his in-
clination toward music, along with his mother's gift for
song. John MacMillan was not talented as a musician
and could not carry a tune, but had great interest in music as an important part of worship and a mark of the
Spirit-filled life, which he imparted to his son.

After his mother's death Buchanan became closer to his father, developing "a genuine and rich friendship." Buchanan writes of his father,

> He was constantly active in the Lord's work in a variety of ways. He developed a virile, strong, disciplined, consistent Christian character *that I have never seen surpassed, and rarely equalled.* When I came to read Matthew Arnold's *Rugby Chapel* in later years, I could think only of him. His discipline was tempered with a rare degree of Christlike gentleness and sympathetic insight that won him an ever widening circle of friends, and of those who harbored a deep sense of admiration and gratitude for his understanding and spiritual counsel.

In 1929, after John and Buchanan returned to North America, Buchanan lived with his aunts at 52 Huntley Street in Toronto and attended school there. (Interestingly, the house was demolished in more recent years to make way for the building complex of the TV ministry of David Mains, known as "100 Huntley Street.") He attended Toronto Bible College, then received a music degree from the University of Toronto (Victoria College). While in college Buchanan gained an appreciation for liturgy, singing in an Anglican church choir and substituting as an organist. He also became active in InterVarsity Fellowship.

Following collegiate studies, he enlisted in the Canadian Royal Air Force and became an instructor in radar for four years in England during World War II. Like most young men, Buchanan was exposed to temptations to sow wild oats, but remained strong in his Christian faith. On one occasion he was offered a cigarette by another soldier in his company, but he declined, saying, "Thanks, I don't smoke." The soldier replied, "You're____ lucky!"[5] The principles that John and Isabel had instilled in him as a child had taken root and were bearing fruit.

He returned in 1946 and proceeded to Nyack to visit his father. During his visit he met Jane Mortenson, a 1945 Nyack graduate who had studied under MacMillan and become a friend of John and Alice. After a short romance, they were married on October 26, 1946 and moved to Toronto, where Buchanan taught for a brief period of time.

Buchanan inherited his parents' love for the Chinese. He desired to return to Chefoo, China, where he had attended school as a child. He and Jane applied through China Inland Mission and traveled to Philadelphia for an interview at the CIM headquarters. However, due to complications caused by his Canadian citizenship, they were not accepted.

They had no choice but to return to Canada, since they could not be employed in the U.S. without special papers. Not knowing what else to do, the bewildered young couple visited his father in Nyack for a time. Dr. Olsen, head of the music department at Nyack, ran into him on campus and encouraged him to join the music faculty. He accepted the offer, returned to Toronto to make the legal arrangements, then returned to join the faculty in 1947.

That began a thirty-three-year tenure as a music professor. Buchanan went on to obtain a master's degree from Manhattan School of Music and a Ph.D. from New York University. As part of his dissertation on "The Calvinistic Hymnody of Claude le Jeuen," he wrote a symphony that won a top award at Harvard.

Buchanan participated in the 1962 revision of the C&MA Hymnal, *Hymns of the Christian Life*. In order to improve the quality of the music, he changed the harmony of some hymns, including some of A.B. Simpson's songs.[6] Former Nyack president Rexford Boda recalled that some

Alliance people at that time did not appreciate his changes, feeling like it was tampering with sacred ground, but his innovations have endured. Thus the MacMillan influence on the Alliance continued through Buchanan's gifting.

Buchanan continued to teach classes faithfully until three years before his death, even through years of suffering from a rare spinal illness, which involved a gradual paralysis. He retired to Orleans, Massachusetts, where he was cared for in a commune where his son Alan was living. He died August 27, 1983.[7] Another MacMillan had completed his course, impacting the lives of scores of students.

Former Nyack College president Rexford Boda, one of those who sat under the ministry and teaching of both MacMillans, said of Buchanan, "He was much respected and admired, a walking encyclopedia of knowledge in many things. I was privileged to have him as a professor in 'Music Appreciation.' " He was described by Marion Howe, another Nyack faculty member, as "of equal stature as his father—but in a different field."

Another student, Richard Barker, notes of Buchanan that he was quiet and unassuming like his father, "but had a different gifting." He disclaimed his father's expertise in spiritual warfare, saying, "I can't preach and pray like my dad." Nyack president Thomas P. Bailey remarked, "Buchanan was a brilliant musician—not in the performing sense, but in the theoretical and historical knowledge which he evidenced. He was well loved by his students in his long tenure at the college."

Buchanan was blessed to see one of his "best" students achieve stature as a musician and scholar. Harold Best, who graduated from Nyack in 1953 with a bachelor of sacred music degree, went on to an illustrious career, joining the faculty at Nyack in 1956 and becoming chairman of the music department in 1968. In 1970 he was appointed dean of the Conservatory of Music at Wheaton College. He acknowledged Dr. J. Buchanan MacMillan as one of the "most influential professors" with "his wide and profound knowledge of music."[8]

The MacMillan heritage has continued to the next generation as well. Buchanan and Jane raised three children. Alan John, born in 1947, shared his father's gift for music, receiving a scholarship in high school to the Interlocken Arts Academy to study music. He received Bachelors and Masters degrees at Boston University, then taught there, going on to Harvard for a Ph.D. Currently he teaches music at Grenville Christian College in Ontario, Canada, following in his father's footsteps.

Janet, born in 1948, also followed her father, obtaining a Masters degree in music from Temple University in Philadelphia and the Kark Orf Institute. She teaches elementary music and gives private music lessons. Both Alan and Janet became skilled violinists. Lois, born in 1952, attended Moravian College, majoring in German. For a time she lived in Germany and is currently raising four children at home.

Buchanan and Jane lived up the hill nearby, so John and Alice had frequent contact with their grandchildren. John and Alice loved gardening, and their lawn on South Boulevard was covered with flowers, to the delight of their grandchildren. Alan remembers his grandfather as old-fashioned and formal. He almost always donned a felt hat, and often wore a vest with a silver pocket watch on a chain (which Alan later inherited).

John earned a new nickname when, as a young child, Alan's attempt at saying "Grandpa" came out "Da," just as Grandma came out "Gammy." "Da" loved to play games with his grandchildren; even at his advanced age, he played baseball with Alan. He also took him to watch the construction of the nearby Tappan Zee Bridge. Alan would sometimes spend the night with his grandparents and John told him bedtime stories about the cartoon character, Bowser the dog, and also made up stories. Alan sometimes asked his grandfather questions to avoid going to sleep; John probably wasn't fooled, but he loved to answer them.

Alan recalls that his grandfather never got angry, but he could be stern. On one occasion, Alan swung a play sword and hit Da so hard that it drew blood. John stared at him sternly and admonished, "Alan, you musn't do that!" At heart, Da was quite tenderhearted, not only to his grandchildren, but to everyone. Alan remembered that students would often stop by to chat.

Alan recalled that his grandfather drove a 1939 Buick with running boards. While some people thought he overdid it, MacMillan would never pull it out of the garage without praying for the car and protection while traveling. This was not done out of fear, but out of an awareness that Satan sometimes wreaks destruction through what he called "raging chariots." As was his practice he believed in claiming Psalm 91.

> The children of the Lord have not been exempt from accident, and some have suffered severely. Do we all fully realize that the element of chance does not exist for the believer. . . . True it is that the angel of the Lord encamps round about them that fear Him, with a view to their deliverance. But the child of God is personally responsible for the definite claiming of such protection, and also for abiding within the circumscribed limits wherein it is effective. . . . Therefore, it is vital that every true servant of God learn the secret of dwelling "in the secret place of the Most High," thereby in all the going out

and coming of life, experiencing the security of
those who "abide under the shadow of Shaddai."[9]

Thus he believed in bathing everything he did in prayer
and resting in the security of God's promises. Alan was impressed with his grandfather's breadth of knowledge and
godliness, calling him "a spiritual light in my life."

Alan also inherited his father's and grandfather's love
for the Far Eastern peoples. As a professor he has had contact with many Asian students and says he has a "magne-
tism for the Chinese." John MacMillan's godly heritage
and heart for people has been passed on from generation
to generation. MacMillan wrote that the "principle of heredity" was not only reflected in the sins of the parents
transferred to the children, but also "it was meant unto
good—the righteous parent passing on to his children
what was best."[10] This principle was indeed displayed in
his own family legacy through his son and grandchildren.
Referring to Proverbs 17:6, MacMillan commented,
"When children's children show outstanding powers and
attain to honorable positions, the progenitor shares in the
glory; to him they become a crown of blessing and
thanksgiving."[11] Though John did not live to see them
come into their places of honor, he shared in their glory
from among the heavenly cloud of witnesses.

The First John 4:1-3 Testing of Spirits

I N VERY QUESTIONABLE CASES of spiritual manifestations, MacMillan advised the use of two scriptural tests: "Wherefore I give you to understand, that no man speaking by the Spirit of God calleth Jesus accursed: and that no man can say that Jesus is the Lord, but by the Holy Ghost" (1 Corinthians 12:3) and "Hereby know ye the Spirit of God: Every spirit that confesseth that Jesus Christ is come in the flesh is of God: and every spirit that confesseth not that Jesus Christ is come in the flesh is not of God" (1 John 4:2-3). MacMillan asserts, "Whenever any power gains control of our minds or any part of our body, we are instructed to test its origin (1 John 4:1-3; 1 Cor. 12:3)."[1] While he recognized both Scriptures as valid tests for distinguishing spirits, First John 4:1-3 became his trademark in deliverance ministry. MacMillan explains his reasoning for the use of this procedure:

The New Testament warns against the acceptance
of what is supernatural without conclusive proof of
its authenticity. "Believe not every spirit [or revelation purporting to come from God]," warns the Apostle John (1 John 4:1), "but try the spirits whether
they are of God," adding significantly, "because
many false prophets are gone out into the world."
When some unusual manifestation is seen, it is not to
be received without question on the supposition that
it must be of the Spirit of God. The Holy Spirit Himself commands that it be definitely tested; to fail to
do so is disobedience, and is the source of much dis-
order in many groups of even sincere servants of the
Lord.[2]

Because of his emphasis upon the use of this tool in
spiritual warfare ministry, we turn to a history and discussion of this methodology.

Its Usage in Early Nineteenth-Century Irvingism

The use of First John 4:1-3 as a testing device for supernatural manifestations has strong and long support from
the evangelical community, contrary to the reports of
Brotherton and others that Archie Ruark was the first in
1946.[3] The earliest known usage of First John 4:1-3 to test
for spurious demonic manifestations occurred in the
1830s during the days of Edward Irving's emphasis on the
charismatic gifts of the Spirit. On one occasion when
someone was prophesying, the spirit of the prophecy was
challenged with the question, "Wilt thou not confess that
Jesus Christ is come in the flesh?" The spirit responded
loudly, "I will not!" The demon was then cast out and
never returned.[4]

Later Nineteenth Century—Scholar George Pember

Near the end of the nineteenth century George Pember, in his treatise on modern spiritualism and theosophy, wrote that First John 4:1-3 applies to the testing of supernatural utterances:

> The apostle is *clearly legislating for those cases of prophetic utterance and speaking with tongues* which were then common in the church. . . . Therefore the duty inculcated by John is that of testing the spirits of prophets, to discover whether they are influenced by the Spirit of God or by demons. And the Ephesians seem to have obeyed the precept when they tried those who said they were apostles, but were not, and found them liars" [italics added].[5]

Here in the nineteenth century, Pember applies this scriptural test specifically to tongues and prophecy. Though he does not mention Irvingism, it is quite possible he may have known of that incident of testing. He wrote this many years before the outbreak of the Pentecostal movement. This evidence thus controverts Brotherton's hypothesis that the procedure as used by Archie Ruark was "historically inevitable" *as a result* of the error of the evidence doctrine of the Pentecostal movement.[6] The application of the First John 4 test to tongues and prophecy predates the evidence doctrine by decades.

Early Twentieth-Century Testing of Spirits—A.B. Simpson

A.B. Simpson, commenting on this text in his 1900 publication *Messages of Love* (the epistles of John in his *Christ in the Bible Commentary*), acknowledges Pember's work, and asserts the need to try the spirits. He does not specifically apply First John 4:2-3 to the testing of tongues as does Pember, but he does allude to the need of testing prophecy, which he calls "*inward visions and revelations*," by "the simple test" of "the Word of God [1 John 4:2-3], and the practical test of righteousness and holiness."[7] He exhorts, "Let us be prepared for false spirits and let us not fear to try them, for if God is giving us any *message or revelation*, He will always give us ample time to be quite sure that it is God" (italics added).[8] Both Simpson and Pember were writing before the outbreak of Pentecostalism.

China Inland Mission

An edition of Pember's work was published in Toronto during the first decade of the twentieth century, so it is possible MacMillan came in contact with the concept in Pember's book at least by then, if not through Simpson. As mentioned in chapter 3, an editorial in *China's Millions* in 1907, written probably by MacMillan's future wife Isabel Robson, advocates the technique for testing the spirits in general, and prophecy in particular: "These words [1 John 4:1-3] were for the Church of the first century; but they are pre-eminently for the Church of the twentieth century. . . . Let us ever remember that the divine test in all cases is one and final, namely, does the prophet confess that Jesus Christ has come in the flesh?"[9] Since both Pember and Hudson Taylor were partial rapturists, Taylor could have been familiar with Pember's work. Since Taylor was involved in deliverance ministry as well, it is not inconceivable that he himself may have introduced the procedure as advocated by Pember to the China Inland Mission. At any rate, apparently by 1907 some in the ministry of the China Inland Mission employed the procedure.

C&MA Missions

The test was not universally practiced in missions, however, for also in 1908, *China's Millions* reported discernment by C&MA missionary William Christie (later C&MA treasurer and a member of the board of managers along with MacMillan) of a spurious tongues manifestation, but not by using the First John 4:1-3 technique.[10] About the same time, Robert Jaffray, later field chairman of the C&MA mission in China who had received the gift of tongues, was evidently aware of the procedure and approved its use as needed specifically for the testing of tongues and prophecy, declaring, "Only by a God-given supernatural instinct, only by 'trying the spirits' in the Scriptural way [1 John 4:1-3], may we be saved from evil influences that fill the 'air' in these last days."[11] He avowed that "a God-given, supernatural instinct" was needed with the test. He also cautioned that those testing a spirit need to take care that they "be separated from and not in any sense under the influence of the spirit at the time of the trial (cf. 1 John 4:1-3). It is no light or trifling thing thus to come into the very presence of supernatural beings."[12]

The British Keswick and Overcomer Movements

Jessie Penn-Lewis had recognized the technique by 1910, reporting in her publication *The Overcomer* an incident in Germany in which a tongues spirit responded to the question "Has Jesus Christ come in the flesh?" by answering, "Cursed be Jesus Christ."[13] Curiously, however, in their 1912 book *War on the Saints* Penn-Lewis and Evan Roberts write about the need to try the spirits, but do not mention confronting spirits with this test. Rather, they seem to view it as a test of doctrinal orthodoxy, as traditionally viewed, distinct from the gift of discerning spirits.[14] So at that time it was apparently not recognized and practiced universally as a valid testing procedure.

By 1925, however, D.M. Panton, who had been strongly critical of the Pentecostal movement, insisted that *all* tongues be tested according to First John 4:1-3: "No spirit-movement or spirit-action must ever be accepted without submission to, and authentication by, the Divine Tests."[15] He even criticized C&MA evangelist F.F. Bosworth for not having his tongue or those of others for whom he prayed tested by this procedure.[16] Panton appears, however, to have revised and moderated his viewpoint somewhat in later years, also allowing for the use of First Corinthians 12:3, Matthew 7:15-20, Galatians 1:8, and Second John 7 as other valid tests, and even encouraging the supernatural gifts of the Spirit, advising not to forbid tongues.[17]

Also in 1925, the technique was advocated for the testing of prophecy in China by independent missionary Margaret E. Barber, who was sponsored by Panton's church. She cited an actual incident in which a clearly supernatural audible voice spoke prophetically and seemingly scripturally from the house of a deceased preacher, but was found to be counterfeit.[18] This is the sixth application of the test to prophecy and the second real-life illustration (along with the Irvingism incident). Barber was a mentor to Chinese leader Watchman Nee, but Nee does not mention the practice. Since he was an avid reader of Pember, he would be familiar with Pember's understanding of First John 4:1-3. However, Nee would appear to view aberrant tongues more often as the use of "latent power of the soul," rather than outright demonic manifestations, though the use of soul power could revert to demonic influence.[19] MacMillan evidently leaned in that direction as well.

Not a Litmus Test

Alliance missionaries and ministers, including Mac-Millan and his colleague George Strohm, employed this technique in discernment from time to time, but evidently did not view it as necessary in all cases as a "litmus test" for true and false manifestations. Contrary to Panton, who interpreted First John 4:1-3 as commanding the testing of *all* spirits, C&MA leaders appeared to understand that the Scripture does not state that all spirits are to be tested, but rather that this criterion is applicable to *all spirits which are tested* as such. Paul Rader, who succeeded A.B. Simpson as president of the C&MA, himself spoke in tongues and preached in Pentecostal circles. He encouraged people not to be afraid of tongues and the gifts of the Spirit, and advocated the testing of tongues or prophecy if there is any question:

> Paul tells us how to regulate the gifts, not to eliminate them. . . . It is time to let people know that they need not be afraid of anything that comes as a gift, if it comes from God. . . . The saints should test the spirits. Here is God's written method of testing. 1 John 4:1, 2, 3. . . . Men and women filled with the Holy Ghost will testify and talk of Christ coming in the flesh; filled with other spirits a damper will fall on the enthusiasm or emotions when His coming in the flesh is spoken of. There is certain safety, for this is God's own acid test given to us by Him. This is the proper test to use to find if the spirit speaking in any person or through any person is the Holy Spirit or some other speaking spirit. . . . Most Christians who have spoken in tongues feel like they are special targets to be hit at by many Bible teachers—yet they

are saints who walk orderly and believe in the
Blood, the Book and the Blessed Hope.[20]

He did recognize that some supernatural utterances of
tongues and prophecy could come from demons, and affirmed that the scriptural test is First John 4:1-3 if there is
any doubt of the source. Those indicators, according to
Rader, can come in the form of a dampened atmosphere, a
check in the spirit or a hesitant response when Jesus' "coming in the flesh is spoken of." Yet he also affirmed that he believed the majority of speaking in
tongues was genuine.

Dr. T.J. McCrossan, a former Greek professor and Presbyterian pastor who joined the C&MA in 1924, authored
Speaking with Other Tongues: Sign or Gift—Which?, which
was published by the Alliance in 1927. This further expanded and expounded upon the position of Simpson and
the early Alliance, thus becoming *ipso facto* the official
C&MA position. McCrossan warns against forbidding
tongues, but also recognized the possibility of demonic
manifestations:

> Sometime some one may speak with tongues in
> your meeting, and you will feel at once that it is not
> of God. It will be harsh and repelling; your spiritual
> nature will revolt. Then just quietly place your hand
> upon such an one and ask to rebuke the evil spirit,
> and you will have very little trouble.[21]

McCrossan states that spurious tongues may be discerned by several signs, but he does not mention the
First John 4:1-3 testing technique. Perhaps, being relatively new to the C&MA, he may not have been familiar
with the methodology, but it would seem likely he would
have been informed of it before the publication of the
book unless it was not widely advocated in the Alliance.
It is also possible that, as a Greek scholar, he may have

had exegetical and hermeneutical concerns about the use of the procedure. At any rate, though the procedure had evidently been known and practiced for a number of years in the C&MA, it was not practiced universally, nor regarded as a litmus test as Panton advocated.

Expanded Usage of the Technique

Dick Hillis, a missionary to China through Orient Crusades, utilized the technique probably in the 1930s.[22] He shared his experiences with other missionaries in Japan, who then also used the procedure in the mid-twentieth century. Missionaries to South America also made use of First John 4:1-3 for testing spirits.[23] A.E. Ruark began using the procedure in Canada in 1946, as a result later coming to believe, like Panton, that most tongues were demonic and insisting that all tongues be tested through this procedure.[24] Since the history behind its use had not been known, the testing of tongues by First John 4:1-3 has become known as the "Ruark Procedure." In actuality, at least five people had applied the text specifically to the testing of tongues decades before: Pember, Jaffray, Penn-Lewis, Panton and Rader. MacMillan could be added to this list, since he applied it to supernatural manifestations, which included tongues. Of these, only Panton advocated its use in all cases. Additionally, as we have seen, the test was applied to prophecy in the time of Irving, as well as by Pember, Simpson, Robson, Barber and Rader. We will see below that MacMillan does as well.

George A. Birch, a missionary to China and Borneo with China Inland Mission, wrote of using the technique in his book *The Deliverance Ministry*.[25] He had joined together with Ruark in deliverance ministry in the late 1960s, coming to much the same conclusion as Ruark.[26]

With the inclusion of stories using the First John 4:1-3 procedure in *Demon Experiences in Many Lands*, published by Moody Press in 1960, it is evident that by the mid-twentieth century the practice had spread throughout evangelical missions worldwide.[27]

Though ordained with the C&MA, Ruark never served in its ministry, and was thus on the fringe of mainstream Alliance doctrine and practice (exemplified by MacMillan), which took a much more moderate and conciliatory attitude toward Pentecostals.

Ernest Rockstad, who, according to Alliance Theological Seminary professor John Ellenberger, was influenced by MacMillan, also made use of the First John 4:1-3 procedure. Though he was also influenced by Ruark's writings, Rockstad himself practiced *glossolalia* and, according to K. Neill Foster, did not believe that the majority of tongues was demonic as did Ruark.[28] Ed Murphy, whose mentors Don Hillis and Ernest Rockstad used the technique, does not discuss the First John 4:1-3 test in his comprehensive treatment of spiritual warfare.[29] However, in a personal conversation with Murphy, he revealed that he does use the technique and wrote about it, but that section was edited out due to space limitations. He also acknowledged his indebtedness to MacMillan.

Dissenting Voices

Not all evangelicals agree that the use of First John 4:1-3 for discernment of demonic spirits is valid or appropriate. C&MA minister Albert Runge is a notable example who questioned MacMillan's use of the procedure, believing it to be an arbitrary formula. He also believed that demons can lie, making the test unreliable.[30] Christian psychologist/theologian John White finds fault with the concept on such hermeneutical grounds:

> Diagnosis presents us with a thorny problem. John's reference to "trying the spirits" (1 John 4:1-3) can hardly be taken as a rule of thumb for detecting demons. It seems rather to be directed at the "spirit" underlying anti-Christian teaching. In any case, in the Gospels, demons seemed ready enough to confess that Christ was come in the flesh (e.g., Luke 4:33-37). In the absence of scriptural diagnostic principles we are forced to fall back either on the direct illumination of the Holy Spirit to guide us in a given case, or else devise rules based on experimental evidence.[31]

Dave Hunt, who stands at the opposite end of the theological spectrum from MacMillan, nevertheless agrees with White on this point: "This scripture has nothing to do with exorcism or conversing with evil spirits, but with identifying false prophets and their false teaching. Already in John's day there were 'many false prophets,' and John is declaring that false prophets are inspired by deceiving spirits."[32]

An Apologetic for the Practice

Anticipating such opposition, C&MA leader K. Neill Foster addressed some of the concerns, providing an insightful theological and practical apologetic for the practice in his Ph.D. dissertation at Fuller Seminary's School of World Mission.[33] He considers this approach as a simple, literal, supernaturalist hermeneutic as opposed to a non-supernaturalist hermeneutic:

> If we are able to demonstrate that the Ruark procedure is essentially biblical, and that it is in harmony with other closely related passages in the New Testament, we will establish the biblicity of a procedure which strikes at the root of the modern absorption with signs, wonders and speaking in tongues.

At the same time we will have established the
biblicity of a procedure which immediately implies
supernatural Christianity, that immediately involves exorcism, and by implication applies a
supernaturalistic hermeneutic to all of Scripture.[34]

Until Foster's dissertation, there does not appear to
have been a scholarly, exegetical defense of the use of First
John 4:1-3 in this manner. It has simply been assumed to
be a legitimate hermeneutical and exegetical application of
the passage and practiced with apparent observable results
for at least a century. Foster's study, while not without its
questions and weaknesses, presents a strong case for the
legitimate use of First John 4:1-3 as a testing procedure for
spirit utterances and manifestations.

Gerald McGraw, C&MA professor at Toccoa Falls College, has also written articles to authenticate the practice,
though his rejoinder has been more empirical and prag-
matic than theological and exegetical.[35] McGraw seems to
believe, like Ruark and Panton, that the vast majority of
tongues are demonic and that virtually all tongues need to
be tested.[36] However, even some who do use the First John
4:1-3 test, such as Keith Bailey, who was tutored by
MacMillan, do not advocate using it in all situations, nor
do they insist that all tongues be tested according to this
Scripture. MacMillan himself did not use the test in all situations, although he may have made use of it increasingly.
Also he noted that First Corinthians 12:3 could also be
used as a valid test, though he apparently made more frequent use of First John 4:1-3.[37]

In actuality, McGraw and Ruark would appear to dem-
onstrate significant historical drift from the historic
C&MA position, which recognized that some tongues and
other phenomena may be demonic, but did not regard all
such manifestations as suspicious until proven innocent

by such a test. There is no present evidence that C&MA leaders who spoke in tongues, such as Paul Rader, Harry L. Turner, Mrs. William MacArthur, Robert Jaffray, F.F. Bosworth or Ira E. David, ever had their tongues experience tested or that they believed all tongues *must* be tested in this way, even though the procedure was known to them.

When the Test Should Be Used

MacMillan's position, as cited above, is that the test should be used whenever an "unusual manifestation" occurs. What does he mean by "unusual manifestation"? He explains:

> In speaking through His people the Spirit of God does not force upon the individual speaker words or messages apart from the yielded will. Should such occur, and the personality of the prophet be submerged to such a degree that he is unconscious of what he is uttering, the time has come when the putting of the test is imperative. In such a case, the challenge to the spirit, "Has Jesus Christ come in the flesh?" will almost always bring forth a negative answer, no matter how apparently orthodox the message itself may seem to be. The Spirit of God does not forcibly take possession of the mind and the intelligence. Rather He enhances the natural powers of His people, so that they have freedom and clarity of utterance to an unusual degree.[38]

MacMillan clarifies further that a supernatural manifestation is suspicious when

> . . . the personality of the individual is completely lost for a time, and he is not conscious of what is happening to him during the time of such working. This is dangerous, and does not correspond to the Pentecostal experience of Acts, when the disciples

were fully alert in mind and body, though acting under divine infilling. Whenever any power gains control of our minds or any part of our body, we are
instructed to test its origin (1 John 4:1-3; 1 Cor.
12:3). The Spirit of God does not take away our in-
dividuality, but makes it more keen.[39]

He appears to be speaking particularly of prophetic or
tongues utterances taking place in a passive or trancelike
state. As mentioned earlier, MacMillan used this technique when a student who spoke in tongues had lost consciousness. MacMillan's statement is quite similar to
Watchman Nee's definition of a passive state, "allowing
our mind or body to sink into a coma-like state, ceasing to
exercise conscious control over the mind, and inactivating
the proper functions of the will, conscience and memory."[40]

Other occasions for the test would be occurrences of
what Carrie Judd Montgomery in *The Alliance Weekly* described as "peculiar motions," such as writhing like a ser-
pent.[41] MacMillan also advises that other unusual
phenomena such as trancelike states, loss of consciousness, convulsions, roaring, questionable visions, etc.,
should be submitted to First John 4:1-3.[42] Other occasions where he suggested the use of the technique are
when a questionable teaching or prophetic utterance has
been given in a conscious state [43] or when someone has
been intensely seeking a manifestation and opening
himself up to receive anything.[44]

To sum up, the application of First John 4:1-3 to testing
supernatural manifestations can be traced back at least as
far as the 1830s. Robson and the China Inland Mission, as
well as MacMillan, applied it generally to the testing of
spirits. The test was applied specifically to prophecy in the
time of Irving, and also by Pember, Simpson, Robson,

Barber, Rader and MacMillan. It was applied also to the testing of tongues by Pember, Jaffray, Penn-Lewis, Panton, Rader and also later by MacMillan. Ruark picked up the practice, advocating imperative and universal use of the test as Panton did, though this was not the position of the C&MA or most who advocated the test. It would appear from the evidence that of all those who have advocated the practice up to the time of Ruark, MacMillan made the most frequent reference to and use of the procedure.

Endnotes

List of Abbreviations used in
A Believer with Authority

AAR   *Alliance Academic Review*

AOB   *The Authority of the Believer*

AW   *The Alliance Weekly*

C&MA   The Christian and Missionary Alliance

CIM   China Inland Mission

CITB   *Christ in the Bible*

CM   *China's Millions*

EEA   *Earth's Earliest Ages*

EWD   *Encounter with Darkness*

OMF   Overseas Missionary Fellowship

SSQ   *The Adult Full Gospel Sunday School Quarterly*

Introduction

1. Paul L. King, "A.B. Simpson and the Modern Faith Movement," *Alliance Academic Review*, Elio Cuccaro, ed. (Camp Hill, PA: Christian Publications, 1996), 1-22.
2. K. Neill Foster with Paul L. King, *Binding and Loosing: Exercising Authority over the Dark Powers* (Camp Hill, PA: Christian Publications, 1998).
3. Two sub-problems of pursuing this investigation have been (1) finding information about a relatively unknown man who has been deceased for forty years, (2) analyzing a massive amount of unsigned editorials (over 1,500 pages) from 1934 to 1950, believed to be predominately MacMillan's writing, and comparing them with over 1,800 pages of writings already identified as MacMillan's. The former, identified as MacMillan's through external and internal writing analysis, combined with the latter, has uncovered a vast treasure of MacMillan's works that could be published. This will enrich the C&MA and the general Christian public, and also provide further insights into his life, ministry and impact. Dr. K. Neill Foster, President of Christian Publications, Inc., has asserted that because of this research MacMillan could emerge as the third major writer of the C&MA (after A.B. Simpson and A.W. Tozer), and that this research may result in the publication of additional writings by MacMillan. Those who are interested in the authorship analysis and listing of all of MacMillan's writings can consult my dissertation (see note 6).
4. Marion Howe, e-mail correspondence to author, January 14, 1998.
5. Donald Kenyon, letter to author, January 16, 1998.

6. Paul L. King, "A Case Study of a Believer with Authority: The Impact of the Life and Ministry of John A. MacMillan" (D.Min. diss., University Microfilms International #9975204, 2000).

Chapter 1—Formative Years

1. Unless otherwise noted, the information in this book was obtained from the MacMillan family, including his daughter-in-law Jane, his grandson Alan and the handwritten notes of his son J. Buchanan MacMillan, entitled "J.B. MacMillan: An Acct. of Family and Self," written in 1964-65. For more detailed geneological information on the family, see my dissertation, Chapter 2.
2. *Scots Kith and Kin* (Edinburgh, Scotland: C. J. Cousland & Sons, n.d.), 74.
3. "Old Testament Thanksgiving," *The Alliance Weekly* (AW), November 19, 1938, 741.
4. "Freedom of the Skies," *AW*, December 19, 1942, 803.
5. "The Problem of Korea," *AW*, July 31, 1948, 482; John A. MacMillan, "A Standard Bearer Fallen," *AW*, November 28, 1936, 762.
6. "Revealing the Lord," *AW*, January 5, 1935, 3; "Anglo-Saxon Declension," *AW*, December 4, 1937, 771.
7. John A. MacMillan, *The Full Gospel Adult Sunday School Quarterly* (SSQ), July 4, 1943, 1. All references to *The Full Gospel Adult Sunday School Quarterly* in this thesis are authored by MacMillan.
8. Determined by comparison of Buchanan's family notes with Toronto city directories; also both John MacMillan and John Arbothnot are listed together at elder session meetings of Westminster Presbyterian Church.
9. "The Evangelical Christian," *AW*, May 1, 1937, 275.
10. Lindsay Reynolds, *Footprints* (Beaverlodge, Alberta, Canada: Buena Book Services, 1981), 179-188.
11. "Summer Responsibilities," *AW*, July 28, 1934, 466.
12. Ibid.
13. Ibid.

Chapter 2—Spiritual Development and Ministry

1. "Saving the Young," *AW*, November 4, 1939, 691; "Child Conversion," *AW*, November 15, 1947, 722.
2. "Religion in the Home," *AW*, August 11, 1945, 242.
3. Membership records, West Presbyterian Church, Toronto, Ontario, 1887.
4. *AW*, November 6, 1943, 707, 711.
5. Toronto city directory, 1888.
6. Membership records, West Presbyterian Church, 1888.
7. Membership records, Westminster Presbyterian Church, Toronto, Ontario, 1891; list of members, Women's Missionary Society minutes, Westminster Presbyterian Church, Toronto, Ontario, 1896.
8. Membership records, Westminster Presbyterian Church, 1899.
9. *SSQ*, August 10, 1947, 19; compare *SSQ*, September 22, 1935, 41, and *SSQ*, August 15, 1954, 20, where he mentions the same incident, but makes no reference to himself; session minutes, Westminster Presbyterian Church, March 4, 1898; September 4, 1898; September 26, 1898.
10. Membership records, Westminster Presbyterian Church, April 1900.

11. Ibid., January 1903.

12. Ibid., June 24, 1904.

13. "Rev. Dr. Neil's Jubilee," newspaper clipping, no date or source, 1909; obituary, newspaper clipping, no source or date, 1928; "Rev. Dr. John Neil a Veteran with All the Ardor of Youth," newspaper clipping, no source, June 28, 1919.

14. Session minutes, Westminster Presbyterian Church, January 15, 1908.

15. Ibid., November 12, 1912.

16. J. A. MacMillan, "Salvation," *AW*, April 27, 1935, 258; "American Youth," *AW*, March 11, 1939, 147; "Attending the Theater," *AW*, September 21, 1940, 594; "Religious Movies," *AW*, January 1, 1949, 4; "National Child Training," *AW*, July 14, 1945, 210.

17. "Blood Lust," *AW*, August 10, 1946, 499.

18. Lindsay Reynolds, *Rebirth* (Beaverlodge, Alberta, Canada: Evangelistic Enterprises, 1992), 71; Robert L. Niklaus, John S. Sawin, Samuel J. Stoesz, *All For Jesus* (Camp Hill, PA: Christian Publications, 1986), 270-271.

19. "The Strength of Fundamentalism," *AW*, January 18, 1947, 34; "Belligerent Fundamentalists," *AW*, April 12, 1941, 227; "Companions of Gallio," *AW*, November 10, 1945, 354.

20. Reynolds, *Rebirth*, 10, 46; Niklaus, et al., *All for Jesus*, 50, 62.

21. William Linder, *Andrew Murray* (Minneapolis: Bethany, 1996), 124; Leona Choy, *Andrew Murray: Apostle of Abiding Love* (Fort Washington, PA: Christian Literature Crusade, 1978), 226-227.

22. "Spiritual Reading," *AW*, November 15, 1947, 732. He also refers to Andrew Murray in "Longing for Revival," *AW*, March 11, 1950, 146.

23. Andrew Murray, "The Sovereign Healer," *AW*, March 30, 1935, 199, 206; Andrew Murray, "Health and Salvation," *AW*, August 24, 1935, 543, 547, 550.

24. "The Beauty of Humility," *AW*, June 8, 1940, 354.

25. Andrew Murray, *Holy in Christ* (Toronto, Ontario: Willard Tract Depot, 1888); "The Evangelical Christian," *AW*, May 1, 1937, 275.

26. "The Old Helmet," *AW*, October 22, 1938, 674; "Expounding the Word," *AW*, August 3, 1946, 482. As further circumstantial evidence, in "The Old Helmet," MacMillan cites Pierson's teaching on the premillennial Second Coming of Christ, a theme on which Pierson taught in Ontario.

27. George D. Watson, *White Robes and Spiritual Feasts* (Cincinnati: God's Revivalist, n.d.), preface, n.p.

28. George D. Watson, *Bridehood Saints* (Cincinnati: God's Revivalist, n.d.), 117-118, 120-122. See also George D. Watson, *Steps to the Throne* (Cincinnati: Bible School Book Room, n.d.); George D. Watson, *Holiness Manual* (Boston: McDonald, Gill, & Co., 1882).

29. Mary N. Garrard, *Mrs. Penn-Lewis: A Memoir* (Bournemouth, England: Overcomer Book Room, 1930), 182-183. Two months later in October Penn-Lewis spoke at A.B. Simpson's Gospel Tabernacle in New York and addressed the students at the Missionary Training Institute at Nyack. She also had tea with Simpson and his wife. Ibid., 188. See also Brynmor Pierce Jones, *The Trials and Triumphs of Mrs. Jessie Penn-Lewis* (New Brunswick, NJ: Bridge-Logos, 1997), 101-102.

30. Jessie Penn-Lewis, *The Warfare with Satan* (Dorset, England: Overcomer Literature Trust, 1963), 63, 65.

31. A.B. Simpson, *Christ in the Bible* (*CITB*) (Camp Hill, PA: Christian Publications, 1992), 5:413-414.

32. John A. MacMillan, *The Authority of the Believer* (*AOB*) (Harrisburg, PA: Christian Publications, 1980).
33. "The Reality of Religion," *AW*, October 24, 1936, 682.
34. Reynolds, *Footprints*, 106-136.
35. Ibid., 460-462.
36. *AW*, January 26, 1935, 50.
37. "Investing in Souls," *AW*, March 19, 1938, 178; *SSQ*, February 2, 1936, 18.
38. Reynolds, *Footprints*, 461-462.
39. *SSQ*, March 17, 1935, 34. Like A.B. Simpson, he regarded the experience as a work of the Holy Spirit which empowers, sanctifies and transforms through the habitation of Christ, in contrast to Wesleyan eradication and suppressionism, the view taught by many in the Keswick movement. See "Christ for Us," *AW*, October 4, 1948, 642.
40. *SSQ*, May 22, 1949, 24; see also *SSQ*, May 19, 1935, 24.
41. *AW*, August 6, 1910, 309.
42. Carrie Judd Montgomery, "Witchcraft and Kindred Spirits," *AW*, October 15, 1938, 660; "Serving the Lord with Joyfulness," *AW*, October 18, 1941, 662.
43. A.W. Tozer, *Let My People Go: The Life of Robert A. Jaffray* (Harrisburg, PA: Christian Publications, 1957), 16, 19.
44. Membership records, Westminster Presbyterian Church, Toronto, Ontario, 1903.
45. "A Quarter Century," *AW*, March 4, 1939, 130.
46. "Salute . . . My Kinsmen," *AW*, February 16, 1935, 99.
47. "Investing in Souls," *AW*, March 19, 1938, 178; see also *SSQ*, February 2, 1936, 18.
48. *SSQ*, October 24, 1943, 13.
49. J.A. MacMillan, "Dependable Ones," *AW*, October 13, 1934, 642.
50. Annual Reports, *Presbyterian Church in Canada, General Assembly*, 1910; Annual Reports, *Presbyterian Church in Canada, General Assembly*, 1920-21, 148.
51. "A Hopeless Method," *AW*, August 28, 1937, 54.
52. "The Day of Atonement," *AW*, November 15, 1941, 727; repeated in "The Day of Atonement," *AW*, September 23, 1944, 387.
53. "Jewish Heart Hunger," *AW*, January 12, 1946, 19.
54. Annual Reports, *Presbyterian Church in Canada, General Assembly*, 1910, 141.
55. *SSQ*, October 6, 1935, 2; *SSQ*, November 13, 1949, 21; see also "Our Great Redeemer," *AW*, April 1, 1950, 194; *SSQ*, March 2, 1947, 27.
56. "Healing in the Early Church," *AW*, August 17, 1936, 522.
57. *SSQ*, September 12, 1937, 34.
58. "No Condemnation," *AW*, April 5, 1941, 210; "No Condemnation," *AW*, March 25, 1944, 178.
59. Ibid.
60. John A. MacMillan, *Encounter with Darkness* (*EWD*), (Harrisburg, PA: Christian Publications, 1980), 44.
61. George H. Pember, *Earth's Earliest Ages and Their Connection with Modern Spiritualism and Theosophy* (*EEA*) (Toronto, Ontario: A. Sims, n.d.), n.p.
62. "Divine Ordination," *AW*, May 28, 1938, 338-339.
63. "The Perfect Messenger," *AW*, May 22, 1948, 322.
64. "The Cooperative Disciple," *AW*, November 6, 1948, 706.

Chapter 3—Isabel Robson—A Divine Match

1. The information about Isabel Robson MacMillan is compiled from MacMillan family records, recollections and the Personnel Record, China Inland Mission, OMF International Archives, Toronto, Ontario, courtesy of Percy Page, OMF archivist.

2. Reynolds, *Rebirth*, 50-51.

3. Reynolds, *Footprints*, 236-237.

4. *China's Millions* (*CM*), Toronto, December 1895.

5. Dr. J.A. Anderson, "Ta-ku-t'ang," *CM*, Toronto, November 1897, 142-143.

6. *CM*, Toronto, July 1896, 93.

7. *CM*, London, March 1897, 37; *CM*, London, May 1897, 68; Anderson, "Ta-ku-t'ang," 143.

8. A.J. Broomhall, *Hudson Taylor and China's Open Century—Book Seven: It Is Not Death to Die* (London: Hodder & Stoughton, Ltd., 1989), 209; Roger Steer, *J. Hudson Taylor* (Singapore: OMF, 1990), 350; *CM*, London, August 1899, 130.

9. *CM*, London, October 1900, 154.

10. *CM*, London, September 1905; *CM*, London, December 1906; *CM*, Toronto, October 1906, 120.

11. *CM*, Toronto, January 1929, 15; *CM*, Toronto, October 1914, 139; *AW*, February 23, 1929, 120-121.

12. *CM*, Toronto, June 1907, 85.

13. "Deliverance from Demons," "Demon Possession," *CM*, September 1908, 102-103. William Christie, who would later serve on the C&MA Board of Managers with MacMillan, and also as vice president of the C&MA, is mentioned in the article as one of the leaders in the exorcism.

14. Mrs. Howard Taylor, *Pastor Hsi (of North China): One of China's Christians* (London: Morgan & Scott, 1900, 1907).

15. John Nevius, *Demon Possession and Allied Themes* (Chicago, IL: Fleming H. Revell, n.d.), 85; "The Love of Money," *AW*, July 6, 1946, 418; *EWD*, 77.

16. Minutes, Young Women's Missions Band, Westminster Presbyterian Church, Toronto, March 2, 1914.

17. John MacMillan, letter to Thomas Robson, March 6, 1914.

18. *CM*, Toronto, January 1929, 15.

19. "Asleep in Jesus," *AW*, February 23, 1929, 121.

20. *CM*, Toronto, January 1929, 15.

21. *CM*, Toronto, October 1914, 139.

22. Minutes, Young Women's Missions Band, Westminster Presbyterian Church, Toronto, February 15, 1995; on Amy Carmichael's *Lotus Buds* see Elizabeth Elliot, *A Chance to Die: The Life and Legacy of Amy Carmichael* (Old Tappan, NJ: Fleming H. Revell Co., 1987), 176.

23. Session Minutes, St. John's Presbyterian Church, March 16, 1916. Courtesy of David Pratley, Clerk of Session.

24. Reynolds, *Footprints*, 237.

25. Lloyd Robertson, personal interview by author, St. John's Presbyterian Church, Toronto, July 12, 1998.

26. Session minutes, St. John's Presbyterian Church, Toronto, May 30, 1918; June 19, 1918; July 10, 1918; July 28, 1918.

27. *Annual Reports, Presbyterian Church in Canada, General Assembly*, 1920-1921, 149.

28. Reynolds, *Footprints*, 397; *Annual Reports, Presbyterian Church in Canada, General Assembly*, 1910, 141.

29. Rev. Jay Smith (C&MA chaplain), letter to author, September 24, 1998. Smith, as a student at Nyack, lived with the MacMillans from 1952 to 1956.

30. "Raging Chariots," *AW*, May 15, 1937, 307; see also *SSQ*, December 27, 1936, 40.

31. Jessie Penn-Lewis, *Prayer and Evangelism* (Dorset, England: Overcomer Literature Trust, n.d.). Coincidentally (a divine coincidence?!), the same year Carrie Judd Montgomery published her book *The Secrets of Victory*, in which she devoted a chapter to binding and loosing. Carrie Judd Montgomery, *The Secrets of Victory* (Oakland, CA: Triumphs of Faith, 1921), 67-74.
32. Jessie Penn-Lewis, "How to Pray for Missionaries," *AW*, June 12, 1937, 373-375; *AW*, June 26, 1937, 406-407; *AW*, July 26,1941, 468-469.
33. "In the Mount of the Lord," *AW*, October 30, 1943, 694.
34. Reynolds, *Footprints*, 352, 364, 366, 389, 391.
35. *AW*, June 28, 1919, 209; see also Reynolds, *Rebirth*, 46.
36. Reynolds, *Footprints*, 386-387, quoted from reports in the April 25 and 26, 1921 issues of *Toronto Globe*. For testimonies of healings in Toronto see also F.F. Bosworth, *Christ the Healer* (Grand Rapids, MI: Fleming H. Revell, 1973), 231-236. For sermon on healing in 1923 at Toronto, see pp. 207-212.
37. Reynolds, *Footprints*, 392, quoted from a report in the May 6, 1922 issue of *Toronto Star*.
38. Notes from C&MA archives, Colorado Springs, Colorado, courtesy of Dr. Joseph Wenninger, Archivist; A.W. Tozer, *Let My People Go!*, 28-30.

Chapter 4—Call to China

1. Session minutes, St. John's Presbyterian Church, Toronto, Ontario, December 28, 1922.
2. "Journal of John A. MacMillan, January 16, 1923-August 26, 1928." The information for MacMillan's ministry in China and the Philippines will be gleaned from MacMillan's journal and information from family members unless otherwise noted. Consult my dissertation for detailed journal dates.
3. "Buddhist Rapprochement," *AW*, May 11, 1935, 291; "Resurrection," *AW*, April 20, 1935, 242.
4. Robert Jaffray, Annual Foreign Report, *AW*, June 28, 1924, 301.
5. "Spiritual Illumination," *AW*, December 9, 1939, 770; *SSQ*, June 29, 1947, 37; *SSQ*, October 29, 1950, 14.
6. *SSQ*, June 5, 1938, 30.
7. *SSQ*, July 11, 1943, 7.
8. *SSQ*, June 8, 1952, 29.
9. *SSQ*, June 20, 1948, 34.
10. "The Parched Land," *AW*, July 16, 1949, 450.
11. *EWD*, 32, 33.
12. "The Religious Outlook," *AW*, January 2, 1937, 7; Robert Ekvall, "Monologues from the Chinese," *AW*, February 27, 1937, 138.
13. "Marching into Eternity," *AW*, July 12, 1941, 435; see *SSQ*, April 20, 1952, 8-9, for another account of a contact of a more positive nature with a Presbyterian missionary in North China.
14. "Islam Invigorating Itself," *AW*, July 12, 1947, 434.
15. *SSQ*, May 16, 1937, 22.
16. "The Test of Liberalism," *AW*, August 9, 1947, 498.
17. "Misunderstandings," *AW*, September 21, 1946, 594.
18. "Human Nature," *AW*, August 7, 1943, 498; *SSQ*, May 8, 1938; see also *SSQ*, April 17, 1949, 8.
19. "God's Hungry Heart," *AW*, July 1, 1939, 402.

Chapter 5—Spiritual Warfare in China

1. "Spiritual Illumination," *AW*, December 9, 1939, 770.
2. *EWD*, 92-93.
3. Notes from C&MA Archives. MacMillan wrote a decade later regarding an almost identical circumstance:

   A young man left for the foreign field, thinking himself rich in this world's goods. Three months after his arrival there, he received a letter from his lawyer, stating that all that he had possessed was gone. He spread the letter before the Lord. Immediately the answer came: "He that forsaketh not all that he hath cannot be my disciple." With deep feeling the disciple replied: "Lord, I am glad that I am Thy disciple; but I fear, if I had known beforehand, I might not have yielded all." As the years have passed since then, the life has deepened; and though one of entire dependence on the Lord, it has realized the richer blessing. The man has wondered if the rich young ruler had been tested as he has been, if he would have come through. God only knows—but God knows so thoroughly that no mistake is made. (*SSQ*, April 22, 1934, 13.)

   The episode is so strikingly similar that one wonders if MacMillan may have written in disguise about himself, as he did at other times. The time frame of three months does not appear to coincide with his journal, though it is periodic, leaving many gaps. He may have received an earlier letter not recorded in his diary. In 1926 he does write that had had been praying for resolution for three years, which would fit the chronology of this incident. Regardless, the incident obviously reflects MacMillan's personal attitude toward the unjust and seemingly devastating loss.
4. "A Spiritual Challenge," *AW*, July 1, 1939, 403.
5. *EWD*, 55-56.
6. Rev. Paul Valentine, phone interview, October 23, 1998.
7. See Paul L. King, "The Restoration of the Doctrine of Binding and Loosing," *Alliance Academic Review* (1997) (Camp Hill, PA: Christian Publications, 1997), 57-80; Foster with King, *Binding and Loosing*.
8. *EWD*, 56-57.
9. Foster with King, *Binding and Loosing*, 247-248. Compiled from MacMillan's Journal and from Jaffray's account as described by Tozer in *Let My People Go!*, 43-49.
10. *AOB*, 53. Rev. Jay Smith, who boarded with the MacMillans as a student three decades later, related that MacMillan had told him that he personally had to apply pressure to the jugular vein to stop the bleeding.
11. Robert Ekvall, et al., *After Fifty Years* (Harrisburg, PA: Christian Publications, 1939), 231-233; Buchanan MacMillan's summary notes on his father's Philippine ministry, C&MA Archives, Colorado Springs, Colorado, courtesy of Dr. Joseph Wenninger, Archivist.
12. Buchanan MacMillan's Philippine Archive Notes; C&MA Annual Reports, 1924-1925, 61-63.

Chapter 6—Ministry in the Philippines

1. Dr. Keith Bailey, phone interview, August 8, 1998, in which he recounted that this was reported to him by Rev. George Strohm; Buchanan MacMillan's summary notes of John MacMillan's ministry in the Philippines, C&MA Archives, Colorado Springs, Colorado, courtesy of Dr. Joseph Wenninger; A.W. Tozer, *Let My People Go!*, 104.

2. David Lloyd Rambo, "The Christian and Missionary Alliance in the Philippines, 1901-1974" (unpublished doctoral dissertation, New York: New York University, 1975), 94-96.

3. Buchanan's Philippine Archive Notes; MacMillan's journal, April 21, 1927, December 16, 1927.

4. John A. MacMillan, "Many Tribes and Tongues in the Philippines," *AW*, June 9, 1928, 371; John A. MacMillan, "Giving the Word to Mindanao," *AW*, August 4, 1928, 504; C&MA Annual Reports, 1924, 60-61; C&MA Annual Reports, 1925, 60-61; C&MA Annual Reports, 1926, 75-77.

5. Buchanan's Philippine Archive Notes.

6. MacMillan, "Many Tribes and Tongues in the Philippines, *AW*, January 9, 1928, 371.

7. Benjamin Y. Mendoza, *The Philippine Christian Alliance: First Seventy-Eight Years* (self-published and printed in the Philippines, 1985), 45; Robert Ekvall et al., *After Fifty Years: A Record of God's Working Through the Christian and Missionary Alliance* (Harrisburg, PA: Christian Publications, 1939), 162-163. Rambo and Mendoza (who is dependent on Rambo) have a variant chronology with the Williamses leaving and the MacMillans coming to the Philippines in 1927. Rambo, "The Christian and Missionary Alliance in the Philippines," 94-96. That MacMillan came to the Philippines in August 1926, is certain from MacMillan's journal and *After Fifty Years*. The confusion may stem from Snead's reticence to appoint MacMillan to the field permanently. It appears that the permanent appointment was not reaffirmed by the board of managers until January 1927. (Rambo, 94). The other seven missionaries from China did arrive in 1927—the Strohms in April 1927, the other five in December.

8. Buchanan's Philippine Archive Notes and MacMillan Journal. John believed that a woman could be called to preach or prophesy. See John A. MacMillan, "Inquirer's Corner," *AW*, April 20, 1935, 251.

9. Buchanan's Philippine Archives notes and MacMillan Journal.

10. Laubach was acquainted with the C&MA work in the Philippines. See Frank Charles Laubach, *The People of the Philippines* (New York: George H. Doran, 1925), 73-74, 344, 386.

11. *AW*, April 20, 1940, 249. He also visited the Alliance school in Africa while writing his now famous Prayer Journal in 1937. Frank Laubach, *Frank Laubach's Prayer Diary* (Westwood, NJ: Fleming H. Revell, 1964), 33-37.

12. Rev. Jay M. Smith, letter to author, September 24, 1998. Smith was living with the MacMillans as a student and recalls having dinner together with them and Dr. Laubach. In later writings Laubach advocated a type of "prayer telepathy" which MacMillan would have disapproved of, calling it "soul power." Contrast Laubach's *Prayer: The Mightiest Force in the World* (Old Tappan, NJ: Fleming H. Revell, 1946), 53-66, with MacMillan's article "Soul Power," *AW*, November 9, 1935, 719. In spite of this, they apparently remained friends.

13. *SSQ*, August 24, 1947, 25.

14. Compiled from Buchanan's Philippine Archive Notes and MacMillan's Journal.

15. C&MA Annual Reports, 1929, 48.

16. C&MA Annual Reports, 1926, 76.

17. *SSQ*, June 6, 1954, 31.

18. Ibid.

19. "Called, Not by Man," *AW*, March 26, 1938, 195.

20. "Know Your Alliance Weekly," *AW*, October 29, 1949, 692.
21. "The Native Churches," *AW*, July 24, 1945, 466-467.
22. "The Lord's Mother," *AW*, July 20, 1935, 455.
23. *SSQ*, April 29, 1945, 15-16; *SSQ*, September 12, 1937, 33; *SSQ*, March 10, 1946, 31.
24. John A. MacMillan, "Making the Earth Tremble," *AW*, April 6, 1929.
25. "Rome and the Bible," *AW*, August 22, 1936, 535.
26. Ibid.
27. *SSQ*, June 7, 1942, 31; *SSQ*, June 14, 1936, 37.
28. Don Richardson, *Peace Child* (Glendale, CA: Regal Books, 1974); Don Richardson, *Eternity in Their Hearts* (Glendale, CA: Regal Books, 1981).
29. *SSQ*, August 22, 1937, 25.
30. *SSQ*, February 17, 1935, 21.
31. "Free from Care" *AW*, July 4, 1942, 418; *SSQ*, March 31, 1935, 43.
32. "Islam in the Far East," *AW*, June 27, 1942, 406.
33. "Is Islam Reviving?," *AW*, April 16, 1949, 242; John A. MacMillan, "Our Mohammedan Problem in the Philippines," *AW*, June 22, 1929, 401.
34. "The Koran in Chinese," *AW*, January 15, 1949, 34; "Reading the Word," *AW*, December 4, 1943, 711.
35. MacMillan, "Our Mohammedan Problem in the Philippines," *AW*, June 22, 1929, 401.

Chapter 7—Spiritual Warfare in the Philippines

1. Rev. George E. Lang, letter to author, March 19, 1998. Lang was a student 1936-1939 at the Missionary Training Institute. He and his wife were students in MacMillan's class "Alliance Truth and Testimony."
2. "Cleansed Within," *AW*, January 14, 1939, 19.
3. Ibid.
4. *SSQ*, August 9, 1953, 17-18.
5. "Healing for the Saint," *AW*, February 24, 1940, 114.
6. MacMillan, "Making the Earth Tremble," *AW*, April 6, 1929, 217.
7. Ibid.
8. Rev. Otto Bublat, letter to author, January 7, 1998. Bublat was a student of MacMillan's at Nyack 1938-1941. Bublat could not remember positively whether this incident took place in China or the Philippines, but he believed it was the latter. For this reason, and the fact that the details fit the location, the anecdote is placed here. Bublat commented, "Mr. MacMillan related this experience in MEEKNESS, and I've never forgotten it."
9. *AOB*, 50-51.
10. Ibid., 52.
11. Ibid.
12. Rev. Richard Barker (retired C&MA pastor), phone interview, January 19, 1999. Rev. Barker was a student of MacMillan's in the early 1950s.
13. *AOB*, 57.
14. *SSQ*, February 23, 1936, 27.
15. Barker interview.
16. Keith Bailey interview. Bailey was personally mentored by MacMillan in deliverance ministry and also talked with Rev. George Strohm about their ministry of exorcism in the Philippines. Bailey believes the source of MacMillan's use of the First

John 4:1-3 methodology came from Penn-Lewis' influence. However, as noted in Chapter 3, he may have become familiar with the practice from Isabel as early as 1907. This will be discussed further in a later chapter.

17. Jerry McGarvey letter to author, January 18, 1998. McGarvey was present and observed this occurrence as a student at Nyack in 1951.
18. Keith Bailey interview.

Chapter 8—The Loss of His Beloved Isabel

1. "Asleep in Jesus," *AW*, February 23, 1929, 121; Buchanan's Philippine Archive Notes.
2. *SSQ*, November 23, 1941, 24.
3. Mendoza, 46.
4. Buchanan's Philippine Archive Notes, MacMillan Journal, August 26, 1928.
5. Buchanan's Philippine Archive Notes.
6. "Asleep in Jesus," *AW*, February 23, 1929, 121.
7. John A. MacMillan, "Resurrection," *AW*, April 20, 1935, 242.
8. *SSQ*, March 20, 1938, 36.
9. "The Mysteries of Prayer," *AW*, May 20, 1944, 242.
10. *SSQ*, January 28, 1951, 13.
11. *SSQ*, November 23, 1941, 25.
12. *SSQ*, May 7, 1939, 19.
13. MacMillan, "Making the Earth Tremble," *AW*, April 6, 1929, 216-217.
14. MacMillan, letter to his sister Bessie, September 11, 1928.
15. MacMillan, "Making the Earth Tremble," *AW*, April 6, 1929, 217; MacMillan, "Our Mohammedan Problem in the Philippines," *AW*, June 22, 1929, 396ff.
16. MacMillan, letter to his sister Bessie, October 24, 1928.
17. Buchanan's Philippine Archive Notes.
18. According to Mendoza (p. 46), MacMillan returned to the United States due to ill health, but there is no other verification that he was ill. He was scheduled for a 1929 furlough even before Isabel died, and other indicators would make it appear that he was in overall good health.
19. Rambo, 96. Again, as mentioned in endnote 7, Chapter 6, Rambo's chronology is in error; MacMillan's term in the Philippines was nearly three years. The discrepancy may be due to the fact that Strohm arrived later and worked with MacMillan for only two years.
20. Mendoza, 46.
21. "To Every Tribe," *AW*, February 3, 1940, 67; compare John A. MacMillan, "The Shame of It," *AW*, February 2, 1929, 72.
22. MacMillan, "Our Mohammedan Problem in the Philippines," *AW*, June 22, 1929, 404.
23. *SSQ*, August 9, 1953, 18; for more on MacMillan's pioneering concept of "territorial spirits" and "spiritual mapping," see "Praying Geographically," *AW*, September 14, 1946, 579.
24. John A. MacMillan, "Let Down Your Nets for a Draught," *AW*, December 28, 1929, 833.
25. Mendoza, 46-47; Ekvall, et al., 234.
26. Ekvall, 233-234.
27. Helen M. Roberts, *Champion of the Silent Billion: The Story of Frank C. Laubach "Apostle of Literacy"* (St. Paul, MN: MacAlester Park, 1961), 68-69; Marjorie Medary, *Each*

One Teach One: Frank Laubach, Friend to Millions (New York: David McKay, 1954), 28ff.

28. Frank Laubach, *Channels of Spiritual Power* (Westwood, NJ: Fleming H. Revell, 1954), 159, 171.

29. "What Is the C&MA?," promotional video, Colorado Springs, Colorado: The Christian and Missionary Alliance, n.d.

Chapter 9—North American Ministry 1929-1934

1. C&MA Personnel Archive Notes.
2. Buchanan's Philippine Archive Notes.
3. *SSQ*, November 30, 1947, 26.
4. *AOB*, 47-48.
5. Reynolds, *Rebirth*, 245; J.A. MacMillan, "A Great Door and Effectual—The Canadian West," *AW*, December 27, 1930, 848-849.
6. MacMillan, "A Great Door and Effectual—The Canadian West," 848-849.
7. "The Reality of Religion," *AW*, October 24, 1936, 683; see also "Seeing God," *AW*, May 27, 1939, 323, where he writes "we have seen the bitter railing of an atheist silenced by the personal testimony of a soldier who had been delivered from a life of sin, and had been spiritually transformed."
8. J.A. MacMillan, "The Christian Creed," *AW*, October 6, 1934, 627; *SSQ*, April 7, 1935, 1.
9. *SSQ*, September 26, 1948, 39; *SSQ*, December 24, 1939, 40.
10. *SSQ*, June 23, 1940, 37.
11. C&MA Personnel Archive Notes.
12. "Quarterly Board Meeting," *AW*, April 9, 1934, 211, 215.
13. *AOB*, 49-50.
14. John A. MacMillan, "The Authority of the Believer," *AW*, January 9, 16, 23, 30; February 6, 13, 20, 27, 1932.
15. *AW*, March 9, 1935, 147.
16. Jessie Penn-Lewis with Evan Roberts, *War on the Saints—Unabridged Edition* (Ninth Edition) (New York: Thomas E. Lowe, Ltd., 1973), n.p.
17. *AOB*, 70-71.
18. Reynolds, *Rebirth*, 186. Reynolds uses a variant spelling "MacMillen."
19. Ibid.
20. Reynolds, *Rebirth*, 185; C&MA Personnel Archive Notes.
21. John A. MacMillan, "Which Shineth More and More," *AW*, March 12, 1932, 168, 174; "Three Amens," *AW*, July 30, 1932, 485ff.; "In the House of the Potter," *AW*, June 18, 1932, 388ff.; "The Grace of Love," *AW*, February 6, 1932, 81; "Heart Rest," *AW*, July 9, 1932, 433.
22. C&MA Personnel Archive notes; John A. MacMillan, "The Spirit-Filled Life," *AW*, February 10, 1934.
23. C&MA Personnel Archive Notes; Smith letter.
24. "Jewish Evangelization," *AW*, March 29, 1941, 194.
25. J. A. MacMillan, "In Every Way," *AW*, July 28, 1934, 471.
26. *SSQ*, November 9, 1941, 18; *SSQ*, August 23, 1942, 24; *SSQ*, October 8, 1950, 5; *SSQ*, December 25, 1949, 39; *SSQ*, July 11, 1954, 5-6.
27. John A. MacMillan, "The Spirit-Filled Christian," *AW*, February 10, 17, March 3, 10, 17, April 7, 14, 1934.

Chapter 10—Macmillan as Writer and Editor

1. *AW*, July 8, 1939, 419.
2. *SSQ*, July 5, 1953, 1.
3. *AW*, April 13, 1940, 227.
4. Comparison of the *Adult Sunday School Quarterly* and the *Home Bible Study Quarterly* shows them to be identical.
5. Smith letter; Harold M. Freligh, "A Prince in Israel: John A. MacMillan," *AW*, June 27, 1956, 10, 15. A search of the libraries of Canadian Theological Seminary and Nyack College, as well as the records of Christian Publications, Inc. and the C&MA Archives in Colorado Springs, Colorado did not locate the Quarterlies for 1955 and 1956.
6. *AW*, June 16, 1934, 371.
7. "The Conflict of Truth and Error," *AW*, June 9, 1934, 354.
8. H.M. Shuman, "Council Elects Dr. Tozer Editor," *AW*, May 27, 1950, 322. During the first year of his tenure, MacMillan shared editorial duties with other C&MA leaders. Several members of the editorial staff would contribute short editorials in each issue, with the writer normally identified by his initials at the end of his editorial. An apparent pattern soon emerged: The first editorial would almost invariably be written by MacMillan. By 1936, he had become the regular writer for almost all the editorials, leaving his editorials unsigned, while other occasional contributors (including Shuman) signed their initials or received a byline. MacMillan's name did not appear on the masthead as assistant editor until 1936—unceremoniously, with no explanation. Yet Shuman and the C&MA personnel records confirm that he was the assistant/associate editor as early as 1934 (H.M. Shuman, "Council Elects Dr. Tozer Editor," *AW*, May 27, 1950; Personnel Record, C&MA Archives). The masthead in 1940 lists MacMillan as assistant editor, but Shuman and others several times called him "associate editor" (*AW*, June 26, 1937, 404; *AW*, July 13, 1940, 436; *AW*, December 21, 1940, 802; Shuman, "Council Elects Dr. Tozer Editor," *AW*, May 27, 1950, 322; H.M. Shuman, "John A. MacMillan," *AW*, July 15, 1950, 436). The titles apparently were used interchangeably.

   See my dissertation, Appendix 5, on authorship analysis that explains in detail the procedure for identifying and verifying MacMillan's authorship of the unsigned editorials. See Appendix 7 of the dissertation for an index, classification and verification of all editorials and articles believed to be written by MacMillan.

   With his dual obligations, MacMillan sometimes overlapped his two major writing projects by including the same illustrations, content or themes in both *The Alliance Weekly* and the *Sunday School Quarterly*. Compare MacMillan, *SSQ*, January 1, 1935, 1, with J.A. MacMillan, "Like a Shadow," *AW*, August 11, 1934, 498; compare "Christian Communism," *SSQ*, April 12, 1951, 24, with "Apostolic Communism," *AW*, September 3, 1949, 562, and J.A. MacMillan, "Post-Pentecostal Communism," *AW*, September 3, 1949, 563ff. See table in Appendix 6 of the dissertation: "A Sampling of Parallels between *The Alliance Weekly* and *Sunday School Quarterlies*."
9. "Redemption and Release," *AW*, December 21, 1940, 803.
10. *AW*, July 21,1934 to July 6, 1935.
11. H.M. Shuman, "John A. MacMillan," *AW*, July 15, 1950, 436.
12. Smith letter; Bublat letter; Lang letter.
13. *AW*, August 21, 1937, 541; *AW*, March 15, 1947, 172.

14. David J. Fant, "The Publication Department," *AW*, July 16, 1938, 452. A search of the libraries of Canadian Theological Seminary and Nyack College, as well as the records of Christian Publications, Inc. and the C&MA Archives in Colorado Springs, Colorado did not turn up an extant copy of this course.

15. "A Catechism," *AW*, June 8, 1940, 355.

16. *AW*, April 18, 1942, 242; John A. MacMillan, "Preface," Charles G. Finney, *Christ Our Sanctification* (Harrisburg, PA: Christian Publications, 1942), 3-4.

17. Smith letter.

18. John A. MacMillan, "The Authority of the Intercessor," *AW*, May 23, 1936, 334.

19. John A. MacMillan, "The Authority of the Rod," *AW*, May 18, 1940, 309-311, 314. A later editorial entitled "The Authority of Darkness" (*AW*, February 5, 1944, 82) and a Sunday school lesson entitled "The Authority of the Word" (*SSQ*, October 29, 1950, 14-15) were never published with the others.

20. John A. MacMillan, "Modern Demon Possession," *AW*, July 24, July 31, September 4, September 11, September 18, 1948.

21. *EWD*, 9.

22. This will be explored further in the chapters on "MacMillan's Twentieth- Century Impact."

23. *EWD*, 10; also Keith Bailey interview.

24. Circulation increased from 8,500 in 1933 to 9,200 in 1934; to 10,000 in 1935 to 10,700 in 1936; to 18,000 in 1937 to 19,000 in 1938; in 1940 from 21,900 to 23,800 in 1941; from 28,900 in 1942, to 36,900 in 1943, to 48,000 in 1944. *AW*, June 2, 1937, 404; July 16, 1938, 452; July 5, 1941, 423. After World War II the circulation leveled off, then decreased for a time, probably due to price increases.

25. *AW*, June 2, 1937, 404.

26. "Increasing Our Circulation," *AW*, October 23, 1948, 674, 686.

27. "A Bestower of Blessing," *AW*, October 30, 1948, 690.

28. Kenneth MacKenzie, "My Memories of A.B. Simpson," *AW*, July 3, September 11, 1937.

29. "Christianity's Records," *AW*, October 23, 1937, 674.

30. Jessie Penn-Lewis, "How to Pray for Missionaries," *AW*, June 12, 1937, 374; Jessie Penn-Lewis, "How to Pray for Missionaries (concluded)," *AW*, June 26, 1937, 406; Jessie Penn-Lewis, "How to Pray for Missionaries," *AW*, July 26, 1941, 468.

31. "A Bestower of Blessing," *AW*, October 30, 1948, 690.

32. *AW*, June 11, 1938, 370; January 11, 1941, 18; March 24, 1945, 83.

33. *AW*, September 27, 1941, 611; "Invitations to 1943 Council," *AW*, October 4, 1941, 626.

34. *SSQ*, June 30, 1940, 38; J.A. MacMillan, "Ancient Bible Manuscripts," *AW*, June 30, 1934, 402.

35. "The Unhurried Christian," *AW*, September 11, 1948, 580; "The Unworried Christian," *AW*, September 17, 1948, 594.

36. "Increasing Our Circulation," 674.

37. *SSQ*, April 12, 1951, 24; J.A. MacMillan, "Post-Pentecostal Communism," *AW*, September 3, 1949, 572; "The Growth of Communism," *AW*, October 1, 1949, 629-630; "A Labor Sunday Litany," *AW*, August 31, 1935, 554-555; "Civilization's Last Phase," *AW*, August 31, 1935, 558-559; "Goat Nations," *AW*, December 10, 1938, 794; "Growing Hate," *AW*, April 1, 1939, 194; "The Philosophy of Force," *AW*, April 8, 1939, 211; "Passing Shadows," *AW*, September 9, 1939, 563.

38. "The Christian Soldier," *AW*, November 12, 1938, 723.

39. "The Only Solution," *AW*, May 1, 1937, 288.

40. "The Present Crisis," *AW*, February 24, 1940, 115.

41. "Abraham Lincoln," *AW*, February 8, 1947, 82.

42. "Capital Punishment," *AW*, August 17, 1935, 522-523.

43. "A Christian Nation," *AW*, September 17, 1949, 594, 606.

44. "Old Mss. of Daniel," *AW*, December 10, 1949, 798.

45. "Roman Statecraft," *AW*, July 23, 1938, 467.

46. "Stern Justice," *AW*, July 23, 1938, 466.

47. "Prayer for the Jews," *AW*, December 24, 1938, 819.

48. "White Supremacy," *AW*, August 24, 1935, 538-539; "Increasing Anti- Semitism," *AW*, August 13, 1938, 514; "Anti-Semitic Agitation," *AW*, December 3, 1938, 770-771; "Dark Days for Israel," *AW*, October 19, 1940, 658.

49. "The Final Word," *AW*, April 15, 1939, 227.

50. "Crime Consciousness," *AW*, October 17, 1936, 662; "Gambling," *AW*, March 9, 1946, 147; "Divorce and Remarriage," *AW*, May 8, 1937, 290; "Looser Divorce Laws," *AW*, July 31, 1937, 482-483; *SSQ*, July 15, 1951, 8-10.

51. "Blood Lust," *AW*, August 10, 1946, 499.

52. *SSQ*, July 8, 1951, 5-7.

53. "Juvenile Delinquency," *AW*, August 6, 1938, 499.

54. "A Divine Perogative," *AW*, February 22, 1935, 115.

55. *AW*, October 31, 1942, 691.

56. *SSQ*, January 5, 1936, 2-3; John A. MacMillan, "Honoring the Lord's Mother," *AW*, November 16, 1935, 730.

57. John A. MacMillan, "British-Israelism—A Latter-Time Heresy," *AW*, September 1, September 8, September 29, 1934.

58. John A. MacMillan, "A Labor Sunday Litany," *AW*, August 31, 1935, 554-555; "First Things," *AW*, April 13, 1940, 227.

59. "Einstein's Atheism," *AW*, November 2, 1940, 691.

60. "Companions of Gallio," *AW*, November 10, 1945, 354; see also "Belligerent Fundamentalists," *AW*, April 12, 1941, 227.

61. "The Strength of Fundamentalism," *AW*, January 18, 1947, 34.

62. "Are We Intolerant?," *AW*, September 3, 1938, 563.

63. "Modern Hymns," *AW*, February 24, 1940, 115; see also, "Religious Enthusiasm," *AW*, May 14, 1938, 307.

64. *SSQ*, November 25, 1951, 24.

65. *SSQ*, July 7, 1940, 4.

66. "Praying Geographically," *AW*, September 14, 1946, 579; *SSQ*, August 9, 1953, 18. This is not to say that he would embrace all that is taught and practiced regarding these concepts today.

67. *AOB*, 71.

68. Ibid., 26. See also article with his byline: J.A. MacMillan, "Spiritual Energy in the Word," *AW*, October 20, 1945, 325.

69. *SSQ*, September 22, 1935, 41; *SSQ*, August 15, 1954, 20; compare *SSQ*, August 10, 1947, 19, where he makes reference to himself.

70. *Reader's Digest*—"Prayer Answers," *AW*, January 25, 1941, 51; "An Imperial Communist," *AW*, May 18, 1940, 306; *British Weekly*—"First Things," *AW*, April 13, 1940; *New York Times*—"The Reality of Heaven," *AW*, April 20, 1940, 242; "The Narcotic Rings," *AW*, April 3, 1937, 211; *New York Herald- Tribune*—"Heathen in

America," *AW*, March 30, 1946, 195; "Jewish Evangelization," *AW*, April 27, 1946, 259; "The Hope of the World," *AW*, October 19, 1946, 658.
71. "A Modern St. Augustine," *AW*, May 18, 1946, 3; "Bond or Free," *AW*, August 19, 1939, 514; "The Evangelical Christian," *AW*, May 1, 1937, 275.
72. For examples, see "The Abundance of Grace," *AW*, August 27, 1938, 546; September 30, 1939, 610; "Paying Taxes," *AW*, July 19, 1941, 450; "Keeping Covenant," *AW*, October 20, 1945, 322.
73. John A. MacMillan, "Rapture!," *AW*, February 3, 1934, 71; John A. MacMillan, "The Grace of Love," *AW*, February 6, 1932, 81; John A. MacMillan, "Heart Rest," *AW*, July 9, 1932, 433; John A. MacMillan, "The Tides of Life," *AW*, February 4, 1933, 69; "A New Year Meditation," *AW*, January 4, 1941, 2.
74. MacMillan, "Heart Rest," 433. See also "Soul Rest," *AW*, June 2, 1937, 402.

Chapter 11—Alice Sherwood—A Second Divine Match

1. *AW*, October 29, 1980, 28; Dr. Maurice Irvin, letter to author, June 30, 1998.
2. Alice E. Sherwood, "He Asks Us to Believe," *AW*, June 18, 1932, 395.
3. Smith letter.
4. *AW*, September 19, 1936, 609.
5. Smith letter.
6. *EWD*, 17-22.
7. Merrill F. Unger, *What Demons Can Do to Saints* (Chicago: Moody Press, 1977), 94-95.
8. Rev. Gerald E. McGarvey, letter to author, January 18, 1998.
9. Smith letter.
10. *AW*, October 29, 1980, 28.
11. Ibid.
12. Ibid.
13. Alice S. MacMillan, "My Lord Will Come Some Day," *Hymns of the Christian Life* (Camp Hill, PA: Christian Publications, 1978), #127.

Chapter 12—MacMillan as Professor

1. Dr. John Sawin (C&MA historian and 1935 Nyack graduate), phone interview, February 28, 1998; Valentine interview.
2. Bublat letter.
3. Sawin interview; Thomas P. Bailey, letter to author, February 9, 1998; F. Paul Henry, letter to author, March 12, 1998.
4. Smith letter.
5. T. Robert Brewer (Nyack, 1942), phone interview, February 19, 1999.
6. Charles Gifford, phone interview, February 21, 1998.
7. Betty Knopp (Nyack, 1936-39), letter to author, March 3, 1998.
8. Gifford interview; L.L. King, phone interview, March 14, 1998; Howard Emary, phone interview, February 4, 1999.
9. McGarvey letter.
10. Cliff Westergren, phone interview, February 28, 1998, just weeks before he died in March 1998.
11. Gifford interview; Thomas Bailey letter; L.L. King interview; Gerald McGraw, letter to author, May 26, 1998; Rev. Jay Smith, phone interview, October 9, 1998; John Nevius, phone interview, April 13, 1999; McGarvey letter; Brewer interview; Rev.

Richard A. Herritt, letter to author, January 13, 1998; George E. Lang, letter to author, March 19, 1998; Knopp letter; Ross Ingraham, phone interview, March 11, 1998.

12. McGarvey letter.
13. Knopp letter.
14. Ibid. See also "Praying Geographically," *AW*, September 14, 1946, 579.
15. McGarvey letter.
16. Smith letter.
17. Ellenberger interview.
18. Richard Barker, letter to author, December 21, 1998; phone interview, December 21, 1998.
19. Nevius interview.
20. McGarvey letter.
21. Nevius interview.
22. Gifford interview.
23. Henry letter; Fye interview.
24. Knopp letter.
25. Smith letter.
26. Rex Boda, letter to author, January 30, 1998.
27. Ingraham interview.
28. Barker interview and letter.
29. Nevius letter.
30. Nevius interview; Gifford interview; L.L. King interview; McGraw letter; Lang letter; Emary interview; Kenyon letter.
31. "Federal Council Doctrine," *AW*, February 12, 1949, 98.
32. *SSQ*, February 21, 1943, 25.
33. "Revival at Nyack," *AW*, October 12, 1940, 643.
34. Ibid.
35. "Nyack Revival Continues," *AW*, November 30, 1940, 755.
36. Ibid.
37. *The Missionarian* (Nyack, NY: The Missionary Training Institute, 1950), n.p.

Chapter 13—MacMillan as Speaker and Evangelist

1. *AW*, September 18, 1937, 595; *AW*, October 4, 1941, 635.
2. *AW*, October 11, 1941, 652.
3. Lang letter.
4. *SSQ*, January 23, 1938, 13.
5. Barker letter and interview.
6. Rev. John Stirzaker, phone interview, May 7, 1999.
7. "Inviting to the Church Service," *AW*, May 22, 1948, 242; *SSQ*, May 27, 1934, 27-28.
8. "The Necessity of Repentance," *AW*, May 25, 1935, 322; also "Heart Trouble," *AW*, July 20, 1946, 451; *SSQ*, January 8, 1950, 7; *SSQ*, April 19, 1936, 10; *SSQ*, October 8, 1950, 5-6.
9. *SSQ*, October 8, 1950, 6.
10. "Assurance of Salvation," *AW*, May 11, 1946, 291.
11. "Heaven's Message to Youth," *AW*, January 22, 1949, 50.
12. *SSQ*, May 26, 1946, 25.
13. "Jewish Evangelization," *AW*, March 29, 1941, 194.

14. *SSQ*, December 22, 1946, 37.
15. "Wider Evangelism," *AW*, January 3, 1948, 2; *SSQ*, September 5, 1954, 29-30.
16. Anita Bailey, phone interview, February 8, 1998. Miss Bailey died just a few months after this interview with her.
17. "The Editorial Sanctum," *AW*, October 25, 1941, 674.
18. Smith letter.
19. Anita Bailey interview.
20. "The Open Door," *AW*, February 24, 1945, 50; repeated "Depression," *AW*, May 18, 1946, 307; "Songs in the Night," *AW*, June 13, 1936, 375.
21. "Depression," *AW*, May 18, 1946, 307.
22. *SSQ*, November 26, 1943, 27.
23. *SSQ*, October 1, 1950, 1.
24. Emary interview.
25. *SSQ*, October 25, 1942, 12.
26. *SSQ*, March 7, 1943, 30.
27. *SSQ*, August 16, 1936, 22; *SSQ*, February 2, 1941, 14-15.
28. *SSQ*, October 10, 1943, 6.
29. Ibid.
30. Smith letter.
31. *SSQ*, February 2, 1941, 15.
32. *SSQ*, October 19, 1947, 10; *SSQ*, March 19, 1950, 37; *SSQ*, August 15, 1954, 22.
33. *SSQ*, August 9, 1953, 18.
34. *AW*, November 24, 1954, 3.

Chapter 14—MacMillan's Ministry of Spiritual Warfare

1. Gifford interview.
2. Barker letter.
3. Smith letter.
4. Brewer interview.
5. Smith letter.
6. Ellenberger interview.
7. Westergren interview.
8. *SSQ*, March 27, 1940, 40.
9. *EWD*, 87-88.
10. "Mental Medicine," *AW*, July 11, 1936, 438.
11. *EWD*, 51.
12. Ibid.
13. Ibid., 51-52.
14. Ibid., 53.
15. Ibid., 52.
16. Ibid., 52-53.
17. Neil T. Anderson, *Helping Others Find Freedom in Christ* (Ventura, CA: Regal Books, 1995), 16.
18. Ibid.
19. Neil T. Anderson, *Setting Your Church Free* (Ventura, CA: Regal Books, 1994), 271-272.
20. Penn-Lewis asserted, "There is a fundamental principle involved in the freeing power of truth from the deceptions of the devil. Deliverance from believing lies must be by believing truth. . . . The great need of all believers is that they should eagerly

seek truth for their progressive liberation from all Satan's lies." (Penn-Lewis, *War on the Saints*, 58-59). We already know MacMillan was strongly influenced by Penn-Lewis. Anderson shows support for her teaching by quoting from *War on the Saints* in his book *The Bondage Breaker* (Eugene, OR: Harvest House Publishers, 1990, 1993, 78). While Anderson does not quote this particular statement of Penn-Lewis, his concept of truth encounter has obvious influence from Penn-Lewis.

21. Anderson opts for "truth encounter" over "power encounter." (*Helping Others Find Freedom in Christ*, 16). Gerald McGraw asserts that power encounter is superior to "truth encounter" ("An Effective Deliverance Ministry: Then and Now," *Alliance Academic Review* (1996), Elio Cuccaro, ed. [Camp Hill, PA: Christian Publications, 1996], 151-170).

22. *EWD*, 17-18.

23. Ibid., 18-21. This is likely the same encounter he writes of in 1949: "The writer has seen as many as thirty demons cast out of a single person in this country" (*SSQ*, Feb. 6, 1949, 18). This also may have been the same incident he refers to in *Encounter with Darkness*, 82-83.

24. McGraw letter.

25. J.A. MacMillan, "The Letters of the Lord," *AW*, Sept. 13, 1947, 582.

26. Kenyon letter.

27. *EWD*, 83-85.

28. Herritt letter.

29. Valentine interview.

30. Ingraham interview; Valentine interview; McGraw letter; Emary interview.

31. Ingraham interview; McGraw letter; Ellenberger interview; Valentine interview; McGarvey letter.

32. Ellenberger interview.

33. McGraw letter.

34. Valentine interview.

35. Ibid.

36. Herritt letter.

37. McGarvey letter.

38. Valentine interview.

39. Emary interview.

40. Valentine interview.

41. Ibid.

42. Emary interview.

43. Ingraham interview. Other students had noticed that his hands sometimes shook in class, which they assumed was due to his age; some erroneously thought he had Parkinson's disease (Robert Niklaus, personal interview, June 27, 1998). However, Jane MacMillan and Jay Smith assured me that he did not have Parkinson's disease and did not normally shake.

44. Ingraham interview. This is similar to an incident mentioned by modern Third Wave leader John Wimber, in which a demon responded with an unidentifiable utterance which through further probing was revealed to be "Pain" (John Wimber with Kevin Springer, *Power Healing* [New York: HarperCollins, 1987], 232).

45. Valentine interview.

46. Unger, *What Demons Can Do to Saints*, 94-97.

47. Ibid., 97.

48. Ingraham interview. Not all students viewed this as a positive experience, however. From the perspective of one student, Albert Runge, this drawn-out deliverance was a ruse of Satan. Years later he wrote an article on the incident entitled "Exorcism: A Satanic Ploy?" (*His Dominion* [Spring 1987], 8:4:13-14). For a discussion of Runge's concerns and criticisms, see my dissertation pp. 242-246.
49. Emary interview.

Chapter 15—The Sunset Days

1. "A Goodly Assembly," *AW*, May 6, 1950, 274.
2. Boda interview.
3. *AW*, March 3, 1954, 12.
4. J.A. MacMillan, "Thankfulness and Thanksgiving," *AW*, November 24, 1954, 3.
5. Harold M. Freligh, "A Prince in Israel: John A. MacMillan," *AW*, June 26, 1956, 10.
6. Smith letter.
7. Ibid.
8. *SSQ*, April 6, 1952, 1; *SSQ*, October 26, 1952, 22; *SSQ*, May 17, 1953, 22; *SSQ*, May 31, 1953, 27, 28; *SSQ*, December 19, 1954, 37.
9. Lulu Jordan Cheesman, "Oppression, Obsession, and Possession," *Herald of His Coming*, August 1953, 7.
10. Bailey discusses his experiences in detail in his book *Strange Gods* (Camp Hill, PA: Christian Publications, 1998).
11. Keith Bailey interview.
12. Smith letter.
13. McGarvey letter.
14. Smith interview.
15. *EWD*, 85; Barker also recounts this incident, Barker letter.
16. McGarvey letter.
17. Smith interview; John A. MacMillan, "The Spirit-Filled Christian V: The Home of the Holy Spirit in Man," *AW*, March 17, 1934, 166, 167.
18. Smith letter.
19. McGraw letter.
20. Smith letter.
21. Ibid.
22. Ibid
23. McGraw letter.
24. Smith interview.
25. Ibid.
26. Keith Bailey interview.
27. McGraw letter.
28. Smith interview.
29. Smith letter and interview.
30. Rexford A. Boda, "J.A. MacMillan and Spiritual Warfare," *Communicate*, May 1998, 8:1:1.
31. Regina Jagst Fischer, letter, August 17, 1998.
32. Freligh, 10.
33. "Grace's Consummation," *AW*, December 8, 1945, 423.
34. Smith interview.
35. Freligh, 10.
36. Smith letter.

37. Freligh, 10, 13.
38. Ibid., 13.

Chapter 16—Twentieth-Century Impact

1. Freligh, 13.
2. Much of the information for MacMillan's impact on the C&MA, as well as all the quoted material in this section, are gleaned from personal interviews and letters from the individuals cited.
3. Penn-Lewis and Evan Roberts, *War on the Saints*, 9th edition (1933), n.p.
4. "A Reprint," *AW*, March 9, 1935, 147.
5. Bailey first became acquainted with MacMillan's articles on the believer's authority in the 1940s when someone gave him copies of *The Overcomer* from the 1930s in which he discovered MacMillan's series.
6. MacMillan, "The Authority of the Intercessor," *AW*, May 23, 1936, 334; John A. MacMillan, *The Authority of the Intercessor* (Minneapolis, MN: Osterhus Publishing Co., n.d.).
7. *AW*, September 18, 1948, 604.
8. J.A. MacMillan, "The Authority of the Intercessor," *Herald of His Coming*, June 1952, 11. The editors mistakenly listed his byline as "*James* A. MacMillan."
9. Lulu Jordan Cheesman, *Herald of His Coming*, April 1952, 12.
10. Lula Jordan Cheesman, "Oppression, Obsession, and Possession," *Herald of His Coming*, August 1953, 7.
11. J.A. MacMillan, "The Authority of the Believer," *Herald of His Coming*, April 1954, 4.
12. *Herald of His Coming*, April 1956, 7; also *Herald of His Coming*, September 1956, 6.
13. Paul E. Billheimer, "Deliverance from the Hands of Our Enemies," *Herald of His Coming*, January 1952, 3.
14. A comparison of Billheimer's article and MacMillan's *The Authority of the Believer* shows much similarity in wording. Some citations are a shortening or paraphrase of MacMillan; others are virtually word for word. On the face of it, it would appear that Billheimer has plagiarized MacMillan. However, in light of the godly reputation of Billheimer and the content of his other writings on the deeper life, such a charge is incongruous. Rather than impugn the integrity of Billheimer, it would seem prudent to consider other more valid explanations. It is possible, for example, that Billheimer read from MacMillan in his radio address without citing him by name; then when it was transcribed and published MacMillan did not get the credit. MacMillan himself quoted from other authors without mentioning their names (though he usually put such statements in quotation marks, indicating they were not his own), and used distinctive words and phrases from other authors without noting the source—accepted publishing practices in the 1950s. One would think that the editors of *Herald of His Coming*, who were familiar with MacMillan's work, would have recognized the parallels and dealt with the issue if it had not been acceptable then. Since Billheimer is no longer living and unable to respond to the allegation, it is best to give him the benefit of a doubt regarding his motives, while at the same time recognizing that the practice would not be legally acceptable today.
15. Paul E. Billheimer, "Man Was Made to Have Dominion Over the Works of God's Hands," *Herald of His Coming*, July 1951, 4; see also Paul E. Billheimer, "Prayer Controls Events," *Herald of His Coming*, June 1951, 2. After MacMillan's "The Authority of the Believer" was republished by *Herald of His Coming* in April 1954, an article by

Billheimer on authority and deliverance was published a month later as a follow-up. Paul E. Billheimer, "Awake, Awake . . . ," *Herald of His Coming*, May 1954, 6-8.

16. Paul E. Billheimer, *Destined to Overcome* (Minneapolis, MN: Bethany House, 1982), 10.

17. Paul E. Billheimer, *Destined for the Throne* (Ft. Washington, PA: Christian Literature Crusade, 1975), 57-81.

18. *AOB*, 22.

19. "Commanding God," *AW*, October 7, 1939, 626; "The Kingdom of the Messiah," *AW*, February 17, 1940, 98; "Behavior in the House of God," *AW*, October 29, 1949, 690.

20. MacMillan, *SSQ*, September 4, 1949, 31.

21. Billheimer, *Destined to Overcome*, 36. Again he does not mention MacMillan, but later in the book he cites an article by Jessie Penn-Lewis in *Herald of His Coming* in 1951 entitled "Overcoming the Accuser" (p. 42) and discussing the subject with C&MA missionary Paris Reidhead (p. 52).

22. "Facing Deadly Foes," *AW*, June 3, 1939, 338.

23. Billheimer, *Destined for the Throne*, 40. It is possible that Billheimer read *The Alliance Weekly* and gleaned his ideas from MacMillan's writings, but did not associate them with MacMillan since there was no byline.

24. F.G. Huegel, *Forever Triumphant* (Grand Rapids, MI: Zondervan, 1955; reprinted Minneapolis, MN: Bethany House, n.d.). See also Billheimer, *Destined to Overcome*, 10-12.

25. Huegel, 52-58.

26. J.A. MacMillan, *Demon Experiences in Many Lands* (Chicago, IL: Moody Press, 1960), 132-136.

27. Merrill F. Unger, *What Demons Can Do to Saints*, 94-97; Merrill F. Unger, *Demons in the World Today* (Wheaton, IL: Tyndale House, 1971), 122, 123, 193-195, 199, 203, 204, 207. Unger does not refer to MacMillan in his earlier work, *Biblical Demonology. The Authority of the Believer* was not directly relevant to his study in that book. He may not have been familiar with MacMillan's *Modern Demon Possession* when he first wrote the book in 1952. Merrill F. Unger, *Biblical Demonology* (Wheaton, IL: Scripture Press, 1952).

28. Unger, *What Demons Can Do to Saints*, 94-97.

29. Ed Murphy, *Handbook of Spiritual Warfare* (Nashville, TN: Thomas Nelson, 1993, 1996), 477.

30. Dorothy Brotherton, *Quiet Warrior* (Beaverlodge, Alberta, Canada: Spectrum Publishing, 1991), 29.

31. K. Neill Foster, "Glossolalia and the Ruark Procedure: Distinguishing Between True and False Utterances," a lecture delivered at the Evangelical Theological Society, Jackson, MS, November 1996.

32. J. Dwight Pentecost, *Your Adversary, the Devil* (Grand Rapids, MI: Zondervan, 1969), 156-165.

33. Ibid., 156, 159-162.

34. Mark I. Bubeck, *The Adversary* (Chicago: Moody Press, 1975), 115.

35. John Richards, *But Deliver Us from Evil* (New York: The Seabury Press, 1974), 233.

36. Samuel Wilson, "Evangelism and Spiritual Warfare," reprinted on the Internet (http:// www.episcopalian .org/TESM/writings/spirwil.htm) from the *Journal of the Academy of Evangelism in Theological Education*. Wilson served as a C&MA missionary in Peru and as research director at World Vision's MARC and the Zwemer Institute

    for Islamic Studies. He is currently Director of the Stanway Institute for World Mission and Evangelism.
37. C.S. Lovett, *Dealing with the Devil* (Baldwin Park, CA: Personal Christianity Chapel, 1967), 140, 141.
38. Timothy Warner, *Spiritual Warfare: Victory over the Dark Powers of Our World* (Wheaton, IL: Crossway Books, 1990), 74.
39. Murphy, 300.
40. Ibid., 20, 49-51, 277, 539, 541, 542, 544, 545.
41. Charles Kraft, *Defeating the Dark Angels* (Ann Arbor, MI: Servant Publishing, 1992), 79-98.
42. Ibid.
43. Wayne Grudem, *Systematic Theology: An Introduction to Biblical Doctrine* (Grand Rapids, MI: Zondervan, 1994), 426-428.
44. Ibid., 435.
45. Richard J. Foster, *Prayer: Finding the Heart's True Home* (San Francisco, CA: HarperCollins, 1992), 229-242.
46. See my dissertation, pp. 280-286.

Chapter 17—The Authority of the Believer

1. This chapter focuses on a synopsis of MacMillan's theology and exercise of the authority of the believer. I have noted the influences upon MacMillan's concepts that have been discovered, as well as relevant theology or practice of these concepts that arose after MacMillan's writings. These principles are compiled from *The Authority of the Believer* as well as from his writings in *The Alliance Weekly* and *The Full Gospel Adult Sunday School Quarterly*.
 2. A.J. Gordon, *The Ministry of Healing*, quoting Trudel in *Healing: The Three Great Classics on Divine Healing* (Camp Hill, PA: Christian Publications, 1992), 215.
 3. Andrew Murray, *With Christ in the School of Prayer* (Springdale, PA: Whitaker House, 1981), 136; see also 116-117, 178.
 4. Ibid., 136.
 5. A.T. Pierson, *The Acts of the Holy Spirit* (Camp Hill, PA: Christian Publications, 1980), 92.
 6. Arthur T. Pierson, *Lessons in the School of Prayer* (Dixon, MO: Rare Christian Books, n.d.), 59. This was republished in *Herald of His Coming* under the title of "The Authority of Faith." A.T. Pierson, "The Authority of Faith," *Herald of His Coming*, July, 1953, 7.
 7. A.B. Simpson, "The Authority of Faith," *AW*, April 23, 1938, 263.
 8. A.B. Simpson, "Spiritual Talismans," *AW*, June 14, 1919, 178.
 9. Simpson, *CITB*, 4:338.
10. *AOB*, 11-12.
11. Jessie Penn-Lewis, *The Warfare with Satan* (Dorset, England: Overcomer Literature Trust, 1963), 63.
12. Ibid., 65.
13. Penn-Lewis and Roberts, *War on the Saints*, 259-262.
14. Simpson, *CITB*, 5:413-414. For more on this, see Paul L. King, "The Restoration of the Doctrine of Binding and Loosing," *Alliance Academic Review* (1997), Elio Cuccaro, ed. (Camp Hill, PA: Christian Publications, 1997), 57-80.
15. *SSQ*, October 28, 1934, 12.
16. *AOB*, 49.

17. Ibid., 55.

18. Ibid., 93, 96.

19. George B. Peck, *Throne-Life*, or *The Highest Christian Life* (Boston, MA: Watchword Publishing, 1888), 171, 174-175, 177.

20. Watson, *Steps to the Throne*.

21. Jones, 136; see also Penn-Lewis and Roberts, *War on the Saints*, 183.

22. "Inheritors of Glory," *AW*, August 17, 1946, 514.

23. "Shaming Our God," *AW*, February 23, 1946, 114.

24. "Family Privileges," *AW*, August 7, 1937, 498.

25. "The Manifestation of God," *AW*, July 30, 1949, 482; see also *SSQ*, October 3, 1937, 2, 3.

26. "Inheritors of Glory," 514.

27. "The Victory of God," *AW*, April 22, 1944, 210.

28. "The Son of Man," *AW*, October 25, 1947, 674.

29. *AOB*, 20. MacMillan explains further:

> Calvary was the crisis at which Satan's rights and powers were terminated, though his actual incumbency of the rule of rebellious mankind continues until that body of overcoming saints who will receive and administer the authority of the kingdom is fully complete. For it must be clearly understood as the teaching of the Word that the power and authority of the risen Head will come in due time to full development in the body. . . . It is the privilege and the duty of us as believers to seek that likeness and the authority of divine power and its outflow of heavenly blessing into our spirits. ("The Authority of Christ," *AW*, October 2, 1948, 626.)

30. "Christian Duty," *AW*, October 30, 1943, 690.

31. "Raging Chariots," 307. He cites examples from World War II:

> Not a few instances have been recorded of the stopping of a bullet by a Bible or Testament in the pocket of a soldier. We do not believe that these were "spent" bullets; rather in the grace of God there has been a divine interference with the swift messenger of death. "The arrow that flieth by day" has been turned back by the interposing of the shield of the Almighty.
>
> God's protective promises, such as those set forth in Psalm 91, have been claimed by many of His children and have been found effective in places of imminent peril. But the effort to make the Scripture promise more effective by encasing it in steel will not, we fear, deepen the faith or help the morale of the soldier. ("Armored Bibles," *AW*, November 4, 1944, 435.)

32. "The Family Altar," *AW*, May 5, 1945, 130; compare *SSQ*, December 23, 1934, 36.

33. *SSQ*, December 23, 1934, 36.

34. *SSQ*, November 26, 1939, 28; see also "Bearing Our Sicknesses," *AW*, June 21, 1941, 386; *SSQ*, March 15, 1942, 33-34.

35. "Divine Protection," *AW*, December 6, 1947, 770.

36. "Go Forward!" *AW*, May 11, 1946, 290; see also "Towards the Horizon," *AW*, October 18, 1941, 659.

37. *AOB*, 23.

38. "Authority," *AW*, June 19, 1937, 386.

39. "Broadening Sympathies," *AW*, December 10, 1938, 787.

40. Jones, 282-283.

41. "The Goodness of God," *AW*, November 20, 1948, 743.

42. "Towards the Horizon," *AW*, October 18, 1941, 659.

43. *SSQ*, October 15, 1939, 10.
44. "It is not the function of the Church of Christ to interfere in world government. Hers is a distinctly spiritual ministry for the salvation and sanctification of men. But there is through prayer a spiritual authority granted to her which she has never learned rightly to exercise. What an opportunity is given in these days of unrest and distrust and perplexity to take a supernatural part, through laying her hand on the throne of the King of kings, and gaining from Him the turning of the hearts of earth's rulers as the watercourses whither He will (Prov. 21:1)." ("Those in Authority," *AW*, May 4, 1946, 275.)
45. "The Oppression of the Enemy," *AW*, June 21, 1947, 386.
46. *SSQ*, November 22, 1942, 25.
47. "The Cooperating Spirit," *AW*, May 4, 1936, 275.
48. *AOB*, 81; see also *AOB*, 38, 40, 46, 47, 54, 69-71.
49. *SSQ*, January 14, 1940, 6.
50. Murray, *With Christ in the School of Prayer*, 115.
51. Carrie Judd Montgomery, *The Secrets of Victory* (Oakland, CA: Triumphs of Faith, 1921), 67-74; Penn-Lewis, *Prayer and Evangelism*, 53-62.
52. Penn-Lewis, "How to Pray for Missionaries," *AW*, June 12, 1937, 373-375; *AW*, June 26, 1937, 406-407. A comprehensive discussion of the history of binding and loosing appears in the article "The Restoration of the Doctrine of Binding and Loosing," by Paul L. King in *Alliance Academic Review* (1997), and in the book *Binding and Loosing* by K. Neill Foster with Paul L. King.
53. Penn-Lewis, *The Warfare with Satan*, 20.
54. Foster and King, 253-254, 266-267.
55. "The Weakness of Power," *AW*, April 2, 1938, 211.
56. Ibid.
57. "Our Most Stubborn Foe," *AW*, June 27, 1942, 402.
58. Ibid., 402-403.
59. J.A. MacMillan, "Islam in the Far East," *AW*, June 27, 1942, 407.
60. MacMillan, "Our Mohammedan Problem in the Philippines," *AW*, 404.
61. "Praying Geographically," *AW*, September 14, 1946, 579.
62. Ibid.
63. Ibid.
64. *AOB*, 38.
65. "All Authority," *AW*, March 2, 1940, 130.
66. *AOB*, 67-68.
67. *SSQ*, May 3, 1936, 17; see also *SSQ*, May 13, 1934, 19.
68. Arthur T. Pierson, *Lessons in Prayer* (Dixon, MO: Rare Christian Books, n.d.), 59-60.
69. *AOB*, 60; see also "Commanding God," *AW*, October 7, 1939, 626.
70. Matthew Henry, *A Commentary on the Whole Bible* (Old Tappan, NJ: Fleming H. Revell, 1935), 4:253-254.
71. John D.W. Watts, *Word Biblical Commentary*, ed. David A. Hubbard and Glenn W. Barker (Waco, TX: Word, 1987), 25:151.
72. Some put it into the form of a question ("Will you command me?"), rather than imperative. The Hebrew verb form is a piel imperfect, which can be expressed either in an imperative or a question, although the wording suggests that the imperative is the most likely. The Septuagint translates with an imperative, showing that to be the understanding by Jewish exegetes 200 B.C. (Watts, 151-153.)

73. George Rawlinson, *The Pulpit Commentary: Isaiah*, eds. H.D.M. Spence and Joseph S. Exell (Chicago: Wilcox and Follett, n. d.), 174.

74. Albert Barnes, *Notes on the Old Testament: Isaiah* (Grand Rapids, MI: Baker Book House, 1851, reprint 1985), 1:154.

75. Charles Spurgeon, *The Power of Prayer in a Believer's Life*, compiled and edited, Robert Hall (Lynnwood, WA: Emerald Books, 1993), 67.

76. Pierson, *Lessons in the School of Prayer*; 60-61; see also, "Clearing the Ground," *AW*, January 26, 1946, 51.

77. Simpson, *CITB*, 3:498. MacMillan expands upon Simpson's teaching on this, though he does not mention him by name. ("Commanding God," 626.)

78. *SSQ*, August 9, 1942, 19.

79. *AOB*, 73.

80. Foster and King, 202.

81. Penn-Lewis and Roberts, *War on the Saints*, 260.

82. *AOB*, 8.

83. "Heavenly Quickening," *AW*, September 21, 1946, 594.

84. "Fasting as an Aid to Prayer," *AW*, March 4, 1950, 130.

85. *AOB*, 96.

86. "Love at Its Flood," *AW*, December 11, 1943, 786.

87. "A United World," *AW*, September 14, 1946, 578.

88. "Mount of Transfiguration," *AW*, July 21, 1934, 450.

89. *SSQ*, May 3, 1936, 17.

90. J.A. MacMillan, "Israel's Night of Remembrance," *AW*, November 22, 1941, 754.

91. "The Power of the Air," *AW*, August 28, 1948, 546.

Epilogue—MacMillan's Family Legacy

1. "Religion in the Home," *AW*, August 11, 1945, 242.

2. "Spiritual Heredity," *AW*, July 5, 1941, 418.

3. Ibid.

4. Ibid.

5. "Slavery Days," *AW*, April 29, 1950, 258.

6. He translated Martin Luther's paraphrase of the Lord's Prayer: "Our Father, Who in Heaven Art," *Hymns of the Christian Life* (Harrisburg, PA: Christian Publications, 1978), 34. Hymns to which he wrote new harmonies included "Joyful, Joyful, We Adore Thee," "Majestic Sweetness Sits Enthroned," "Hark! Ten Thousand Harps and Voices," "Come, Sevenfold Holy Spirit," "Sweet Will of God," "Breathe Upon Us," "Stretch Forth Thy Hand," "Even As He," "Go and Tell Them" and "Come, Labor On." He also composed the music for A.B. Simpson's "Healing in His Wings."

7. *The Alliance Witness*, October 26, 1983, 28.

8. *The Path*, Nyack, NY: Nyack College, 8:1:7, Winter/Spring 1998.

9. "Raging Chariots," *AW*, May 15, 1937, 307.

10. *SSQ*, October 10, 1943, 6.

11. *SSQ*, August 3, 1947, 16.

Appendix—The First John 4:1-3 Testing of Spirits

1. *SSQ*, March 29, 1942, 40; see also February 18, 1951, 22; April 22, 1951, 13.

2. *SSQ*, December 6, 1942, 30; see also October 1, 1950, 4; April 8, 1951, 7; April 22, 1951, 13; April 6, 1952, 1; May 17, 1953, 22.

3. Brotherton, 31, 102; Keith Bailey informed me of some of his research uncovering earlier usage of the technique, which started my search.

4. D.M. Panton, "Testing the Supernatural," *The Dawn: An Evangelical Magazine*, May 15, 1925, 64; Edward Miller, *The History and Doctrines of Irvingism* (London: Thynne and Jarvis, Ltd., n.d.), 1:101.

5. Pember, *EEA*, 342-343.

6. Brotherton, 29, 31.

7. A.B. Simpson, *CITB*, 6:374-375. Though he does not mention Pember by name, it is obvious he is referring to Pember's *Earth's Earliest Ages* when he says, "A distinguished writer, who has become familiar with the subject of demonology by much contact with it, has suggested that they may be the spirits of a former human race before the fall of Adam."

8. Ibid., 375.

9. *CM*, Toronto, June 1907, 85.

10. *CM*, Toronto, September 1908, 102-103.

11. R.A. Jaffray, " 'Speaking in Tongues'—Some Words of Kindly Counsel," reprinted in Richard Gilbertson, *The Baptism of the Holy Spirit* (Camp Hill, PA: Christian Publications, 1993), 348-349.

12. Ibid.

13. *The Overcomer*, January 1910, n.p.; Panton, "Testing the Supernatural," 64.

14. Penn Lewis and Roberts, *War on the Saints*, 23-24, 53, 186-187.

15. Panton, "Testing the Supernatural," 63.

16. D.M. Panton, "Outlook of the Hour," *The Dawn*, February 15, 1926, 483; Panton, "Testing the Supernatural," 62, 67.

17. D.M. Panton, "If the Gifts of Miracles Are the Alps of the Church—Grace and Love Are Her Himilayas," *Herald of His Coming*, July 1951, 1.

18. Margaret E. Barber, "Testing the Supernatural," *The Dawn*, September 15, 1925, 285. According to Barber, a voice of a former preacher who had died was heard in his house giving proclamations: "The utterances were extraordinary—full of Scripture; exhortations to live a holy life were frequent; and people of evil character dare not go, because no sooner were they seated, than the voice would address them by name, and ask them to repent of their sins. In most cases, sins known only to the person and the spirit addressing them were revealed." Yet when the First John 4:2 test was applied, there was no positive response, but rather silence for half an hour, followed by the voice saying, "Read First Corinthians 13:13." This demonstrated an avoidance of answering the question with a "Yes" or a "No," indicating a false spirit.

19. Watchman Nee, *The Latent Power of the Soul* (New York: Christian Fellowship Publishers, Inc., 1972), 54-56.

20. Paul Rader, *Harnessing God* (New York: George H. Doran Co., 1926), 99-101.

21. McCrossan, *Speaking with Other Tongues: Sign or Gift—Which?*, 42-43.

22. *Demon Experiences in Many Lands*, 40.

23. Ibid., 72, 93, 94.

24. Brotherton, 93-107, 153-161.

25. George A. Birch, *The Deliverance Ministry* (Camp Hill, PA: Horizon House Publishers, 1988), 141, 145-170.

26. Brotherton, 114, 121.

27. *Demon Experiences in Many Lands*, 40, 72, 93, 94.

28. K. Neill Foster, "Discernment, the Powers and Spirit-Speaking," unpublished dissertation, Fuller Theological Seminary, 1988, 193-196.

29. Murphy makes reference to this passage of Scripture five times, but never mentions it as an actual test for spirit manifestations in the text, though he believes it is a valid means of discernment when used with discretion. Murphy, 164, 361, 381, 401, 419.

30. Albert Runge, "Exorcism: A Satanic Ploy?" *His Dominion* (Spring 1987), 8:4:13-14. See also chapter 13, note 23. For a discussion of Runge's concerns and criticisms, see my dissertation, chapter 14.

31. John White, "Commentary on Psychological Observations on Demonism," *Demon Possession: A Medical, Historical, Anthropological and Theological Symposium*, ed. John Warwick Montgomery (Minneapolis, MN: Bethany, 1976), 253.

32. Dave Hunt, "Q & A," *The Berean Call*, May, 1999, 7.

33. K. Neill Foster, "Discernment, the Powers, and Spirit Speaking," 161. Foster argues contra White that, according to the Greek tenses, a confession must be continual or repeated in order to be valid.

34. Ibid., 149. When writing his dissertation, Foster was not aware of the significant history of the test as presented here, and thus calls it the "Ruark procedure."

35. Gerald E. McGraw, "An Effective Deliverance Methodology: Then and Now," *Alliance Academic Review* (1996), Elio Cuccaro, ed. (Camp Hill, PA: Christian Publications, 1996), 151-170.

36. Gerald E. McGraw, "Tongues Should Be Tested," *The Alliance Witness*, June 5, 1974, 3ff.

37. *SSQ*, February 18, 1951, 22; *SSQ*, April 22, 1951, 13.

38. *SSQ*, April 6, 1952, 1.

39. *SSQ*, March 29, 1942, 40.

40. Watchman Nee, *The Spiritual Man* (New York: Christian Fellowship Publishers, Inc., 1968), 3:124.

41. Carrie Judd Montgomery, "Witchcraft and Kindred Spirits," *AW*, October 15, 1938, 660-661.

42. "Demon-Energized Cults," *AW*, February 2, 1946, 66.

43. Regarding First John 4, MacMillan comments:

It is evident that in the church at Ephesus many professed to have the gift of prophecy. Messages were given to the assembly by these men, which purported to be from the Holy Spirit. John refused to receive these unless they passed the test of definite confession of the deity and humanity of Christ. Every teacher claiming inspiration from the Holy Spirit must prove it by submitting to be proved by his brethren with the question directed to the spirit within him, which is given in chapter 4:2. It is a procedure that would eliminate the false working from those churches that accept without hesitation whatever professes to be the manifestation of the Spirit. (*SSQ*, August 31, 1941, 27.)

These cases he distinguishes from separating the wheat from the chaff in imperfect prophecy, as mentioned earlier.

44. *EWD*, 85.